GARLAND STUDIES ON

INDUSTRIAL PRODUCTIVITY

edited by

STUART BRUCHEY
ALLAN NEVINS PROFESSOR EMERITUS
COLUMBIA UNIVERSITY

A GARLAND SERIES

GLOBAL PRODUCTION AND DOMESTIC DECAY

PLANT CLOSINGS IN THE U.S.

BRIAN PHILLIPS

GARLAND PUBLISHING, INC.
A MEMBER OF THE TAYLOR & FRANCIS GROUP
NEW YORK & LONDON / 1998

Library of Congress Cataloging-in-Publication Data

Phillips, Brian, 1956–
    Global production and domestic decay : plant closings in the
U.S. / Brian Phillips.
        p.   cm. — (Garland studies on industrial productivity)
    Includes bibliographical references and index.
    ISBN 0-8153-3196-7 (alk. paper)
    1. Plant shutdowns—United States. 2. Displaced workers—
United States—Psychology. 3. Employees—Relocation—United
States—Psychological aspects. 4. Early retirement—United
States—Psychological aspects. 5. Foreign trade and employment—
United States. 6. Plant shutdowns—New York (State)—Syra-
cuse—Case studies. 7. Automobile industry and trade—New York
(State)—Syracuse—Case studies. 8. General Motors Corporation.
I. Title. II. Series.
HD5708.55.U6P48 1998
338.6'042—dc21
                                                    98-29072

Printed on acid-free, 250-year-life paper
Manufactured in the United States of America

"The reason jobs are hard to find is, you know the answer, I don't know how many companies are moving outside the United States, but, possibly thousands. In the near future you will need a college education to mop floors or wash dishes."

. . . Dislocated General Motors Automobile Worker

"People have to be taught about the things displaced workers face everyday. I'm very discouraged to find out the number of people who are ignorant on this matter or just don't care. I can't wait to retire so I can stop working for one of the most inept, unpatriotic companies in recent memory."

. . . Dislocated General Motors Automobile Worker

Dedicated to the former General Motors Syracuse Plant Employees, whose cooperation and assistance made this research possible.

Contents

Tables

Appendix F

Foreword

Brian Phillips has written an important study. His contribution lie in three areas: theoretical, empirical, and public policy. At the theoretical area he anchors the problem of "downsizing" within a broader context of the trends toward the internationalization of capital flows and the accompanying transfer of profits upward into the corporate coffers and outward to overseas investments. His case study of the closing of an auto plant in upstate New York is thus illustrative of larger historical changes that are affecting the U.S. working class. The changes are part of corporate strategies that are shaped more by profit calculations than by abstract notions of "rationality," "efficiency" or "competitiveness." As the study demonstrates, the workforce was productive and efficient within the competitive realm.

The second major contribution of this study is the multiple level of analysis; it moves from a general analysis of global trends using aggregate data through a description of "enterprise" performance and organization to the "micro-impact" on personal and family relations, friendships and community ties. Professor Phillips' analysis of the inter-face of macro and micro relations is carried out through rigorous empirical analysis and participant observation. The result is a brilliant portrayal of the human cost of corporate restructuring.

This is a different story then appears in the business section of our daily newspapers: of family tension, psychological disorders, forced abandonment of communities and the break-up of long-standing friendships. Phillips' sociological perspective informs us that family values are not simply a question of "personal responsibility" as some conservative ideologies would have it, but of corporate decision-making.

The third significant contribution of Phillips' study is the different responses and impacts that the shock of downsizing has on workers. The study describes both the flexibility and adaptability of some workers under adverse circumstances as well as those who are unable to "move on." The problem of flexibility, however, as Phillips demonstrates, is not simply a question of personal will, an individual socio-psychological attribute, but a function of age, family commitments and trade union agreements. The impact of corporate downsizing is thus seen in a matrix of other social forces, personal loyalties and demographic factors.

Professor Phillips' focus on the social impact of corporate relocation and the multiple negative impact that it has on U.S. workers suggests the need to call into question the rules and operational procedures that govern an unrestricted free market capitalist economy. The study points to the need for laws or regulations that protect workers' rights, that limit capital movements and that establish rules of corporate responsibility for the labor force. These policy issues are not fully explored yet they are clearly implied in the course of Phillips' study. The basic point is that this book presents, in a clear and rigorous fashion, the "workers' side" in the process of "globalization" and seriously calls into question the facile assumptions of economists who claim that the free market left to its own devices will benefit everyone.

James Petras
Binghamton University

Preface

This book explores some of the explanations for and consequences of globalized production by transnational corporations. A review of the theoretical underpinnings of the reasons for corporate overseas expansion precedes a discussion of transnational corporation overseas production facilities. The literature reviewed supports the position that the exodus of manufacturing capital has been assisted by state policy which has encouraged capital flight, and that corporate efforts to downsize manufacturing operations in the United States have added to corporate profitability and championed profits over the strengthening the domestic economy.

These actions produced higher corporate profits in the 1990s than at the end of the post World War II recovery period. At the same time, the systematic de-industrialization of the United States has resulted in significant social costs, with growing income inequality and continued wage deterioration as many Americans fall out of the middle class ranks.

As manufacturing corporations in both heavy and light industries continue to expand overseas and simultaneously close and/or downsize domestic operations, American workers and their families experience unemployment, low wage re-employment, early retirement and relocation. The consequences of plant closings on workers have been more than economic costs. Many workers have experienced mental and physical health problems, and have seen adverse effects on families and friends.

Continued overseas expansion by the General Motors Corporation and its re-importation of products to the United States as well as its closing of domestic operations are used as examples of the actions of many manufacturing industries in their search for profits.

The results of research into the closing of a General Motors parts plant in upstate New York underscore the consequences that manufacturing workers and their families may experience. The statistical analysis of 119 returned questionnaires and the information gathered in over 20 interviews on the effects the closing has had on early retirees (n=88) and relocatees (n=31) are presented. The study shows that both groups of workers have suffered as a result of the shutdown. It also shows that the relocatees may have suffered more then the early retirees in relation to mental and physical health issues and have experienced more negative effects on family and friends.

Acknowledgments

I would like to acknowledge the following individuals who have made my education possible and my life more interesting:

Harold Clapper

Professor James Geschwender
Binghamton University

Professor David Hakken
SUNY Institute of Technology, Utica/Rome

Professor Bill Jack Harrell
SUNY Institute of Technology, Utica/Rome

Professor Muto Ichiyo
Binghamton University

Professor James Petras
Binghamton University

Professor Richard Rehberg
Binghamton University

Mustafa Saatci

I would particularly like to acknowledge the support and
encouragement of my late friend and associate
Dr. Steven Vieux.

Introduction

Capital formation and accompanying class struggles have for centuries shaped the economic, social and political fabric of societies. The development of capital formation is itself a process of accumulation, reproduction and expansion, and, as capitalism evolves and changes, so too does this process.

For the past few years in the United States, capital's search for profits has been quite successful. Capital's after-tax profits during the mid 1990s have been the highest in 25 years and greater then at the end of earlier postwar recoveries[1] (Baker and Mishel 1995, p. 1). Higher profits have been achieved, in part, by the migration of U.S. manufacturing capital overseas, downsizing manufacturing operations in the U.S. and "draining" the domestic economy. This strategy has been assisted by state policy which has encouraged capital migration and domestic decay. The results have been a systematic disinvestment of the nation's basic productive capacity, which is known as deindustrialization, and a variety of hardships for millions of Americans.

Deindustrialization, with respect to the massive capital migration of productive manufacturing from the United States to other countries, has sparked a plethora of literature as to the reasons for and explanations of manufacturing relocation. Within the international division of labor, many countries increasingly have become sites for profitable manufacturing which is competitive on the world market.[2] Transnational corporations,[3] the single most important factor in creating shifts on global economic activity, have relocated to specific sites around the globe depending on the type of manufacturing process involved.

Overseas expansion has been at the expense of the domestic economy. United States international trade policy has been quite favorable to overseas expansion, and domestic U.S. taxes laws have encouraged corporations to operate overseas. As a result, corporations no longer invest in this country's infrastructure, capital equipment and human capital. The path chosen to assist the transfer of operations overseas is to depress wages and downsize the workforce in the U.S. The outcome of these actions has meant record breaking corporate profits at the expense of American jobs.

In the past few years, relocation and domestic decay have affected millions of American workers through plant closings in many heavy and light industries across the country. Permanent layoffs in the 1990's are occurring amid claims of United States economic recovery and by corporations that are economically successful.

Between 1981 and 1991, a total of 1.8 million manufacturing jobs vanished in the United States-a decline of nine percent. In the 1950s, one-third of all jobs in the United States were in the manufacturing sector. By the early 1990s a mere 16 percent of the American workforce was involved in manufacturing (Barnet and Cavanagh 1994, p. 275). The loss of manufacturing employment for many workers has meant layoffs, unemployment, declining incomes, relocation and early retirement. For some workers, these consequences have had severe adverse effects on their health and family relations.

This book explores the causes and consequences of industrial relocation and domestic decay. Aggregate data is supplied to position the reader within the larger general context of the activities of transnational corporations. Numerous industries, including the automobile industry and General Motors in particular, fit center stage in the causes and consequences of industrial relocation.

The closing of a General Motors Inland Fisher Guide components plant facility located in Syracuse, New York is exemplary of United States domestic decay through plant closings. The case study of this particular closing reviews, in detail, the effects the shutdown has had on the hourly workforce. In some sense, the shutdown of the GM-Syracuse facility can be viewed as a best-case scenario, since all the workers were offered either the option to transfer to other GM facilities or take early retirement.

The organization of the book is as follows. Chapter 1 addresses the causes and implications of transnational corporations (TNC's) transferring their manufacturing operations overseas. Discussion begins by reviewing the debates surrounding an international division of labor. The theoretical underpinnings of this section highlight several theories that attempt to explain capital's overseas expansion. The extent and depth of corporate transnational relocation are also reviewed.

Chapter 2 is a thorough investigation of the consequences of deindustrialization. Several transnational corporations and export firms have had record breaking profits in the past few years. Profits have been made possible, in part, by U.S. policies that have encourage capital flight and domestic decay. Other economic actors have suffered as a result. Many of the middle and lower economic classes have experienced declining manufacturing employment in specific industries, which has meant numerous plant shutdowns at dramatic social costs.

Chapters 3 and 4 deal explicitly with the plant shutdown case study. Chapter 3 introduces background information on the closed plant as well as the events that occurred shortly after notification of closure was given. The responses to the shutdown by the groups involved are also reviewed.

Chapter 4 is an analysis of the data collected from two questionnaires that were distributed to 275 early retirees and relocatees (transferred workers) from the closed GM-Syracuse components plant. The experiences of these workers will parallel the aggregate data on the effects of plant closings.

Chapter 5 relates the closing of the General Motors components plant to United States domestic decay and the international context.

Just as it is important to review what the book is about, it is equally important to highlight what it is not. The author recognizes the many reasons for U.S. deindustrialization, with industrial relocation being only one. This book does not explore at any length the researchers, authors and academicians who see capital flight and disinvestment as "essentially groundless" (Mckenzie 1979; Branson 1984) or that the U.S. economy is not only *not* in decline, but is more robust now than ever before (Nau 1990; Lawrence 1984). Nor is the nonexistence of a more global or world economy argued.

The author duly recognizes the many ways one can conceptualize the approaches to an international division of labor, ones that encompass parameters other than the theories explored in this work.

The present U.S. economic condition in parallel with advancing globalized production makes an inquiry into overseas industrial relocation, and domestic decay important areas for review. When numerous plant shutdowns occur, millions of workers are "emptied into the streets." Exploration into the hardships that many workers experience due to plant shutdowns may shed light on potential solutions. While many U.S. citizens and some government officials voice concern over the economy, the loss of high paying jobs and numerous plant shutdowns, it is difficult for many to understand how and why, in the face of these problems, corporate profits and overseas expansion coupled with domestic decay continue to accelerate.

A PERSONAL NOTE FROM THE AUTHOR

I take a personal interest in the closing of the General Motors Inland Fisher Guide Division components plant. For several years during the late 1970s and then again during the late 1980s, I was employed at the General Motors components facility. In the late 1970s, as a member of the United Automobile Workers (UAW), I worked as a injection machine mold operator. For three years during the late 1980's as a member of management, I was employed at the same facility as a production control scheduler.[4] I was responsible for subcontracting automobile component parts throughout North America and parts of Europe.

As an hourly employee for General Motors I have gained firsthand experience and understanding of the meaning behind being a autoworker. Threats of the plant closing, hard work, violence, anger, frustration, camaraderie, monotonous and at times dangerous work, and "cooperation" programs etc. etc. etc., have all assisted in my understanding of the "labor process."

As a member of the GM management "team," I gained a very clear understanding of the meaning behind profitability. Plant closings, corporate subcontracting, and capital relocation, as well as the seriousness and silliness of corporate power, have all increased my awareness of capital's search for profits.

NOTES

1. For a more historical view of capitals search for profits (post-W.W.II), see appendix A.

2. Workers in developing countries who are employed by transnational corporations have fallen victim to somewhat different hardships. Low wages (sometimes below subsistence), together with high rates of industrial accidents and related illnesses, are but a few problems encountered.

3. I use the terms transnational and multinational corporations somewhat interchangeably in referring to American-based corporations doing business abroad.

4. For a narrative of the authors GM production control experience see Appendix B

Global Production and
Domestic Decay

CHAPTER 1

Relocation Abroad

TRANSNATIONAL CORPORATIONS AND AN INTERNATIONAL DIVISION OF LABOR

Over the past twenty years a debate over the reasons for manufacturing moving abroad (more or less centered on the left)[1] has been taking place. This debate has been encompassed in the term NIDL and can be divided into three general categories.[2] The first includes those researchers who emphasize the sphere of exchange; the second, those who highlight production-oriented theories; and third, researchers and academics who locate themselves within the circuits of capital in the internationalization of capital.[3] What most of these researchers show is that contemporary capitalism is in a variant stage which is either some entirely new form of "regime of accumulation" or is a mere extension or transformation of traditional capitalism.

Theories of Exchange and Distribution

The New International Division of Labor. The ground-breaking book that stimulated much of the debate in the area of an NIDL is *The New International Division of Labor* (Frobel, Heinrichs and Kreye, 1980). Its main premise is that capital relocates to areas around the globe in search of lower labor costs. Thus, the reason for an NIDL is the development of the world market for labor power and production sites. An NIDL will be established if three preconditions are met (Frobel, Heinrichs and Kreye 1980, p. 178):
- Development of transportation and communication technology to assist capital's relocation to other areas of the globe.

- Development of production process technology in manufacturing that fragments and standardizes job tasks (deskills) which can use unskilled labor.
- Emergence of a worldwide reservoir of potential labor power.

In attempts at substantiating their theory regarding an NIDL, Frobel, Heinrichs and Kreye underscore the growth and development of "free production zones or Export Processing Zones (EPZs) and contract processing.[4] EPZs and contract processing areas are "industrial estates" designed for the optimal utilization of the labor force. They are geographically located in the developing or underdeveloped areas of the globe (Asia, Latin America, etc.) and are designed to attract capital by offering low wage costs, tariff and tax exemptions, subsidized imputs and a infrastructure of factory walls, energy supplies, deep water harbors, airports, etc. (Frobel, Heinrichs and Kreye 1977, p. 86).

Frobel et al. also have documented long working hours, extreme intensity of work, physical and mental exhaustion among workers (typically women from 16 to 24) who labor in these free trade zones (Frobel, Heinrichs and Kreye, 1977, p. 81). These factors are claimed to bring about a international solidarity of the working class (Frobel et al. 1980, p. 405-406).

A variation of an NIDL focuses on the fall of the rate of profit where industrial relocation is a specific response to a profit "squeeze." This line of argument states that the post-World War II period has witnessed a strengthening of the working class in relation to capital, and, as a result, capital has been unable to increase its rate of profit through the exploitation of the working classes in industrialized countries. Hence, capital relocates to the periphery in search of lower wages (Arrighi 1978).

Limitations of a NIDL and the profit squeeze: The NIDL and the variant *profit squeeze* have come under criticism. Some researchers claim that the significance of the NIDL should not be over generalized and state that more than 90 percent of manufactured exports from the periphery nations originated in only 16 countries, and that five peripheral countries account for nearly 75 percent of all manufactured exports. A sizable number of peripheral or developing countries (an estimated 60 countries) are still dependent on the extraction of raw materials and agricultural exports. Although TNCs do relocate to low wage sites, not all third world countries meet the required conditions of social, political, and physical infrastructure (Ross, R. and Trachte, K. 1990 p. 111).

Other researchers have noted that the NIDL is too one-dimensional because it focuses too much on low wages as the overwhelming consideration for TNCs to move abroad (Dicken 1992, p. 125). The NIDL and the variant *profit squeeze* also have been further criticized for paying exaggerated attention to industrializing those countries that have allowed TNCs to operate.[5]

Furthermore, these theories not only neglect the role that technological change plays in increasing labor productivity, but overemphasize the role of capital in increasing its rate of profit by reducing labor costs. Reducing labor costs is only one means by which capital can increase its rate of profit and should not be seen as the only one.

In conclusion, the NIDL and the *profit squeeze* deny the importance of certain independent dynamics, for example; the role that governmental policies (in both home and host countries) may play in serving the interests of the ruling classes, and also, the importance's that class struggles can play in conditioning capital's relocation (Jenkins 1984, p. 34).

Arguing in a somewhat similar vein as the NIDL theorists, the world systems perspective also recognizes the importance of the growth of world markets and the rapid expansion of manufacturing production outside the industrialized core. One major difference between the two theories is that the world systems perspective does not view the rapid growth of manufacturing leaving the core countries and moving toward the developing countries as indicative of a new stage of labor-capital relations. In fact, capital relocation, for the world system theorists is nothing more than the cyclical movement of capital.

World System Perspective. World systems theory (mainly credited to Immanuel Wallerstein) claims that there has been a capitalist world economy since the beginning of the 16th century and that individual countries can be understood (in terms of trade and exchange) by their place and function within that world system. Capitalist world economy is thus divided between rich core and poor peripheral regions. The core countries exploits the periphery for commodities, producing unequal exchange and development.[6] The division of labor between the core and peripheral regions facilitates the transfer of value, benefiting the core (Wallerstein 1979 and Wallerstein and Hopkins 1982).

World systems theory does not consider variations of capitalism as being fundamental within the structure of the world economy. Only cycles of expansions and contractions occur within the world system. Within the core countries, some nations reach hegemonic status through a comparative productive advantage and impose "free" international trade. Competition within the core countries begins and eventually the hegemonic nation declines and is replaced by a new hegemonic state (Wallerstein 1979, p. 95).

Within periods of growth and stagnation, for a variety of reasons, a crises of over-production results in the core. To elevate this crisis a rise in real incomes develops. This rise in incomes is accompanied by a transfer of production to lower wage countries partly restoring world demand (Wallerstein and Hopkins 1982, p. 65-70).

The recent economic downturn (Wallerstein dates this around 1967) for the United States is a cyclical phenomenon (Kondretief B-phase) that other hegemonic states have been through. In fact, transnational firms and the growth of the industrial working class in the periphery (developing countries) have existed earlier in capitalism's history (Wallerstein and Hopkins 1982 p. 37-40). It is not uncommon to hear world system theorists draw a parallel to the Dutch East India Company of the 17th century and large transnational corporations of today.

Wallerstein argues that the concept of a NIDL is not a new action by entrepreneurs to restore profits but that it is a cyclical phenomenon. Where the Dutch carried on trade and exchange relations with other areas of the globe, today's TNCs relocate production and manufacturing operations to EPZs and the "new industrializing countries" (NICs) of Singapore, Hong Kong, Taiwan and South Korea (Wallerstein 1979, p. 39).

Limitations of the World System Perspective: A variety of criticism have been leveled against the world systems approach. On a practical note the Dutch companies of the East and West Indies as well as the British Hudson Bay Company are not, arguably, the direct ancestors of the large transnational corporations of today. These companies were not only confined to the colonial territories of their home countries, but also were established for reasons of trade and exchange and not production (Dicken 1992, p. 12). On more theoretical grounds, several authors[7] have criticized the world system theory because it:

- Privileges exchange relations in the marketplace over production relations in the workplace.
- Reduces class relations to the strategies of those in power rather than analyzing the struggles between the capitalist and other classes.
- Neglects the interplay between class conflicts and the dynamics of state formation and policy-making.
- Underestimates the importance of local production conditions and worker resistance in determination of local economies.
- Overlooks cultural diversity and the potential for resistance in and from the periphery (Blim 1992).

The foundation of the world systems perspective stems from the earlier works of Paul Baran's "stagnation thesis" and A.G. Franks "development of underdevelopment."[8] A review of the Baran/Frank "development of underdevelopment" thesis is offered here to further explore the world systems perspective, and, along with Peter Evans "dependent development," theory, to further elucidate the development of contemporary capitalist world economy and the role of TNCs.

The Theories of "the development of underdevelopment" and "dependent development." In response to what has been termed modernization theory (1950s), that focused on the industrial development of the third world through TNC involvement, Paul Baran's "stagnation thesis" and A.G. Franks "development of underdevelopment" postulated that Western commodity production in the Third World constrained effective industrial growth. As capital relocated to low wage havens in Latin America, the market exchanges that developed benefited the core at the expense of the periphery, and held the periphery in a permanent subservient role.

Shortly thereafter, Peter Evans revised the Baran/Frank arguments and claimed that industrialization "in a limited sense" had occurred in areas such as Brazil and Mexico as a result of Foreign Direct Investment (FDI) from the West and TNC involvement. He went on to show how class relations evolved and created conditions permitting industrialization. Evans coined the term "dependent development." It was "development, because it is characterized by capital accumulation and an increasingly complex differentiation of the internal productive structure; dependent, because it is indelibly marked by the effects of continued dependence on capital housed in the current core countries" (Evans and Gereffi 1981, p. 31).

Limitations to the Arguments. Most of the limitations on the theories of the "development of underdevelopment" and "dependent development," lie in the underpinnings of the Baran/Frank arguments. The authors have been criticized for not paying enough attention to internal class relations (the importance of class struggle) as well as for failing to take into account capitalist forces like the IMF and the World Bank. The policies of the IMF and the World Bank have benefited some of the upper classes in both the U.S. and some Third World countries at the expense of many in the Third World (Petras 1984, p. 71). Other researchers have argued that the "development of underdevelopment" thesis is best understood as a regional rather than global theory of imperialism (Blim 1992, p. 4). Evans has been criticized for not considering "the relationships among contradictions of capital accumulation and the dynamics of class conflict in the core and the development process which he observed" (Ross and Trachte 1990, p. 78).

Despite the weaknesses of the market oriented approach, they have offered one view of the international nature of capital accumulation, and its need to maximize profits and transfer production from the core (U.S.) to the periphery. Furthermore, market oriented approaches, and other theories that follow, all attempt to explain some of the major reasons for problems that have developed or are developing in the core; that is, the decline of manufacturing investment and accompanying social problems (such as underemployment) in the U.S.

One main problem that can be inferred with exchange and distribution oriented theories is the attention paid to the international solidarity of the working class (as was seen in the argument behind the *profit squeeze*). At the time of this writing, one can safely assume that international solidarity of the working class is nowhere near the internationalization of capital. As has already been noted, market oriented theories of a NIDL omit from their main focus a host of other important factors that cause and shape the movement of transnational capital abroad. State policies, class struggle, and transnational actors are but a few important aspects of TNC relocation. Another set of approaches, those that fall under production oriented theories, offer a striking contrast to the market oriented approaches.

Production Oriented Theories

One well known researcher whose writings are not directly concerned with a NIDL, but are by implication (Jenkins 1984, p. 31), are the works of Warren (1980). His main concern is with the development of the forces of production. His main argument, in the complete opposite direction from Petras (1986 pp. 48-70), is that capitalism is a progressive force in the third world. Western intervention is seen to allow for capitalism to develop internally to those countries. If problems with capitalism manifest themselves, they are problems of the internal dynamics of that specific country and not a result of external forces. According to Warren, capitalist ties are weakening dependency and opening up backward societies to industrialization. Capitalism should be seen as a progressive and liberating force (Warren 1980, p. 9 and 45).

According to Warren, one finds that manufacturing is becoming diversified into the light and heavy industries in Latin America. Economic power is becoming more dispersed throughout Asia, Africa, and Latin America where many Third World states are exercising more control over the operations of TNCs (Warren 1980, p. 170). In exchange oriented theories, capital accumulation leads to an NIDL that is exploitive to Third World countries. Warren would maintain that it was internal dynamics of the state and not capitalist development that are obstacles (Jenkins 1984, p. 37).

Other production-oriented researchers, cautions use of a specific theory of capitalism that is offered by the market oriented approaches, as well as the use of the term NIDL. Lipietz (1986) argues against the world system perspective and asks why couldn't the world system operate on the basis of a network of hegemonic centers. "Why should we necessarily look for a predecessor to England or a successor to the United States" (Lipietz 1986, p. 24).

In place of the world systems approach, Lipietz (along with others)[9] uses the term "modes of regulation and regimes of accumulation."[10] For Lipietz, capitalism appears differently in different countries. The development of capitalism in each country is the result of internal class struggles, producing outlines of regimes of accumulation that are consolidated by forms of regulation sustained by the state. The goal at hand should be to study each specific national social formation, observe the succession of regimes of accumulation and modes of regulation and to analyze its expansion, crisis and external relations. Lipietz remarks that this is done regularly for the core countries, whereas the treatment of the periphery generally is a consequences of the demands of the core.

Thus, for Lipietz, imperialism is a tool for capitalism to resolve its contradictions. His view is that imperialism could disappear, be modified or hold on "by habit" if other solutions to the contradictions of capital could be found (Lipietz 1986, p. 21).

Lipietz states that the NIDL is not the only product of the organizational activities of TNCs. The objectives of the TNCs are in concert with the ambitions of the dominant class of some national economies. Creation of the NIDL is not the purpose of TNCs; rather, capitalists in the core simply try to get around customs barriers of the periphery and sell manufactured goods according to the logic of an existing division of labor. New trends appear in the division of labor and it is a result of "how every country functions, what it produces, for whom, how, what the forms of wage relations are, what successive regimes of accumulation developed and why" (Lipietz 1986, p. 24-27).

Limitations of Production Oriented Theories. Criticism of Production-oriented theorists (Warren for the most part) is plentiful and is generally as follows: there is a lack of analysis of the form of production of surplus value and accumulation. Because of this, there is a lack of specificity of how industrialization takes place in these Third World countries. Although Warren mentions the roles that host governments play in capitalist development (which he terms internal dynamics), he leaves out the constraints that are placed on many Third World governments (by either home countries of TNCs or by TNCs themselves) to pursue "correct" economic policies. Warren treats productive forces as occurring uniformly in all Third World countries with no mention of the forms of exploitation or the nature of working class struggles. Warren is incorrect not to acknowledge the role that TNCs play in the industrialization process as well as the political, economic and social havoc that accompanies that process (Jenkins 1984, pp. 37-39).

Warren's work has been further criticized because:

"He didn't provide a coherent explanation for the prolonged periods of non industrialization in the Third World; he fails to explain the persistence of a vast number of scarcely industrialize countries; he fails to discuss the different patterns of industrial growth in advance capitalist, Third World, and socialist countries; he fails to provide a comprehensive framework to understand the interrelationship between the changing nature of capital in the West and the process of industrialization in the Third World; finally, he fails to discuss the enormous inequalities in industrial development among Third World countries, both in terms of the changes in productive systems and in terms of industrial growth; moreover, he fails to consider the possibility of the deindustrialization of specific Third World countries" (Petras 1984, p. 72).

It seemed that Warren focused too narrowly on the effects of industrial relocation. He attempted to extrapolate and over generalize specific instances of economic prosperity for some in the Third World and to relate them to capitalist industrialization throughout the Third World. Also, he was incorrect in viewing capital as been dispersed around the globe.

The work of Lipietz has also been criticized. It has been argued that the main problem with his work focuses on the exaggerated treatment of nation states and lack of emphasis on imperialism. Lipietz focuses too much attention on the internal dynamics of the nation state as being the main reason for capitalist development or the lack thereof.

Because of this, he is either unwilling or unable to see the role that imperialism has played not only in capitalist development but also in the ability of some countries (in Latin America) to overthrow capitalism. Capital accumulation is interwoven with imperialist exploitation and oppression and "because of this it has led us to the brink of global environmental destruction and nuclear holocaust" (Broad 1990, p. 57).

Lipietz has also been criticized for applying the term "global Fordism"[11] too generally over all industries across the globe. Some industries utilize a variety of production techniques to harness the maximum amount of benefits. Not all of these production principles can be defined as regimes of "intensive" accumulation (Hill 1989, p. 166).

Together, exchange and distribution-oriented theories and production approaches, illuminate more clearly the dynamics behind industrial relocation. One line of argument that attempts to pull these two theories together is put forth by Marx's "internationalization of capital."

The Internationalization of Capital

A Marxist approach, one that focuses on the "circuits of capital" which emphasizes the unity of production, distribution and exchange, offers a more adequate interpretation of the NIDL. According to Marx, capital must continually restructure and expand itself in search for higher rates of profit.[12] This restructuring and expansion is intended to bring about (for a time) the harmonious relationship between production, distribution and exchange, and occurs through the circuits of commodity capital (labor), money capital and productive capital (means of production, fixed capital). These three circuits of capital have now been internationalized and have been identified with the growth of world trade, international capital movements and the operations of TNCs, as well as the internationalization of products within those firms.

By viewing the NIDL in this way, profitability either can be restored or increased in a number of ways other than through relocation to low wage countries. Profitability can be raised through the increased productivity of mass production and economies of scale; the opening of new cheap sources of energy and raw materials; increasing the intensity of machine use, state subsides, passage of laws favorable to TNCs; and international bank lending (Jenkins 1984, pp. 40-45).

Implications of the Internationalization Approach for an NIDL- This approach makes it difficult to generalize about an NIDL because different countries or areas have been affected by different models of capital accumulation.[13] The internationalization of capital gives importance to specific national conditions and the role of the state in determining patterns of differentiation. For example, protectionism could limit capital in pursuing international reallocation. Yet, the internationalization of capital also affords the possibility of introducing production techniques and manufacturing processes that may be exported back to advanced capitalist countries[14] (Jenkins 1984, pp. 46-49).

Towards a Synthesis of the NIDL Debates

The theoretical underpinnings of the shifting of industrial production abroad have certainly brought forth more information than could be covered in this review. The preceding was intended to highlight some of the reasons for and explanations of industrial relocation. Elements of most of the debates are important factors in the dynamics of a NIDL. Low wages, the strength of the working class, the importance of markets and trade, the exploitation of the periphery to the advantage of the core, the possibility of capitalism developing differently in different countries, and the importance of state policy are all issues to be reviewed in determining the course of industrial relocation.

Marx's theory of the internationalization of the circuits of capital does not champion one circuit of capital over another, but shows the importance and complimentariety of all three (production, distribution, and exchange). Because of this, it seems to offer the best starting point at understanding the dynamics of an NIDL.

One important conclusion that can be drawn from most of the debates is that there is as increasing tendency toward the globalization of production. Whether this phenomenon is a decay or transformation, it appears that capitalism can "no longer [be] well comprehended by conceiving [it as] a system of national oligopolies in which nations are in a fixed hierarchy of international exchange" (Ross and Trachte 1990, p. 5).

The globalization of production threatens national boundaries, exploits both developed and developing economies and diffuses manufacturing around the globe. It leaves in its path, as a result of the disarray brought to social and economic institutions, a mass of unemployed/low paid workers and crumbling communities. Transnational Corporations are at the heart of the globalization of production.

The next section reviews the extent of these moves abroad by U.S. transnational corporations. Issues such as the amount and type of overseas manufacturing investment and overseas employment levels resulting from TNC involvement are discussed as well as the importance that subcontracting plays in the relocation of manufacturing.

TRANSNATIONAL CORPORATIONS AND THEIR RELOCATION

Arguably, transnational corporations may be the single most important factor in creating shifts in global economic activity. Their economic importance is due to the fact that they are able to control economic activity in more than one country. In addition, TNCs can take advantage of geographical differences between countries and influence government policies, and they are able to shift operations and resources on a global scale. A variety of factors have influenced the ease with which these activities can be successfully implemented (Dicken, 1992). Technological advancements (communications, transportation, production), international financial resources, and government as well as non governmental international agencies such as the International Monetary Fund (IMF) and the World Bank, enter into the matrix on TNCs move abroad.

The economic importance of TNCs within the global economy should not be doubted. The worlds largest 600 TNCs account for between one-fifth and one-fourth of value added in the production of goods in the global market economies. Viewed another way, the combined assets of the top 300 firms make up nearly 25 percent of the productive assets in the world (Barnet 1994, p. 15). Their importance as exporters and importers is even greater; for example, 80-90 percent of the exports of the United States is associated with TNCs (United Nations Centre on Transnational Corporations (UNCTC), 1988, p.16).

Overseas Manufacturing Investment[15]

A number of changes have occurred in the relative position of the very largest American TNCs[16]. They no longer dominate the world economy as they did in the late 1960s.[17] Since their growth rate peak in 1968, the rate of new subsidiary formation has fallen substantially. However, throughout the 1970s and 1980s and at the expense of their domestic activities, transnationality during the 1980s has increased. This expansion is due to the rise of smaller and medium size American TNCs. Large U.S. TNCs, although not adding new subsidiary formation, are expanding their existing operations and restructuring their foreign networks. From 1960 to 1988 the growth of U.S. overseas direct investmet in manufacturing increased by nearly $120 billion.[18] "In absolute, if not in relative terms, United States TNCs are more significant today than they were in the past. They constitute the largest and most extensive network of international production facilities in the world" (Dicken 1992, pp. 60-61).

U.S. foreign investment in manufacturing has not been distributed through out all industrial sectors. "Approximately 63 percent of all the overseas assets of United States TNCs in manufacturing in 1988 were in just four categories: chemical and allied products, non-electrical machinery, electronic and electrical equipment and transportation equipment." Within these categories some of the largest industries are automobile production and electronics.[19] Among these industries their geographic spread varies considerably (Dicken 1992, p. 62).

The U.S. automobile industry (General Motors and Ford) concentrates its foreign production facilities[20] predominately in the developed countries. About two-thirds of General Motors and Ford's overseas car production is located in Europe[21] (West Germany, United Kingdom, and Spain). Together, General Motors and Ford (holding the first and second position respectively in world passenger car production) controls nearly 30 per cent of the world market.

Of the 100 largest transnational corporations, General Motors and Ford occupy the fourth and seventh positions,[22] respectively, in their number of total foreign affiliates (UNCTAD 1995, p. 21). General Motor manufactures 42 percent of total car production outside the United States while Ford makes nearly 60 percent of its total production outside the United States.[23] (Dicken 1992 pp. 290 and 298).

For the last ten years, the electronics industry, located in the developing and underdeveloped countries and consisting of semiconductors, computers, telecommunications equipment, consumer goods and professional and industrial electronics, has been, the fastest growing area of economic activity in the world economy.

The semiconductor industry was the first U.S. industry to go abroad on a large scale (Grunwald and Flamm 1985, p. 38). Within the semiconductor industry alone, the largest United States firms had 1986 annual sales of over $4.8 billion (UNCTC 1988, p. 46). In the late 1980s, United States corporations owned over 80 assembly plants. Of these plants, three were located in the U.S., ten were in Mexico, 15 in Europe and 52 were in East and Southeast Asia, concentrated in Hong Kong and Singapore (Dicken 1992, p. 332).

Technological advances in communication and transportation have had an enormous impact on this industry, as have the establishment of EPZs and free trade manufacturing areas. Because of the discrete steps in manufacturing semiconductors the expensive high-tech imputs and R&D (utilizing a low number of highly educated professionals) remain within the U.S. while labor-intensive production is done outside the U.S. borders. Other important factors such as public subsides and a favorable political climate, have been found to be more important concerns for this industry than many of the others operating outside the U.S. (Grunwald and Flamm 1985, p. 78).

Geographical patterns in manufacturing investment have also not been distributed evenly around the globe. There has been faster than average growth rates in Europe and the Far East (Dicken 1992, pp. 62 and 64).

There have also been some changes in manufacturing investment in Europe and other parts of the globe. One half of the total U.S. manufacturing investment in the United Kingdom has moved out (by 1988 investment had fallen to just below 30 percent of all U.S. manufacturing investment in Europe) and towards West Germany,

Spain and Ireland. Overall, some four-fifths of all U.S. TNCs investment in manufacturing (some $140 billion) is in the developed market economies; this degree of concentration has been increasing rather than decreasing.

Among the developing countries, investment has declined in Latin America (with the exception of Brazil and Mexico) and increased in the Far East. Almost 70 percent of the Far East investment went to Singapore, Hong Kong, South Korea and Taiwan (Dicken 1992, pp. 62-65).

The Question of Returning Industries

A number of TNCs in the consumer electronics industry have moved their overseas manufacturing operations back to the United States. RCA has relocated its surveillance camera business from Taiwan to Pennsylvania. Some companies, like Apple Computer, decided not to continue to locate some of their assembly operations in Singapore and Malaysia and opened up plants in the United States instead.

It is important to recognize that when operations move back to the United States, or, like Apple Computer, decide not to relocate portions of the business offshore, it is because technological advancements have made it feasible to automate these new facilities. The need for labor-intensive operations becomes very low. Apple, for example, built a highly automated plant in California that employs 200 workers (of whom 70 are engineers). Their direct labor costs represent 3 percent of total costs. It would be dangerous to generalize from specific cases that jobs in the electronics industry are now coming back to the U.S. In fact, offshore industrial relocation by U.S. electronics firms is expected to rise over the next few years[24] (UNCTC 1988, p. 49).

The return of the garment industry to areas in the U.S., such as NYC, has sparked off a debate around the question of whether manufacturing is returning to the United States. These "sweat shops" utilize low wage (below minimum wage) illegal immigrant and child labor. Rather than being seen as the first of a great influx on industries back to the U.S., the garment industry should be seen as a specific case, one which uses a certain labor process that other industries are unable to mimic.

The garment industry is unlike other labor intensive industries. It utilizes low technology imputs and is able to manufacture with a small number of workers housed within several locations. These unique characteristics allow any number of entrepreneurs to establish a business with low capital start up costs. And because the industry lends itself to housing a small number of workers it makes laws forbidding the use of illegal immigrants and children virtually unenforceable by labor department authorities.

Other industries are unable to produce under the same conditions as the garment industry. For most of its imputs the auto industry utilizes large capital outlays extensively linked to a large labor intensive workforce, in full view of all to see. While subcontracting indeed occurs where parts are made with relatively low numbers of workers, even subcontracting doesn't lend itself to small sweatshops utilizing low tech imputs with little or no capital outlays. U.S. automobile production is mainly housed within core countries. The production process of automobiles cannot and should not be seen as a similar process as shirt making.

The semiconductor industry offers a unique twist. There are four basic steps to semiconductor manufacturing: design, chip fabrication, assembly and testing. Until recently, all but one step (assembly) was done with high technology and large capital outlays. Assembly of semiconductors was, until recently, done with a low technology labor intensive workforce located in developing countries. Two interesting points should be brought up. First, to reach economies of scale, semiconductor assembly was not done with a handful of workers but done with a large workforce. Second, the trend of assembly and packaging that was once labor intensive is now being done with costly high-tech machinery. "As capital becomes cheaper in relation to the cost of labor, automation becomes more and more attractive economically [in chip assembly and packaging] . . . large firms have both large production runs and access to cheaper capital . . . they might be expected to be more highly automated"(Grundwald and Flamm 1985, pp. 49-54).

The return of manufacturing industries may not occur to any large degree. If the production process in question (operating like the garment industry) utilizes low tech, unskilled, labor intensive, low wage jobs with only a few number of workers required for profitable production then industry may return to the U.S. How many industries at present are able to produce under the same conditions as the garment industry today?

Employment in Overseas Manufacturing Plants of the United States

One important way to comprehend the impact of overseas investment is to review data on employment figures.[25] "Overall employment in the foreign affiliates of United States TNCs grew from 2.4 million in 1966 to 4.07 million in 1987, an increase of 68.2 per cent" (Dicken 1992, p. 65).[26]

The fastest rates of employment increases in Europe were in Spain and Ireland. Among the developed economies the fastest rates of growth appeared in Japan. But, the highest rates of employment growth have been occurring in the developing countries of Brazil, Mexico, Singapore, South Korea, Malaysia and Taiwan. Overall, employment in the developing countries grew at almost five times the rate of employment levels in the developed economies. This was in marked contrast to the trend in manufacturing investment. "Presumably, it reflects a difference in the labor intensity of U.S. manufacturing investment in the developing countries compared with that in the developed countries" (Dicken 1992, p. 67).

In terms of both investment and employment, Canada and United Kingdom declined in relative importance. Europe was the dominant focus of about half the world total of both investment and employment. Outside Europe, the countries of Brazil, Mexico,[27] and the NICs (New Industrializing Countries of Singapore, South Korea, Malaysia and Taiwan) had spectacular growth in U.S. manufacturing investment and employment.

A Qualifying Note: Subcontracting

Quantitative analyses are important tools in understanding international aggregates of such things as the amount of foreign manufacturing investment and employment of U.S. TNCs. These figures assist in understanding the nature of TNCs and the depth and degree of their geographical spread. But, in some instances these figures do not illuminate other important factors. Foreign direct investment in manufacturing alone does not reflect the strategic importance that this investment can have on both home and host countries. For example, when the United Auto Workers Union sits down to bargain with the auto industry, management's threat to relocate, if concessions by the union are not given, is a very real cause for concern. The power relations that develop as a result of foreign direct investment remain hidden when merely reporting aggregate figures (Ross and Trachte 1990, p. 7).

Similarly, when FDI in manufacturing is reported as leaving the United States and going to, Mexico for example, one should not immediately assume industrial development for Mexico occurs. United States TNCs have invested nearly $2 billion in the Mexican Maquiladoras (border between U.S. and Mexico). The nearly 1,000 plants in this region employ some 310,000 Mexican workers. Unfortunately, the disadvantage for Mexico, in addition to low pay and horrendous working conditions, is that these plants are 100 percent foreign owned and provide little or no linkage of assembly activities to the Mexican economy (UNCTC 1988, p. 170). The deindustrialization of the U.S., as firms move manufacturing operations overseas, should not immediately infer industrialization elsewhere.

Foreign Direct Investment figures alone do not capture comprehensively the relocation of manufacturing. Subcontracting is a means of capital relocation that is not included in the figures reported as direct investment in manufacturing. Although there is little data on the dollar value and number of subcontracting relationships, research suggests that as a result of the global interconnectedness of TNCs, subcontracting relationships occur at a much larger degree today than several years ago. Subcontracting should be viewed as one of the ranges of possibilities open to firms in organizing production (Holmes 1986, pp. 80-100).

Subcontracting is when a firm has a written agreement with another firm (vendor) to undertake production or subassembly of goods according to the specifications of the firm who has contracted the work out. Four major reasons that relate to the structure and nature of labor supply conditions have been found to influence the extent to which subcontracting will take place in a particular industry:

- Subcontracting to minimize and control labor costs— Subcontracting provides an important means of minimizing the costs of variable capital to the parent firm since it acts as both a mechanism ensuring wage discipline and as a method for segmenting the labor force.
- Subcontracting to retain flexibility with respect to variable capital—Utilization of subcontracting to capture differences in the price of labor and also to treat labor as a variable cost of production.
- Subcontracting to maintain managerial control over the labor process—Used as a weapon against labor to either accept managerial prerogatives or risk capital relocating elsewhere.
- Subcontracting to ensure adequate supply of labor—Tap into sources of labor not normally available (Holmes 1986, pp. 92-94).

The relationship between the contacting firms and their vendors are different than the mere purchasing of goods. The firm contracting the work has a degree of control both directly and indirectly over the other firm. Direct control over the vendor is done under strict specifications and written agreements of how the product is to be made, how much of the product is required and in what time frame, as well as where to ship the finished product.

The contracting firm also has a degree of indirect control over the vendor. If a vendor begins to shift over most of his/her manufacturing capacity to the contracting firm, then the managerial operations of that firm are at the whim of the contracting firm. Eventually the "independent" vendor becomes more of a subsidiary to the contracting firm but bears all the expense of market fluctuations. Contracting relationships have been found to be very uneven between contracting firm and vendor, usually benefiting the contracting firm (Holmes 1986, p. 88).[28]

In the garment and textile industries, firms frequently contract out work to independent "jobbers" located in low-wage countries. These independent work sites are not formal subsidiaries of the apparel firm and the firm makes no investment in plant or equipment. Often, the foreign work site seeks its own capital to finance the equipment needed to do the work.

Global finance also has played a major role in the relocation of manufacturing that does not show up in direct investment data. It is important to underscore the possibility that loans made to Third World countries are going towards the financing of private and state-owned manufacturing facilities that are being used by U.S. TNCs.

Also, practices in the textiles and garment industries cannot be explained simply as a relocation of production from developed to developing countries in the search for lower labor costs. Other factors are involved such as specific markets, subcontracting and licensing, exchange rates and flexibility to react to consumer tastes, all of which are major issues to be considered other than low wages (Elson 1988, pp. 352-376). It is important to note that the number of workers employed in a subcontracting arrangement does not show up in the statistics reported for employment levels of foreign owned manufacturing facilities (Ross and Trachte 1990, p. 87).

Joint ventures are another means of relocating production that does not appear in the figures reported in foreign direct investment. For example, General Motors has a joint venture with a Korean automobile firm by the name of Daewoo. General Motors owns a share of the Korean firm; both have agreed to a joint venture to produce a subcompact car for the American market. In return General Motors shifts some production of its subcompacts from the U.S. to plants in Korea. General Motors investment in the production of this vehicle is considerably less than building a new plant in Korea.[29]

Internationalization of Services

Another important avenue for creating shifts in global economic activity is through the service industries. The service industry is a complement to and not a substitute for manufacturing. Hence, It would be incorrect to assume that service Foreign Direct Investment (FDI) is displacing industrial FDI. But, aside from this fact, there has been a growing interdependency between these two sectors, and, in some ways services have become arenas of capitalist accumulation in their own right.

Before exploring more deeply into the role that services play in the world economy, a review of what services are, in general, is important.

Services can be and often are regarded as intangible, perishable and requiring consumption at the time and place of production. The service industry includes the construction services (site preparation, buildings etc.), transportation (freight and passenger), financial services (banking, credit, securities), trade services (wholesale and retail), communications, insurance and health related services, to name a few (Dicken 1992, p. 351).

As difficult as it is to determine what constitutes a service, other problems arise in classifying them. One way to classify services is to see them in relation to how far removed they are from the earth's physical resources. Problems associated with this type of classification underscore separation between goods and service, and fail to capture any interdependencies.

Another way is to categorize services as either consumer or producer (business) services. These types of classifications focus attention on the final customer of the particular service. Unfortunately, these types of categorization fail to recognize that some services are "mixed," being both consumer and producer oriented (Dicken 1992, pp. 350-352).

Still another way is to view services within the production chain. By viewing services this way, one takes into consideration the imputs prior to production, those integral to the production process as well as the operation of a firm, and those service imputs that are necessary for final sale (UNCTAD 1988, p. 177). This classification also carries with it a number of problems when one considers output that goes to other service industries (Riddle 1986, p. 25).

The definition and classification of services have been part and parcel of several debates that show the importance (or unimportance) of services to manufacturing. It has been argued that services are mere spin-offs of manufacturing (Britton 1990, p. 532) while some see services not as peripheral or supportive to goods production, but enabling the production of goods (Riddle 1986, pp. 21-28).

It has been well documented that many services are imputs to industrial production (Blade 1987, pp. 164-165; Gershuny and Miles 1983, p. 30; Petit 1986, p. 123). As was reported earlier, Cohen and Zysman (1987) argue that 25 percent of the U.S. Gross National Product (GNP) originates in services used as imputs to goods-producing industries. Service imputs to the production process have been in the transportation, construction, utilities and business services sectors (Britton 1990, p. 531).

By the 1970s and 1980s service industries began to internationalize and enter other branches as in financial systems. As a result, the complementariety of services to manufacturing also spread. In fact, many services are owned by manufacturing corporations. This point is evident when reviewing U.S. figures on FDI in services.

FDI in Services. Not only is a significant portion of U.S. FDI made up of services, but the share of outward stocks in services have been on the rise. The total share of services in FDI is about 43 percent. From 1977 to 1986 (and at the expense of the extractive industries), the share of services to total FDI went from $60 billion to $119 billion (UNCTC 1988, pp. 372-373). As can be imagined, the composition of FDI in services varies greatly. More than 80 percent of U.S. FDI in services is in finance (banking, insurance and other financial services) and trade-related services (whole sale and retail). Financial services occupy more than 50 percent of these two sectors (UNCTC 1988, p. 383).

The internationalization of capital that allowed the growth of finance was, in part, a result of the creation of international markets for national currencies. This was made possible by floating exchange rates and Eurodollars;[30] which signaled the creation of more global financial and securities houses. This triggered the proliferation of new financial instruments (Thrift 1989, pp. 34-38).

The Importance of Manufacturing in Services. Industrial corporations have played a dominate role in administering services in other countries. As significant as Transnational Banks (TNBs) has been the growth of finance-related affiliates of non-financial corporations. A example of this can be seen in the diversification of General Electric (GE) into financial services. In 1993, General Electric had revenues of $60.5 billion of which $22.1 billion or 36 percent was made up of GE Capital Services (financial services).[31] In that same year, GE had earnings[32] of $4.3 billion, of which $1.8 billion or 41 percent was from GE financial services. In 1993, GE financial services earnings increased by 21 percent over the previous year (General Electric Annual Report 1993, pp. 26-27). Also, in 1987, Ford Motor Company made 18 percent of its profits from financial services and planned to move further into worldwide finances in the future (Thrift 1989, p. 32).

In the 1980s, marketing affiliates of industrial corporations gained a greater importance in trade-related activities than "stand alone" TNC trading companies (mainly due to the fact that the world's largest manufacturing TNCs have created their own trading departments). Two other important points need to be made. First, about half of all foreign service affiliates are owned by industrial corporations,[33] and second, 4/5 of the U.S. wholesale trade is owned by industrial corporations (UNCTC 1988, pp. 382-396).

In all, industrial corporations of the United States account for 50 percent of the outward FDI stock in services. Whether measured by percentage of assets, sales or employment abroad, United States industrial companies are far more transnational than United States service corporations[34]. Within those service industries controlled by service TNCs, a handful of service conglomerates controls most of the activity (UNCTC 1988, p. 420). Even considering these facts, some service TNCs have become arenas of capitalist accumulation in their own right and there has been a growing interdependency between industrial and service TNCs.

Intermeshing of Industrial and Service Production. American Express (AE) is one of the largest non-bank securities and financial firm on the entire globe. In 1986, its operating capital was $14.1 billion and total assets of $99.4 billion. These figures far surpass the second and third place holders. AE as well as other service industries are also major purchasers of industrial production equipment. AE spends nearly $500 million dollars a year on transnational computer equipment; the Bank of New York spent nearly $1.2 billion dollars in 1985 to revamp its computer and communications networks. The "facilitative ether" that Transnational Banks and non-bank banks offer within the arena of financing international production goes without saying (UNCTC 1988, pp. 119 and 430).

Not only are many service industries spin-offs of manufacturing and other industries, but links within the service industry can offer significant accumulation patterns in their own right. The linkages between finance institutions and legal and accounting agencies or between advertising and marketing consultants with other service firms are very important to the health and vitality of many firms (Britton 1990, p. 534). The accounting firm of Arthur Anderson operates in over 40 countries and employs more than 43,000 people (Thrift 1989, p. 32).

The linkages from goods-producing industries to service TNCs can be seen in the telecommunications industry, which makes it possible for manufacturers to conduct business on a global scale. It might be argued that management consulting firms have indeed contributed to the value added in the production of goods when one takes into consideration the importance that many companies pay to "flexible work systems" (i.e., lean production and post-Fordist manufacturing). Quinn and Gagnon (1986, p. 101) argue that about 75 percent of the total value added in the U.S. goods sector is created by service activities within that sector. In another way, advertising, which does nothing to enhance the value of a commodity, is a vital element in the competition between enterprises.

At the level of capitalist economies, services and goods production can be viewed as interdependent. Firms are better able to compete when a quantity of knowledge (information services) is available. Information and handling technologies have offered many corporations avenues to increase profits. (Britton 1990, p. 543).

Intermeshing services and production increases high wage service jobs attached to production. The internationalization of production means a loss of these positions as a service industry follows manufacturing. It is also true that services have developed as a result of other service industries . And, if the internationalization of services continues, so too will the growth of other U.S. services companies outside the domestic economy. Those services considered "stand alone" will grow in those OECD economies that offer the greatest return on investment, not necessarily in the United States.

The Role of Services in the Internationalization of Capital. The international service industries had significant support from the Reagan Administration, which had a obvious interest in the international services industry. That administration assisted in creating a Services Advisory Committee to offer service industries direct collaboration with the U.S government on issues relating to trade. Also, the Reagen

Administration felt that U.S. international services could assist the president in "throw[ing] its weight on the side of other liberal interests . . . to offset the traditional protectionist lobbies . . . which had been gaining in strength due to the shift of most of organized labor to the protectionist camp" (Gibbs 1985, p. 200).

In international trade negotiations like GATT, the United States government moved to lower barriers for service industries resulting from the clear advantage the U.S. had and has, *vis a vis* other countries (Gibbs 1985, pp. 200-204). During the 1970s, the conventional theory of a post-industrial society[35] (the shifting out of manufacturing) was raised as a answer to the United States economic problems (Bell 1976, p. 14).

One plausible explanation for the move towards the internationalization of services is not so much centered in bolstering the U.S. economy, but on increasing the financial strength of service conglomerates. This line of reasoning is similar to that seen in the internationalization of U.S. manufacturing to increase U.S. profits.

At one high level of abstraction, the difference among manufacturing or service TNCs is academic. The "bottom line" is the balance sheet. General Motors in not in the car making industry, Arthur Anderson is not in the accountancy business and Exxon is not in the oil business. They are all in the profit making business. What TNCs require are a presence in any market that will allow them to make money; the ability to operate free of regulation that puts them at a disadvantage; and the ability to gain access to the lowest cost imputs that allows their respective industries to operate. Unfortunately, so very often these objectives have been met to the detriment of large segments of human population, while at times being "packaged" as being best for "the country."

Recap: Relating the Data to Some of the Theories of Relocation

Together, the quantitative and qualitative data supply evidence as to the reasons why TNCs relocate overseas. The evidence seems to point to the claim that there are a vast number of reasons why relocation occurs (as posited by Marx's' internationalization of capital) other than just to low wage countries. TNCs relocation is also dependent on the type of industrial manufacturing being performed. As industrial manufacturing relocates, the service industry is pulled along facilitating the growth .

Not all TNCs relocate to the same countries for the same reasons. Some of the criticisms leveled against exchange and distribution theories, together with the production oriented approaches, are, for the most part, substantiated by some of the data. A quick review of the automobile and semiconductor industries and, in some respects, the garment industry, reveals some interesting points.

The geographic restructuring of automobile assembly is most telling. Its geographic spread was concentrated within the developed countries and not in the low wage areas of the globe. This fact does not support exchange oriented theories of capital spanning the globe in search for low labor costs. Production in the developed countries took advantage of high skill and technology levels that were conducive to assembly procedures.

Some researchers argue that the "world car" and "global sourcing" of automobile parts production cannot substantiate the production and exchange oriented approaches of Warren (1980) and Frobel et al (1980). The "world car" and "global sourcing" concepts, believed to industrialize many Third World countries and supply lower labor costs to the industrialized countries, were eventually abandon by the auto makers (or used to a less degree than was anticipated). Instead, the automobile companies chose to locate production closer to final markets[36] and use many industrialized countries for the global sourcing of parts (Hoffman and Kaplinsky 1988).

Transnational corporations in general and automobile manufacturing specifically are not following one manufacturing trajectory (i.e., to low-wage countries). Political, technological, economic and social factors influence the varied paths of automobile manufacturing.

In some instances, global sourcing of automobile parts from low-wage countries is economically advantageous. At other times, it may be more advantageous to utilize the "company town" approach, where the fabrication of parts and assembly are confined mainly to one general location. This is done in Japan by Toyota and by the Saturn Corporation in Spring Hill, Tennessee.

Still, in some instances the use of "cross penetration" is utilized. Cross penetration consists of production alliances with rival producers,

(These alliances were pointed out in the pervious discussion on joint ventures). Ford, for example, has an alliance with Mazda (Ford owns 25 percent of Mazda) to standardize major component parts of their new models for sale in Japan, the United States and Europe. General Motors and Toyota have a similar alliance.

The purpose of these alliances is to stimulate technological improvements, reduce production costs without sacrificing model design and performance, and gain the capacity to shift parts supply bases quickly in response to currency movements and trade barriers (Hill 1989, p. 173). At least for the present time in the auto industry, a variety of options (or arsenal of weapons) are available for the automobile TNCs to increase their profits.

The semiconductor industry (chip assembly and testing), operating in some of the East and South Asian countries, supports the claim that capital searches for lower labor costs. But, the evidence also indicates that Warren's argument for industrializing parts of the globe is weak. High technology imputs and most of the R&D in the semiconductor industry, that could be seen to help industrialize many foreign countries, remains in the industrialized countries (as is the case of the United States semiconductor research).

Also, neither the exchange-oriented or production-oriented approaches discussed the possibility of relocating production back to the United States or to other developed countries. As already mentioned one of the criticisms of the exchange oriented-approach dealt with the role that technology could play at increasing the productivity of labor. It is technological advancements that have allowed for a small portion of semi-conductor work to relocate back to the United States and to other locations in the developed countries.

But, as was alluded to earlier, it would be incorrect to assume that a reversal of manufacturing decline will appear in the developed countries. Further investment in the developed countries may have a tendency to displace more jobs than are being added. "Deindustrialization, in the sense of job loss in manufacturing, may paradoxically be as much if not more a result of a certain kind of re industrialization (in investment rather than employment terms) than a result of a dispersal of manufacturing to the Third World" (Sayer 1986, p. 121).

Political and economic considerations within host and home countries have had a very favorable impact in the semiconductor industry. Capital's attraction to these countries also revolves around a "green" labor force, inexperienced in labor organization; laws allowing for the extension of working hours, the scope of multiple shifts, and ease with which the labor force can be replaced; and the state suppression of labor organizations. In the United States the tariff structure makes it very favorable for the re importation of semiconductors from offshore plants (Sayer 1986, p.114).

The industry that best exemplifies exchange oriented theories of capital relocation, is the garment industries. Low wages are a main consideration for this industry. Many of the subcontracting "jobbers" very often are quite similar to the garment sweatshops that were so prevalent at one time in New York City. Although the exchange oriented theories do not address important factors (other than low wages) that have contributed to the location of capital (such as loans to assist the development of subcontracts within the Third World and "favorable" subcontracting agreements), the garment industry still remains a solid example of exchange oriented approaches.

As the shift in manufacturing from the United States to overseas locations continues, growing economic decline in the U.S. is left in its wake. It is to the discussion of these issues and many more that are now reviewed.

NOTES

1.   Theories of location, more or less centered on the (right), are couched in Orthodox economic theories. The theory of "comparative advantage" argues that production location is determined by the relative comparative advantage of producing nations in the production of particular goods. Comparative advantage is a function of relative factor endowments (Howes 1993, p. 50). Theories of these sorts see the world as being free of market "imperfections" and very often do not incorporate the importance of power relations or worker struggles.

2.   The author realizes the variety of different ways a NIDL and the debates can be categorized.

3.   The author would like to acknowledge a number of other scholars who have made important contributions to these debates (NIDL). Time and space have limited a careful review of their work:

Frank, A.G. 1980. "Crisis in the Third World.;" Hymer, S. 1972. "The Multinational Corporation and the Law of Uneven Development" in *Economics and World Order.*; Cardoso, H. 1974. "Dependency and Development in Latin America" in *New Left Review.*; Castells, Manuel. 1985. "High Technology, Economic Restructuring and the Urban-Regional Process in the United States." in Manuel Castells ed, *High Technology, Space. and Society,*.

4. With EPZs, transnational corporations own and manage these production enclaves. Under contract processing, TNCs transmit intermediate products to factories under contract. On sending back these finished products the host country receives a payment.

5. This line of argument (Industrialization thesis) will be more thoroughly explored when reviewing production oriented approaches to a NIDL.

6. Wallerstein has coined the term semi-periphery and defined it as a region between core and periphery that acts not only as a buffer to impede retaliation by the periphery against the core, but also is seen as both exploiter and exploited within trading relations.

7. Skocpol, T. 1977. "Wallersteins World Capitalist System" *American Journal of Sociology*; Brenner, R. 1977. "The Origins of Capitalist Development" *New Left Review.*; and Ross and Trachte, 1990 (see bibliography)

8. Baran, Paul. 1957. *The Political Economy of Growth.* New York: Monthly Review; Frank, Andre Gunder. 1967. *Capitalism and Underdevelopment in Latin America.* New York: Monthly Review.

9. For example: Aglietta, Michel. 1979. *A Theory of Capitalist Regulation*, Norfolk, England: Lowe and Brydone Printers Limited.

10. Defined as follows "The *regime of accumulation* describes the stabilization over a long period of the allocation of the net product between consumption and accumulation; it implies some correspondence between the transformation of both the conditions of production and the condition of the reproduction of wage earners. It also implies some forms of linkage between capitalism and other modes of production .. There must exist a materialization of the regime of accumulation taking the form of norms, habits, laws, regulating networks and so on that ensure the unity of the process ... This body of internalized rules and social processes is called the *mode of regulation.*" (Lipietz 1986, p. 19)

Central to his argument is the use of the terms "bloody Taylorism" and "peripheral Fordism." Bloody Taylorism relates to the exploitation in wages and intensity of work found in EPZs. Peripheral Fordism relates to how qualified positions of employment (engineering) stays in the core while deskilled execution and assembly is moved to peripheral countries. Lipietz describes the entire process with the term "Global Fordism" (Lipietz 1986, pp. 30-33).

11. see footnote 10

12. This is due to the contradictions of capital (the way capital restructures itself) which gives way to a fall in the rate of profit. This body of knowledge is couched in the term "crisis theory." The authors view on crisis theory is discussed in appendix C.

The internationalization of capital provides for a more complex analysis of the NIDL than the more mono-causal explanations that focused on only one moment of the circuit of capital (like market exchange relations). One difference between Marx's "internationalization of capital" and the other approaches is that the internationalization of capital approach gives attention to class relations and accompanying struggles as well as periods of crises resulting from competing international capitals. Both these factors can assist in shaping the unfolding of capital.

13. This point was discussed by Lipietz

14. This point can be seen by viewing the amount of garment manufacturing (clothing) returning to New York city. The author's problem with this example is that it is not production techniques that have allowed for this but low labor costs coupled with the use of illegal immigrant and child labor.

15. Does not include services and extractive industries

16. Those TNCs with a billion dollars or more in sales.

17. This is due in part to the rise of foreign TNCs within the global economy.

18. A growing share of foreign direct investment (FDI) has been going towards services (activities in trading, banking finance and insurance and business and commercial activities). By 1985, it was the service sector and not the manufacturing sector which contained the largest share of FDI (Dicken 1992, p. 58). "However, it would be misleading to think of services FDI as displacing industrial FDI, Rather, what one observes is the growth of a global economy in which an increasing share of both goods and services are being produced by TNCs (UNCTC 1988, p. 372). The internationalization of services will be taken up later.

19. Textiles industry (consisting of the yarn preparation and fabric manufacture) and apparel industry (consisting of the manufacturing of the garment) are certainly important industries that have an enormously important impact in U.S. trade relations and are widely discussed in the literature. But foreign direct investment in these two industries has been quite low compared with the industries of auto and electronics. This is a result of the vast usage of subcontracting within these industries especially in garment manufacturing (see Ross and Trachte 1990, p. 90).

20. This is assembly production facilities only. Both General Motors and Ford utilize parts production from a variety of developed countries around the globe.

21. The remaining one-third was divided up principally between Brazil and Mexico

22. Shell corporation, Exxon and IBM hold the first three spots, respectively, in number of foreign affiliates.

23. 1989 figures

24. This same scenario holds true for the auto industry as well. Numerous articles have claimed that production plants, such as the GM Saturn facility in Tennessee points to industrial rise in the U.S. A few auto plants opening in the U.S. does not even out the over 20 GM plants alone that are/will close. United States manufacturing growth will not offset the number of jobs lost to U.S. TNCs overseas manufacturing.

25. It should be noted that employment figures do not take into consideration non-equity forms of employment and contract employment. As a result employment figures can be seriously understated (UNCTC 1988, p. 211).

26. These figures are close to the ones published by UNCTC (1988, p. 217)

27. Brazil has high employment and manufacturing investment in auto and electronics industries. Mexico has high employment in manufacturing investment in auto and semi-conductor industries.

28. One major drawback for the contracting firm is the loss of control in the manufacturing operations. In the auto industry, for example, parts production can require a vast amount of engineering requirements and timing of the shipment of the finished product is vital to continue assembly line production. If problems should occur in vendor production, that are beyond the technical scope of the vendor, then the engineering department of the contracting firm must offer assistance. One can quickly imagine the difficulty in immediate on site resolutions of the problem if the contracting firm is in the USA and the vendor is a small shop somewhere in Korea. The authors

experience in the automobile industry confirms this issue of concern for the contracting firm.

29. Another similar example of subcontracting that goes unreported in FDI is when a U.S. based firm contracts work out to a firm located in a different country but within the same company. For example, the author worked as a production control coordinator (as seen in Appendix B). The job entailed coordinating manufacturing and transportation of finished automobile component parts. One of the parts plant was another corporate facility located in Logrono, Spain. This plant made and shipped its products to U.S. assembly plants. Arrangements similar to this one are quite common with the corporation and it can reasonably be expected to occur in the other U.S. automobile corporations.

30. Dollars held in banks outside the United States, eventually these dollars were dumped on the international market.

31. figures are rounded

32. All GE earnings are net figures

33. As of 1982, latest data that could be found.

34. A greater share of service TNCs are located in the developed counties as compared with their industrial counterparts. This is mainly a result of following the industries overseas as well as the inability of service corporations to "unwrap" their services and distribute them to low-wage countries.

35. The authors' research does not adhere to the theoretical foundations of a post-industrial society. The conventional theory of a post-industrial economy (shifting from agriculture to manufacturing to services), in case of the United States is theoretically weak. One could argue that the U.S. never shifted out of agriculture, in terms of dollars invested and food produced. Only in employment levels was a marked change noted. For a quick rebuttal of a post-industrial society see Gibb 1985, p. 205.

36. This type of strategy can be seen by viewing the Saturn Corporation were most of the product is made on site and for the U.S. market.

CHAPTER 2

Consequences of Industrial Relocation

THE WINNERS AND LOSERS

Capital in search for ever greater accumulation of profit is one of the main contributors to U.S. deindustrialization. Although the disinvestment of America's basic productive capacity through the relocation of manufacturing has been beneficial to some, it also has had obvious adverse social consequences for many Americans.

Those that Gained the Most

The growth in the international circuits of transnational corporations, accompanied by state policy and international organizations such as the International Monetary Fund (IMF) and the World Bank, facilitated the expansion of overseas investment at the expense of the domestic economy. While the domestic economy declines, a variety of international actors such as export firms, industries and corporate executives are becoming quite monetarily successful.

A number of export processing firms are experiencing growth and prosperity. The value of U.S. exports increased from $201 billion in 1985 to $421.6 billion in 1991 and the volume of U.S. manufactured exports rose by 90 percent between 1986 and 1991. By 1991, more than half of all U.S. exports and imports were transfers of components and services within the same Global corporation, many of them American based (Barnet and Cavanagh 1994, p. 275). In 1991, Hewlett-Packard Corporation had overseas revenues of almost 60 percent of total sales. The U.S. semiconductor industry had its global market share in sales rise from 39.2 percent in 1986 to over 43 percent in 1991 (Petras and Morley 1994, p. 66).

Transnational corporations building overseas are also capturing large profits through their international circuits. Between 1985 and 1987, the Ford Motor Company raised its capital expenditure in Europe by 37 percent, while money spent on their domestic operations fell by 17 percent. General Motors, while losing $2.3 billion between 1980 and 1986, increased their sales in European operations by 60 percent between 1986 and 1991. In 1992, General Motors parts affiliates had sales increases of 18 percent to a total of $4 billion. In the first quarter of 1994, General Motors posted earnings of $1.9 billion. Though this figure is the highest ever recorded in the history of General Motors, they are still closing plants in the United States (Petras and Morley 1995, pp. 82 and 86).

Federal agencies, such as the Agency for International Development and state policy, such as the North American Free Trade Agreemen have not only assisted the expansion of overseas manufacturing but in some ways can be seen as encouraging it. Since 1981 the United States government, through the Agency for International Development, has funneled millions of dollars into the building of EPZs in Central America and the Caribbean Basin. Since 1990, some 30 U.S. apparel manufacturers have shifted their operations into these areas, while about 68 already had their products manufactured there. Domestically, the U.S. clothing industry has closed 58 plants and laid off 12,000 workers (Petras and Morley 1995, p. 85).

The North American Free Trade Agreement (NAFTA) was, at its inception, claimed to create jobs in the U.S. and not encourage manufacturers to relocate to areas such as Mexico. Both the U.S. State Department and the Commerce Department have encouraged capital flight. In December of 1986, appearing before a Congressional subcommittee, Alexander H. Good, director of the U.S. Foreign Service stated: "We are convinced the program has important economic benefits for both the U.S. and Mexican economies ... The Commerce Department supports participation in the Maquiladoras program by U.S. industry because it helps U.S. companies remain healthy in the face of intense international competition and it keeps U.S. employment as high as possible" (Barlett and Steele 1992, p. 35).

There is sound reason to believe that this claim is false. Between 1987 and 1991 U.S. companies have invested $11.6 billion in Mexican plants. While manufacturing jobs increased in these Mexican based affiliates by almost 25 percent between 1986 and 1990, manufacturing jobs in the U.S. rose by less than one percent (Petras and Morley 1995, p. 84). As was mentioned earlier, there is little reason to believe that the Maquiladoras program will industrialize the Mexican economy. It seems more reasonable to assume that the corporations in that area stand to gain the most.

Current supporters of NAFTA now claim that long term benefits will outweigh short term dislocations. Most NAFTA supporters now expect that jobs will be lost, community tax revenues will shrink, and wages will decline. Low U.S. income earners (in the bottom two-thirds of family income distribution) will be hurt worst. But, in the long run, supporters claim that NAFTA will create more jobs and higher wage jobs in the United States and slow emigration from Mexico to the U.S. (Faux 1993, p. 309).

The International Trade Commission made several attempts to show the job growth effects of NAFTA, but concluded that only eight one hundredths of one percent of employment would be added to job growth in the U.S. The study ignored the expected loss of 500,000 to almost a million jobs (Faux 1993, p. 310). A study by The Institute for International Economics, which showed an increase of 170,000 jobs because of NAFTA, was claimed by the Economic Policy Institute to deliberately omit data that showed otherwise. Many projections that do show job increases in the U.S. make assumptions about current trade surpluses with Mexico when these figures are expected to change (Faux 1993, p. 310). A study by economists Timothy Keochlin and Mehrene Larudee reported that an estimated 290,000 to 490,000 jobs would be lost and close to $320 billion in U.S. wages would be lost by the year 2000 (Keochlin and Larudee 1992, pp. 19-24).

The claim that NAFTA will create higher wage jobs in the U.S. should also be viewed with skepticism. Professor Edward Leamer of the University of California, a well known advocate of free trade, estimated that with NAFTA there will be a average wage loss of $1,000 per worker for 70 percent of the labor force.

The NAFTA agreement will not only fail to slow immigration, but may add to it. By drawing Mexican workers closer to the border, paying them low wages and have them work in unsafe and at times unsanitary conditions, could be an incentive for Mexicans to cross into the United States and look for more gainful employment. The NAFTA agreement "is largely an investment agreement designed to protect American investors" and not designed to benefit Mexican or American workers (Faux 1993, pp. 311-313).

Under the direction of the United States government, the World Bank in tandem with the IMF has played a major role in allowing corporations to gain access to Third World economies. These efforts were attempts at bolstering TNCs profits at the expense of many Third World countries and, in effect, contributed to domestic decay in the United States.

The IMF's primary responsibility was to deal with monetary matters with an emphasis on countries suffering from a short term balance of payments problem. Many of the IMF's policies correspond to the policies favored by TNCs. IMF policies were seen to open up the economies of Third World countries and allow for the free movement of goods and money. Transnational corporations, being able to move resources around the world, were eager to move their investment to whichever country offered the best profit potential. Transnational capitalists and local political leaders in host countries have benefited either monetarily and/or politically in aligning themselves with these corporations. TNCs have used their economic and political power to "force" countries to seek IMF assistance and submit to conditions of the IMF (Brett et al. 1983, pp. 18 and 41).

The World Bank was established to provide long term developmental assistance to developing and developed countries. But, like the IMF, it too has been found to benefit large corporations. The World Bank, together with the United States government has successfully forced countries to give up major control of certain projects within their countries to American TNCs. India, for example, was strongly encouraged to give up price controls, marketing rights and the right to use domestic materials over the materials supplied by

TNCs, within their fertilizer and chemical industries (Payer 1982, p. 142).

The World Bank has been further criticized for fostering the growth of local capitalist classes, even in countries where one did not exist; and making sure that the local capitalist class would align itself with international capital. In addition, the World Bank has been accused of pressuring borrowing governments to improve the legal privileges for the tax liabilities of foreign investment, insisting on production for export, which chiefly benefits the corporations that control international trade, opposing minimum wage laws and trade union activity, and opposing all kinds of protection for locally owned businesses and industry (Payer 1982, pp. 19 and 117).

Over the years, the function of the IMF and the World Bank has been one and the same in the international arena . The World Bank together with the IMF used structural adjustment lending (SAL)[1] to pave the way for U.S. corporations to exploit Third World countries. SALs were made available to many Third World countries who were experiencing debt servicing problems.[2] In order to receive an SAL, a country would have to abide by certain conditions which included cutting wages, liberalizing polices to increase imports and establishing incentives for export markets, and removing restrictions to foreign investment, all of which aided U.S. TNC penetration at the expense of the host country[3] (Bello, Cunninghan and Rau 1993, p. 27).

Other international trade agreements, similar to some of the ones negotiated under the General Agreement on Trade and Tariffs (GATT), have reduced tariffs and eliminated some export and import controls. This action has been shown to be in part responsible for the loss of manufacturing employment in the United States (Wood 1994, pp. 175 and 196-210) and at the same time, beneficial to some TNCs (Bello, Cunninghan and Rau 1993, p. 27). For example, in 1991 some 200 Japanese transnationals, operating in Mexico, import products into the U.S. which count as Mexican and not Japanese exports (Barnet 1994, p. 64).

Not only has international trade law aided and abetted international circuits of TNCs, but the U.S. tax code also has encouraged capital flight. The Internal Revenue Service has provided tax credits which allow U.S. subsidiaries to transfer profits from one country to parent companies in the United States without paying taxes on these profits. Pharmaceutical companies such as duPont, SmithKline Beckman,

Bristol Myers-Squibb, and Upjohn, to name a few, have all relocated to Puerto Rico and escaped paying an estimated $14 billion of income and other taxes. Corporations have thus terminated tens of thousands of factory workers jobs in the U.S. (Barlett and Steele 1992, pp. 95-98).

Tax reductions in personal incomes have had very favorable effects for high income earners such as corporate executives. In 1986, just under 200,000 individuals and families with incomes over $100,000 paid an "alternative minimum tax" of $4.6 billion. In 1989, just under 50,000 individuals and families with incomes of over $100,000 paid alternative minimum taxes totaling $476 million. The passage of a adjustment to the alternative minimum tax that was supposed to make everyone pay a "fair share" in taxes resulted in a 75 percent drop in the number of people who paid tax and a 90 percent drop in the amount they paid.

Between 1980 and 1989, the average wage earned by those in the under $20,000 income category (which in 1989 represented nearly 50 percent of all individual returns) rose $123 or 1.4 percent. In that same time period, the average salaries of those with reported incomes of over $1 million rose by 49.5 percent (Barlett and Steele 1992, p. 7).

Between 1989 and 1994, while wages of earners below the 80th percentile declined, the wages or earners in the 90th percentile increased (Baker and Mishel 1995 p. 3). Viewed from another vantage point; between 1979 and 1994 household incomes climbed by 10 percent, but 97 percent of the gain went to the richest 20 percent. Between 1990 and 1994 the percent change in real family income of the top 5 percent of U.S. households went up by 15 percent while family incomes of the lowest 80 percent of U.S. households went down (New York Times 3 March 1996, p. A26; New York Times 8 March 1996, p. A22).

Not only have the incomes of the very rich increased, but so has the number of very rich. In 1981 there were a reported 600,000 millionaires; in 1989 the number of individuals with millionaire status rose to 1.5 million (Phillips, Kevin 1990, p. 156). The top 10 percent of the wealthiest households controlled approximately 68 percent of the nation's wealth in 1986 (Phillips 1990, p. 11).

High paid corporate salaries are also going up. In 1953, executive corporate compensation was equal to 22 percent of corporate profits. By 1987, executive compensation rose to the equivalent of 61 percent of corporate profits (Barlett and Steele 1992, p. 20). During the decade of the 1980s, in one year co-founder of Hewlett-Packard Inc., David Packard, found himself richer by $1.2 billion (Phillips 1990, p. 11).

Since 1986, AT&T has reduced its workforce by 125,000 people but, CEO Robert E. Allen's salary and bonus have increased fourfold, to $3.3 million. Although his salary and bonus was reduced by $200,000 in 1995, he was award options worth $9.7 million (New York Times 9 March 1996, p. A13).

While corporate executive salaries were rising in the 1980s, unionized workers were being forced (through threats of layoffs and plant closings) to negotiate benefit "give backs" and extremely low pay hikes of under 2 percent per year over a three year period, which was below the rate of inflation (Phillips 1990, p. 20). In return for "give backs," management granted job security clauses. Even though many unionized workers capitulated to managerial demands, organized workers across the United States continued to lose their jobs.

Another way corporate salaries and profits have gone up, while disinvestment of the nations productive capacity continued, has been through mergers and acquisitions domestically and globally. The decade of the 1980s has been a time of merger and acquisition mania in the United States. In 1989 alone the value of announced mergers and acquisitions totaled nearly $350 billion. While thousands of workers lost their jobs, as firms cut costs to pay for their mania craze, CEOs and investment bankers and brokers were making handsome profits. Since mergers and acquisitions have been successful for corporate capital in the 1980's, the buying and selling of corporations has continued through the 1990's (Storm 1995, p. A1).

The 1990's wave of mergers will pace ahead of the 1980's. Mergers and acquisitions in 1995 exceed $350 billion. Several mergers and acquisitions have taken place that have been unprecedented in American history, for example:

- Westinghouse acquired CBS for $7.5 billion.
- Southern Pacific Railroad will be absorbed by Union Pacific in a $5.3 billion merger.

- Walt Disney acquired Capital Cities/ABC for an astounding $19 billion.

The banking industry has also been through several mergers and acquisitions:

- Chemical acquired Case Manhattan and cut 12,000 positions
- Wells Fargo acquired First Interstate and cut an estimated 7,000 jobs
- Fleet Financial acquired Shawmut National and severed 2,500 positions

Chief Executive Officer of Chase Manhattan Thomas G. Labrecque commented "If you're doing what you think is right for everyone involved, then you're fine. So I'm fine." Someone is certainly fine at Case but not the workers. From 1985 to 1995 Chase's assets grew by 38 percent while their workforce shrank by 28 percent (New York Times 4 March 1996, p. 1 and A14).

The value of mergers and acquisitions in the United States is only overshadowed by the value of worldwide mergers and acquisitions. In 1995, corporate consolidation worldwide is expected to reach $800 billion, with a two year total of $1.2 trillion (Storm 1995, p. A1).

To further compound matters, Wall Street has given its approval of companies that disinvest in the nations productive capacity. When Sears announced the reduction of 50,000 positions, its stock went up nearly 4 percent. The day Zerox slashed 10,000 jobs its stock climbed 7 percent. AT&T's stock soared when the communications giant announced reducing its workforce by 40,000 workers (New York Times 3 March 1996, p. A28).

The stock market is now booming for some of the largest corporations. Between 1991 and February of 1996 the weekly closings of the Dow Jones average of 30 industrial stocks rose from 3,000 to 5,641.69. In fact, the stock market has reached 81 new highs in 1995. Corporations have found their stocks to rise at the mere mention of downsizing (New York Times 8 March 1996, p. A22).

One way of viewing United States corporate strategy is by seeing it as a catalyst for economic decay, brought about through the elimination of restrictions on corporate activity at home and abroad. Corporate

America's efforts at expanding abroad were to create a global playing field that would be beneficial to a few corporations and a handful of individuals at any expense. The weakness of this strategy was the corporations' preferred mode of regaining competitiveness, which was to cease investment in the country's infrastructure, capital equipment and human capital. The path chosen for restructuring was to depress domestic wages, downsize the workforce and transfer operations abroad.

The Social Indicators of U.S. Economic Decay

The social dislocation resulting from the loss of manufacturing jobs in cities like New York exemplify some of the growing problems in this country:

- Since 1990, New York City has lost an estimated 250,000 jobs . Population is estimated to fall within the decade to 7 million (which is lowest level since the Great Depression), (Fitch 1993, p. 182).
- In 1990, New York City was becoming poorer relative to its suburbs, the state and rest of the U.S. Three of the five boroughs (more than 75 percent of the city's population) have incomes below the national average. An estimated, 6.7 percent of Manhattanites make more than 50 percent of the total personal income in the borough (Fitch 1993, p. 187).
- Crime continues to escalate in New York. It is No. 1 per capita in robbery as compared to the rest of the nation and ranks third in the nation for seven classes of major felonies. Between the late 1950s to 1990 robbery in New York City increased 1600 percent and auto theft increased 1000 percent (Fitch 1993, p. 223-229).
- The level of poverty has soared in New York City. In the 1950s, it was the richest city in the world; by 1990, it became the poorest city in the advanced capitalist world. Nearly one out of every four New Yorkers lives in poverty. In 1950, one out of 25 people was on welfare; in 1990, nearly 1 out of 5 was.
- Housing in the 1990s for New York City residence is scarce and expensive. The Average U.S. renter pays 22 percent of income for rent but, in New York City, 47.5 percent of rental households pay 30 percent of income to rent, nearly one-third

pay more than 40 percent. Fewer housing units are produced now than in the 1950s. One-third of all housing units in New York City were built in the 1920s (Fitch 1993, pp. 242-252).

New York City is not an isolated instance of domestic disintegration but an example of what has occurred in many major cities across the United States. In addition to the decay of many industrial cities there has been a increase of wealth concentrations and income inequalities in the United States.

During the 1980s one of the nation's largest redistribution of wealth occurred. "While overall family after-tax income rose by 15.7 percent, the income of families in the bottom decile fell by 10.4 percent, from $4,791 to $4,295 (in constant 1990 dollars) while the income of those in the top one percent rose by 87.1 percent, from $213,675 to $399,697" (Edsall and Edsall 1992, p. 23). To further emphasizes the problem, the income held by the middle 20 percent of Americans is at the lowest point since 1947, the year at which that data began to be reported.

Wage inequality and wage deterioration continues to plague American families throughout the 1990s. The bottom four-fifths of families had less income in 1993 than in 1989. Between 1989 and 1994 the real wages among the bottom 80 percent of all male wage earners has declined. Adjusted for inflation, the median wage is nearly 3 percent below what it was in 1979. Trends such as these are expected to continue (Baker and Mishel 1995, p. 2).

To further underscore wage inequality and deterioration, between 1990 and 1992, while blue collar workers feared losing their jobs through manufacturing relocation, their incomes rose by a mere 2.6 percent. During that same time the incomes of 360 CEOs from the largest corporations, most of which are transnational, rose by 26 percent (Petras and Morley 1995, p. 119).

The slight rise in the incomes of blue collar was overshadowed by the drastic rise in poverty in the United States. From 1977 to 1988 the number of Americans living in poverty increased five fold to 32 million. By 1991 the figure rose to 35.7 million[4] (Petras and Morley 1995, p. 123). Some figures show that in 1989, 11 million workers (or one in every seven) held year-round, full-time jobs and earned less than

$11,500 annually (Schwarz and Volgy 1992, p. 81). Other figures show that in 1987, roughly two out of every five poor people in the United States had incomes of less than 50 percent of the official poverty line. The probability of poor people escaping poverty dropped sharply in the 1980s, after rising in the 1960s and early 1970s. (Currie 1990, p. 302.).

Another social indicator that rose was the unemployment level of those who worked in well paid blue collar and white collar industrial jobs. Between 1987 and 1991, 5.7 million white collar workers lost their jobs. Factory workers as a percent of the total workforce declined from 20 percent in the 1980s to 17 percent in 1991, and continues to fall (Petras and Morley 1995, p. 124 and 152).

The lack of jobs and a decaying standard of living have brought on a wave of increasing crime rates. Statistics on the rate of violent crimes committed per 100,000 people increased from 364 violent crimes in 1970 to 597 in 1980 to 732 in 1990. Between 1989 and 1990, homicides increased by nine percent to an all time high of 23,440. Within 12 months this record was broken when 24,700 Americans were murdered. As a result of soaring crime rates, the U.S. now incarcerates more people than any other country on the globe, some 455 per 100,000 population. The incarceration rate for black Americans is an astounding 3,370 per 100,000 (Petras and Morley 1995, p. 147).

At the same time the economic conditions mentioned above were worsening, adequate housing was becoming more scarce, homelessness was increasing and the infrastructure (roads, bridges and highways) was decaying, past presidential administrations cut programs that would have mediated their impact. The result was lower unemployment benefits, reduced monies for social programs (such as AFDC[5]), cutbacks in federal food programs, public employment and job-creation efforts, while simultaneously encouraging growth of low wage employment.

Little help seems on the way from the current administration. President Clinton has laid plans to cap the length of time American citizens are allowed to stay on welfare, reduce the amount of money in his economic stimulus package that would have created more jobs and has endorsed policies that continue to aid TNCs in relocating manufacturing abroad. The decade of the 1980s and the early years of the 1990s can be characterized by spreading deprivation amidst selective pockets of rising employment and economic growth for a few Americans.

While spreading deprivation continues to escalate in the United States, it is difficult to imagine how manufacturing employment decline can be stabilized by the globalization of production or offset by job growth in the service sector.

Manufacturing Employment Decline Versus Job Growth

Several industries have closed manufacturing plants throughout the U.S., resulting in the layoffs of thousands of workers. Some federal government studies have concluded that between 1983 and 1989, nearly 10 million workers lost their jobs for these reasons (Portz 1990, p. viii). Other figures report that from 1979 through 1995 and estimated 43 million jobs will vanish in the United States (New York Times 3 March 1996, p. 1). A few key figures highlight the increasing loss of jobs.

- One of the world's largest car manufacturer, General Motors, plans to shut down 23 assembly and components operations which will affect nearly 100,000 workers.
- Throughout the United States, Western Electric eliminated 4,000 from their payroll.
- Allied Signal, the aerospace, automotive and engineered materials company, "restructured" and 5,000 jobs vanished.
- J. I. Case, the construction and farm equipment maker, eliminated some 4,000 workers jobs.
- Computer giant IBM, which had a reputation for guaranteeing job security, will layoff 20,000 of its workforce.

The drive towards the globalization of production is not increasing jobs in the domestic economy but, is in fact, relocating jobs to developed and developing countries. Nor is globalization causing the U.S. economy to grow. "Domestic employment attributable to manufacturing fell from 27 percent in 1970 to 19 percent in 1985. In the same period, the share of the gross national product (GNP) contributed by manufacturing, measured in current dollars, tumbled from nearly 25 percent to less than 20 percent. Even in dollars adjusted for inflation, in every manufacturing industry except computers the contribution to GNP declined" (Harrison and Bluestone 1988, p. 28).

Millions of workers are now competing for a shrinking number of manufacturing jobs. While not all of the job losses can be attributed to overseas relocation, the number of jobs created in developing and developed countries by TNC relocation (4.07 million jobs as of 1987 as reported earlier) certainly would have increased U.S. employment levels if those industries had stayed in their country.

Some researchers such as Grunwald and Flamm (1985) have questioned the effect that the movement of some industries abroad has had on the stability of production employment in the United States. They state "the movement toward more assembly abroad [within the semiconductor industry], however, seems to have had little or no discernible effect on the instability of U.S. production employment . . . " (Grunwald and Flamm 1985, p. 101). They also maintain that an increase in the "nonproductive employment" associated with a shift in production employment of semiconductors abroad, has served to stabilize employment levels.

It is most interesting to note that Grunwald and Flamm, in the second half of their book, qualify their quantitative data and state that their figures "exclude[s] indirect effects on employment in other industries that supply components or use the finished product" (Grunwald and Flamm 1985, p. 222).

These forward and backward linkages that accompany an industry are, in fact, vital factors to be considered in determining employment levels. One only has to study the automobile industry, where hundreds of thousands of people are employed as a result of the industries' presence, to gain a clear meaning of the importance of "indirect" employment levels. For example, it has been estimated that the automobile industry is responsible for one-forth of the value of all retail sales, the jobs of nearly one out of every six American workers and the economic health of one in every six businesses in the United States (Hill 1982, p. 1).

Also absent from Grunwald and Flamm's figures is the possibility of increases in the number of "non-productive" employment levels if the semiconductor industries came back to the United States.

The debate on how foreign direct investment effects employment levels in the United States has been addressed in a book on the power of TNCs entitled *Global Reach*, by Richard Barnet and Ronald Muller. These authors consider the Harvard Business school's claim that foreign direct investment abroad creates jobs in the U.S. on the one hand, and the AFL-CIO's claim that U.S. jobs are being lost by foreign direct investment on the other (Barnet and Muller 1974, p. 290-301).

Although the authors concluded that long term effects of foreign direct investment "seem" to be unfavorable to the creation of jobs, their work was later followed by other researchers who conclusively found that FDI results in a reduction of jobs (Bluestone and Harrison 1982, p. 44).

What Richard Barnet and Ronald Muller did conclude was that even if jobs on the production line were being replaced with jobs within the service sector, this change cannot be justified in any political or human sense. "The changing composition of the workforce and its changing geographical location brought about by the globalization of U.S. industry are affecting the lives of millions of Americans in serious and largely unfortunate ways" (Barnet and Muller 1974, p.302).

The replacement of production employment with service jobs is an important point to be investigated. Several researchers have claimed that industries in the service sector and other white collar high paying positions are employing a large number of workers who lost their jobs in manufacturing . Between 1975 and 1980, some 12 million new jobs were added to the American economy, all within the service sector. Of this 12 million, nearly 10.2 million were in the private sector and concentrated mainly in the retail trades, fast food restaurants, banks and hospitals.

The service industry should not be seen as "replacing" the workers that have been displaced from their manufacturing jobs. Most of the employment in these fields offers low wages and few benefits. For example, in the retail trades, employees earn less than 45 percent of the average weekly wage of a manufacturing worker (Cohen and Zysman 1987, pp. 54-55). And, there is some evidence that shows it is unclear that low paying jobs have proliferated as manufacturing employment declined (Schwarz and Vogly 1992, p. 83).

Although the service sector and other white collar positions may have been an important engine for growth in employment in the 1980s, fully 82 percent of the gain in male employment during this time was in jobs paying below poverty-level wages (Currie 1990, p. 306).

The situation has changed little for the early 1990's. Of the 19.7 million workers who entered the workforce between January of 1990 and January of 1991 an astounding 53 percent were in the employment fields of sales, administrative support including clerical and the services. Within these employment fields the largest concentration of new workers were in occupations such as cashiers, secretaries, receptionists, janitors, cooks, waiters, waitresses, and child care workers (Berman 1993. p. 15).

The service sector itself is now showing signs of employment reductions. The U.S. Bureau of Labor Statistics has reported that by the early 1990's job loss has become more common among white collar workers than it had in the 1980's. In a surveyed population of 2.8 million workers displaced between 1991 and 1992, more than 50 percent last held white collar positions (Gardner 1995, p. 48).

Throughout the 1990's workers with a least some college education make up the majority of people whose jobs were eliminated, out numbering those with a high school education. In fact, white collar positions paying at least $50,000 per year account for twice the share of the lost jobs than they did in the 1980's (New York Times 3 March 1996, p. 1).

Several hundreds of thousands of positions are being shed in the service type positions within major transnational corporations in the United States. In the 1990s, while many of these corporations attempt to streamline (or "rightsize" as opposed to downsize) their managerial staff and technicians in efforts to cut costs, the service sector may no longer offer low wage employment to those feverishly looking for work. Even in some of the lower paying service jobs there have been employment reductions. Some 115,000 jobs were abolished in the financial sector during 1990 and 1991. In this same period, 525,000 retail jobs disappeared (Petras and Morley 1995, p. 160)

Many high wage service-type jobs, such as product design, inventory control, accounting, financing, training, testing etc. are directly linked to manufacturing. Loss of manufacturing means the loss of these types of jobs. Some 25 percent of the U.S. Gross National Product (GNP) originates in services used as imputs by goods producing industries (Cohen and Zysman 1987, p. 22).

A commonly held belief is that the United States can run a trade surplus in services to offset the U.S. merchandise deficit. Financial services (banking) is offered as one main example of the type of service that could offset deficits in the merchandise account. It is clear that financial services will not offset massive American deficits in manufacturing. Service exports were about one-fifth the size of world merchandise exports, and this figure is not expected to change. United States banking services will not offset our merchandise account (Cohen and Zysman 1987, p. 42). Foreign banks are larger and are growing larger at a faster rate than U.S. banks (Dicken 1992, p. 368; Barnet and Cavanagh 1994, p. 391).

Although attempting to do so, U.S. banks are failing to dominate the world market in financial services. Foreign banks are penetrating the U.S. market, accounting for more than 40 percent of large commercial loans in New York City and San Francisco. Although large U.S. Transnational Banks (TNBs) are generating profits, foreign TNBs are providing strong competition for them around the globe (Cohen and Zysman 1987, p. 42).

Charges that American production jobs are being lost to foreign countries are often answered with statistics indicating numbers of new employment positions created in the U.S. However, what is too often not mentioned are the *types* of jobs being created in the domestic market. Very often, these low paying, low quality employment positions are without the benefits package normally associated with production jobs. Also, high tech employment positions merely claim to be the greatest hope in generating employment.

A recent employment trend has been toward the drastic acceleration of part-time and temporary work. "According to federal government statistics, these [part-time and temporary jobs] accounted for about half of all new jobs in 1992, up from less than a quarter of new jobs a decade ago. In the private sector, the figure was closer to two-thirds. And of the 380,000 new jobs created in January 1993, an astronomical 90 percent offered only part-time work." (Petras and Morley 1995, p. 125). Much of this employment pays close to minimum wage levels and is rarely accompanied by benefits such as health and pension plans.

The field of biotechnology was claimed to offer the greatest hopes in generating high employment levels. Biotechnology is anything but labor intensive, in fact, it can be seen as reducing employment levels.

In 1992, the largest biotechnology company (Amgen) employed less than 2,500 people. Biotech products, like genetically engineered food products that bypass farming altogether, could drastically reduce employment levels in crop growing (Barnet and Cavanaugh 1994, p. 426). While debates between manufacturing employment decline and job growth continue, many Americans are subjected to plant closings in several industrial settings. It is to the investigation of plant closings that encompass the remainder of this book.

Plant Closings in Specific Industries

Manufacturing relocation and domestic decay have caused hardships for millions of Americans. All across the United States there has been a transformation of both heavy and light industries that have ushered in a variety of plant closings.

Steel Industry. In the early 1900s, United States steel mills were, in terms of output and technology, far ahead of those in England and Germany. During this time, in efforts to stave off competition, American steelmen organized the United States Steel Corporation. It was a vast holding company of some 200 subsidiaries involved in all areas of steel making which placed some 65 percent of the nation's steel production capacity in the hands of one vast empire. As long as competition was averted, steel companies could charge high prices for their product and saw little reason to modernize steel making. All this worked for nearly 60 years workers (Bensman and Lynch 1989, pp. 80-88).

By the late 1950s, Japan re-entered the steel making business. With inexpensive iron ore from Venezuela and high technology modern steel furnaces, the decline of the American steel industry began. By the late 1960s, U.S. steel companies for the most part were in a quasi permanent recession. In response to the competition, U.S. steel companies began attacking labor in efforts to cut labor costs.

Throughout the 1970s and 1980s, while asking the U.S. government for import restrictions, United States steel companies began shifting their assets out of steel making and into more profitable ventures and enter partnerships with their very competitors. In 1979, U.S. Steel Corporation Chairman M. Roderick commented that U.S.

Steel is in the business of making profits, not steel. In that same year, he ordered 13 steel mills closed and displaced some 13,000 American workers (Bensman and Lynch 1989, pp. 80-88; Camp 1995, p. 92).

In 1981, while the U.S. Steel corporation showed a gain in profits, the steel company moved headlong into diversification by acquiring Marathon oil and later Texas Oil. Together the acquisition cost U.S. Steel about $ 9 billion. In 1978, about 73 percent of U.S. Steel revenues came from steel making; by 1985, the comparable measure was down to 33 percent. The oil and gas segment of the company now accounted for about 54 percent of revenues (Portz 1990, p. 91). Other non-steel activities included investments in plastics, chemicals, shopping malls and hotels (Haas 1986, p. 23).

While United States steelman were demanding import restrictions from the Japanese, they were seeking assistance from the Japanese in maximizing profits. The United States Steel company looked into making technological agreements with Japanese manufactures to modernize existing steel facilities. The owners of the forth largest steel producer in the U.S., National Steel, sold half its shares to Nippon Kokkan. And, the ninth largest steel producer, Wheeling-Pittsburgh, created a joint subsidiary with Nisshin Steel of Japan (Bellon and Niosi 1988, p. 54).

The American steel industry began shrinking to a point were few believed it would ever be able to make a comeback. Between 1979 and 1984, American steel companies shutdown over 20 percent of their productive capacity and permanently laid off 40 percent of their workforce. Some 150,000 Americans were out of a job (Bensman and Lynch 1989, p. 91). By the end of the 1980s the United States Steel corporation, alone, closed some 150 plants.

The American steel industry did not act alone in its re-deployment of industrial assets. Their activities were compounded by U.S. banks, as a result of banking legislation. In the mid 1970s the principal bankers of Ohio's Youngstown Sheet and Tube Company withdrew financial support needed for modernization and increased investments in the Japanese steel industry. Citibank increased its loans to Japan from $59 million to $230 million. Chase Manhattan's support of Japanese steel rose from $59 million to $204 million while Chemical Banks support of Japanese steel climbed from $15 million to $82 million (Haas 1986, p. 19).

Chase Manhattan and Citicorp also invested heavily in the state-owned South African Iron and Steel Corporation (ISCOR) by providing them with 90 percent of their $538 million in U.S. bank loans. The major foreign customers of ISCOR were the same Japanese steel makers who obtained huge loans from the very banks that divested in Youngstown. While many American steel companies were complaining about the lack of needed capital to modernize as well as foreign competition, they, too, were directly investing in South Africas mining and mineral processing enterprises (Haas 1986, p. 19).

Electronics. The transnationalization of the electronics industry illustrates the overseas mobility of capital. The divisibility of the production process into discrete steps aided the mobility of capital to areas such as Taiwan and South Korea. Other factors influencing mobility of the electronics industry overseas included; the lower wages paid in these countries, favorable tariff structures, a docile labor force, and weak unions, as well as military dictatorships that create stable economic climates (Perrucci 1988, p. 27).

Between 1966 and 1975, the sales of televisions and apparatus, radios and parts, semiconductors and consumer electronic products doubled in the United States while offshore production increased ten times. In one area of electronics, radio and television production, domestic employment declined by 250,000 workers between 1967 and 1977. "The experiences of this industrial sector [electronics industry] provides a model of the change in the American economy that bears directly on plant closings and unemployment" (Perrucci 1988, pp. 27 and 29).

Rubber Industry. The rubber industry illustrates the mobility of capital in moving to lower wage havens in the United States as well as shed its operations to overseas investors. That portion of the rubber industry that employs the most workers and has the largest revenues is/was the tire industry.

Akron, Ohio, once known as America's rubber city, at one time produced nearly two-thirds of the nation's tires in 65 plants and more than 50 percent of the nation's non-tire rubber goods. In the 1950s, the industry employed 37,000 workers in Akron; as of 1986, employment was down to 3600. Much of the non-tire production has all but stopped. By 1988 aircraft, truck and passenger tire production had ceased and they were no tire plants operating in Akron. The end result was the closing of several plants as well as the displacement of thousands of unionized workers (Jeszeck 1993, pp. 18-44).

United States tire manufactures were either acquired by foreign manufacturing firms and/or moved to greenfield production sites in the southern and southwestern United States. At present roughly 50 percent of U.S. tire production is done by overseas firms operating in the U.S. Tire manufacturers such as Uniroyal-Goodrich and Firestone are now foreign owned. As of 1987, over 75 percent of United States tire production has been done in Southern United States by nonunionized workers (Jeszeck 1993, pp. 18-44).

The shift in U.S. tire manufacturing (either in ownership or location) occurred not as a result of union wages being to high but as a result of; shortsightedness to market changes in earlier years (i.e. from bias-ply to radial tire production), unwillingness to invest in upgrading workers skills and technology, and the tire corporations simply no longer wanting to deal with a unionized workforce (Jeszeck 1993, pp. 18-44).

Automobile Industry. For most of the twentieth century, the key manufacturing industry throughout the world has been and arguably still is the automobile industry. Some 4 million workers are employed directly in the manufacturing of automobiles throughout the world and an additional 10 million are involved in the manufacturing of materials and components. If those persons involved in selling and maintenance are added to those numbers, the total is nearly 20 million. Organizationally the automobile industry is one of the most global of all manufacturing industries and is predominantly made up of a small number of giant transnational corporations. Ten leading producers account for no less than 76 percent of the world production of automobiles (Dicken 1992, p. 268).

In North America, General Motors and Ford[6] remained the world's leading automobile producers throughout the post-World War II period, although their share of world's market has declined. In the 1960s, the

United States produced more than half of total automobile output in the world (Dicken 1992, p. 272). But by 1992, the United States motor vehicle production had fallen to 20.9 percent of the world's total (Standard and Poors 1994, p. A79). While General Motors and Ford had drastically lost domestic and world market share, by 1994 these firms declared substantial profits. General Motors in particular had record breaking profits in 1994 of $4.9 billion (Bennet 1995, p. D1).

Both Ford's and General Motor's profits have not been entirely a result of diversifying into non-automotive businesses or financial services. Ford derives 84 percent of its sales from its car, truck, automotive parts and glass operations. Most of the balance of profits were from its financial subsidiaries which have contributed to automobile production and sales.

General Motors derives about 80 percent of its sales from its automobile production. Although 15 percent of GM's sales are derived from non-automotive ventures, the corporation has attempted sell some of their non automotive manufacturing facilities (i.e., diesel locomotive manufacturing and Allison Aircraft Engines subsidiary). Included in the 15 percent figure is GM's Electronic Data Systems, which contributes to their automobile manufacturing. The remaining 5 percent of sales is made up of GMs financial operations, which are a vital part of their motor vehicle marketing operations (Standard and Poors 1994, p. A85).

One business area that has contributed to General Motor's and Ford's profit increases has been there overseas production of motor vehicles and co-production and contracting agreements with foreign manufactures. As was mentioned earlier, Ford manufactures almost 60 percent of its cars outside the United States, while General Motor's has over 40 percent production outside the U.S. These percentages have continued to increase (Dicken 1992, p. 290). Areas of American automobile market penetration have been heavy in Spain and other parts of Europe. Also, estimates show that General Motors alone has some 29 plants operating in Mexico (Baldwin 1987, p. 152). By 1993 over 90 percent of General Motors net profits came from their foreign operations (Zajac 1993, p. 276).

As was previously reviewed the United States automobile corporations also have engaged in co-production, contracting relationships and joint ventures with foreign competitors[7] (the very competitors they have asked the U.S. government to impose import restrictions on, i.e. Japan). While GM was laying American workers off, the firm was simultaneously engaged in production agreements with countries like South Korea, which has been notorious for trade union repression (Baldwin 1987, p. 152). While General Motors and Ford have been expanding abroad, they have continue to close domestic automobile assembly and parts plants, displacing workers.

Since the late 1970s, the U.S. auto industry have been "restructuring" its operations to increase their profits. Between 1978 and 1989, employment in the U.S automobile industry fell by nearly 25 percent, from 470,000 to 355,000 (Dicken 1992, p. 306). Employment reductions and plant closings will continue throughout 1996 and possibly beyond (Standard and Poors 1994, p. A83). General Motors typifies the massive downsizing campaign.

From 1980 to the early 1990s, GM reduced its U.S. hourly workforce by more than 45 percent (Leary 1994, p. 28), and, by the end of 1996, they will have a total hourly workforce of and estimated 300,000 workers.[8] By the end of 1996, General Motors will close at least six assembly plants and 15 parts and components plants (Standard and Poors 1994, p. A83).

General Motors. A variety of reasons for restructuring have been cited by the auto industry. GM in particular has cited global competition, excess capacity and a drop in consumer demand as the main motivators in generating its massive downsizing campaign.

On January 26, 1987, a congressional hearing was held by the Senate Subcommittee on Labor in Norwood, Ohio. The hearing was called to review the reasons behind General Motors decision to close 11 plants in four states. The location of the hearing was of particular relevance, General Motors had an assembly plant located in Norwood that closed in the fall of 1987.[9] The following excerpts from that hearing help explain the ways General Motors views its own restructuring program and its movement overseas.

Senator Howard Metzenbaum (chairman of the subcommittee) made the opening statement and was followed by former General Motors President and Chief Executive Officer F. James McDonald and former United Automobile Workers President Owen Bieber. Senator Metzenbaum was very critical of the actions behind GM's plant closings and wondered why the Japanese can come to the United States and open new plants while the American auto makers are taking their operations overseas in order to build cars and then import them back into the United States. He cited numerous facts and figures in efforts to support his position. Senator Metzenbaum raised concern about U.S. small car production leaving the United States and how this action may cause the loss of other American car lines.

Mr. McDonald. "I am Chairman F. James McDonald, President and Chief Operating Officer of General Motors . . . Mr. Chairman, the market for automobiles has become a global one. And today the U.S. automotive industry is facing unprecedented competition . . . I believe that the only way to meet the new global competition is to make strategic investments in new plants, technologies, and enlightened management systems to make our products world-competitive and thereby save American jobs" (United States, Congress, Senate, Subcommittee on Labor of the Committee on Labor and Human Resources 1987, p. 6-7).

Senator Metzenbaum. "Thank you Mr. McDonald. I notice that you have a written statement, and in reading it you left out one particular line. I just want to be certain that this is not an indication that the line is not factual . . . When you were talking about stamping plants [the metal stamping of car parts] you indicated that jobs are not going overseas. You then added another line saying. "General Motors buys no stampings from offshore." Is that a fact?

Mr. McDonald. "That is a fact, yes, sir" (United States, Congress, Senate, Subcommittee on Labor of the Committee on Labor and Human Resources 1987, p. 26).

In response to the metal stampings of car parts, later testimony by Owen Bieber reveals:

Owen Bieber. "Mr. McDonald is right, you don't have to worry about the doors and so on, nobody is going to ship that overseas, because they are heavy and they damage easily" (United States, Congress,

Senate, Subcommittee on Labor of the Committee on Labor and
Human Resources 1987, p. 64).

The dialog was then taken up by Senator Metzenbaum and F.
James McDonald.

Senator Metzenbaum. "Mr. McDonald, You say you established
Saturn corporation to be able to "compete directly in the very
competitive small-car market." Recently you announced that your
initial investment [in Saturn] was being cut by 50 percent . . . Do you
really intended to compete aggressively with the Saturn?"

Mr. McDonald. "Surely. I say that I am a manufacturing man; that
has been by whole life." [Mr. McDonald continues but does not
address Senator Metzenbaum's entire question.]

 Senator Metzenbaum. "But the rest of my question has to do with
whether this auto is a different auto than that which was originally
contemplated. President Le Fauve of Saturn recently announced that
the Saturn car was very different from and larger than the model
shown to the press . . . Isn't the Saturn becoming more of a mid-
sized car rather than the small car you originally planned."

Mr. McDonald. "Well, a great amount of what people might like to
know about the Saturn car we consider proprietary . . . but I will tell
you this . . . it is a subcompact" (United States, Congress, Senate,
Subcommittee on Labor of the Committee on Labor and Human
Resources 1987, p. 26).

Inquiry into the size of the Saturn car, at the time of this writing,
reveals that Saturn Corporation claims that only one line of the Saturn,
the two door coupe is considered subcompact. The remaining lines are
considered something larger.[10]

Senator Metzenbaum. "Now that the Big Three have pretty much
ceded the small car market to the Japanese and others, these same
competitors seem to smell blood and are making inroads in the mid-

size and sports-car market. What are General Motors plans? ..." "Mr. McDonald. "We have invested in the last five years [in] six brand new assembly plants ... I don't think we have abandoned any markets ..."

The former head of the GM Pontiac division, John DeLorean, recalls that as far back as the late in the 1960s, General Motors deliberately refused to make a small cars when demand in the marketplace was growing for those vehicles. Their refusal was based on the fact that General Motors was making more money selling larger cars (DeLorean 1980, p. 39).

Senator Metzenbaum. "Then how do you explain the fact that more and more of your production is being procured overseas and more and more Japanese production is being brought here to this country? There is that inconsistency that I have difficulty with ..."

Mr. McDonald. "Well, if you look at what we are bringing into this country in terms of assembling vehicles, we bring the Sprint from Suzuki, we bring the Spectrum from Isuzu, and we are going to bring the Pontiac LeMans from South Korea. When you put all that volume together and include the portions we get out of our joint venture with Toyota in Fremont, California [NUMMI], you are talking anywhere from 3 to 4 percent of our total volume. So its a very, very small amount, and that is all the plans that we have at the present time for imported vehicles ... [In term of automobile engines we bring a few engines] from Brazil and ... a few [engines] we bring in from Mexico ..." (United States, Congress, Senate, Subcommittee on Labor of the Committee on Labor and Human Resources 1987, p. 27).

General Motors management must have had a change of mind in reference to the percentage of overseas production of imported automobiles and the production of cars at their Fremont, California plant (NUMMI). For the 1992-designated model year, General Motors U.S. production (automobiles made within the borders of the United States and excluding NUMMI) totaled 2,602,434 units. Production of the 1992 NUMMI automobile and the 1992 output of the subcompact (Geo Metro) that is assembled in Canada for sale in the United States together with the 1992 General Motors sales of subcompact car lines imported from Japan and Korea totaled 280,383 units or over 10.5 percent of U.S. production (Wards Automotive Year Book 1993, p. 193, 194, 224). [11]

> Senator Metzenbaum. "How do you explain the fact . . . General Motors, the worlds largest manufacturer, is taking more and more of its production overseas? We know what you are doing in Mexico, you are telling us what you are doing with respect to some of the Japanese manufacturers, you are going to be doing it with the Korean manufacturers, and you are saying it is a low percentage of the total. But the fact is you are doing it . . . (United States, Congress, Senate, Subcommittee on Labor of the Committee on Labor and Human Resources 1987, p. 27).

> Mr. McDonald. "Our intermediate cars or what we call our A-cars . . . our [Buick] Centurys . . . we produce all of those in this country . . . So there isn't-we don't have any thoughts at all of taking those kinds of cars and going offshore. That is just an impossible thing to think about" (United States, Congress, Senate, Subcommittee on Labor of the Committee on Labor and Human Resources 1987, p. 28).

General Motors management must have had another change of mind since F. James McDonald appeared in front of Congress. In 1993, General Motors produced 34,156 Buick Centurys in Mexico. These were export cars produced for sale in the United States (Automotive News 1994, p. 20).

During the testimony, Senator Metzenbaum reads part of Owen Bieber's statement concerning the sourcing of 400,000 vehicles offshore and another 100,000 to 200,000 vehicles from Canada. He raised the issue that GM was using the United States-Canada Auto Pact to ship cars into the United States duty free, which was not the intent of the pact and that, in 1986 while GM was canceling engine programs in the U.S., they were importing 800,000 engines and planned to import more.

Mr. McDonald. "Well, I think, first of all, you will find that, as a percentage of all automobiles, General Motors imports less than any other domestic manufacturer ..."

Mr. McDonald continues and talks about the Saturn car and GM's relationship with the UAW and does not address the issue.

Senator Metzenbaum. "Your words are good, and I like your words, but I am not sure that I like the facts as well as the words" (United States, Congress, Senate, Subcommittee on Labor of the Committee on Labor and Human Resources 1987, p. 28).

Later during the testimony Mr. McDonald attempted to refocus the dialog towards GM's competitiveness in the subcompact car market. He claimed that the Chevrolet Berretta and Corsica are "in the subcompact area" (United States, Congress, Senate, Subcommittee on Labor of the Committee on Labor and Human Resources 1987, p. 29). At the time of this writing, these car lines are not considered subcompacts and, in fact, are two-and-a-half times larger than the accepted size of subcompacts.[12]

Senator Metzenbaum. "Now, I understand that General Motors has 17 production plants in Mexico with 12 more to be opened in the near future.[13] Let me ask you, how many autos does General Motors sell annually in Mexico?"

Mr. McDonald. " Idon't know whether I know the number ..."

Mr. McDonald gave some estimate and then tried to bring in the issue of metal stampings being done in the United States. His answer was met with a statement from a member in the audience who said "You are the biggest employer in Mexico right now." Mr. McDonald did not address the statement and continued to talk (United States, Congress, Senate, Subcommittee on Labor of the Committee on Labor and Human Resources 1987, p. 33).

As the testimony continued Senator Metzenbaum discussed the issue of the balance of trade and how it was a matter of concern to both GM and Congress and said:

Senator Metzenbaum. "But if we do something about the balance of trade and do something about getting those foreign markets open to you but at the same time you take more and more of your production overseas, it may help the shareholders of General Motors, but it won't help the employees of General Motors, and that is our concern." [applause]

Mr. McDonald. "I don't think there is anybody that believes that more than we do in terms of trying to keeps jobs in the United States, and again, I will back up—" (United States, Congress, Senate, Subcommittee on Labor of the Committee on Labor and Human Resources 1987, p. 34).

His statement was meet with boos and remarks of double talk.

During the testimony, Senator Metzenbaum raised the issue of Corporate Average Fuel Economy (CAFE), the federal fuel economy standards and mentioned how General Motors maintained that they would close plants, like the Norwood facility, if the 1986 fuel economy standards were not lowered. Senator Metzenbaum responded that the standards were lowered but GM was going to close the plant anyway.

Mr. McDonald responded by maintaining that the CAFE standards were unfair to GM because they produce a wide range of automobiles where the foreign manufactures serve only the lower end of the market.

Senator Metzenbaum. "How has Chrysler met them."

Mr. McDonald. "Chrysler-this is a prejudiced view point."

Senator Metzenbaum. " . . . If you made [the smaller cars] here you probably would be closer to meeting those standards . . . The CAFE standards which came about were based on the auto manufacturers arguing, 'lets us have a average standard' . . . [Congress did that and we imposed penalties if standards were not met and these penalties] . . . would have cost you, I think, $385 million in 1985 . . . you had said if you had to meet that standard that you 'will be forced to cut production of larger cars and move production out of the United States' ... you recently identified the Norwood plant ... which would be affected if the CAFE is not lowered ... it was lowered ... [and the plant is still going to close]."

Mr. McDonald. "The closing of the Norwood plant had nothing to do with the CAFE standards ... it is purely the market" (United States, Congress, Senate, Subcommittee on Labor of the Committee on Labor and Human Resources 1987, p. 36-37).

The next witness was Owen Bieber. Most of his testimony was a response to F. James McDonald's testimony. Senator Metzenbaum directed few questions towards Mr. Bieber. His statement attested to the lack of commitment General Motors had to the small car line as well as the lack of commitment to American jobs.

Mr. Bieber. "The company [General Motors] is cutting back domestic production and capacity while increasing offshore sourcing of vehicles, offshore sourcing of engines, designs and components ... [They] are cutting deeply into [their] commitment to U.S. production plans ... GM is also starting to outsource engine parts rather than investing in new casting technology ... now that's bad enough but the other problem is when you don't build engines and transmissions and rear axles in America, you soon lose your technology to build those, because no damn fool is going to teach new engineers to build an engine that you don't produce"(United States, Congress, Senate, Subcommittee on Labor of the Committee on Labor and Human Resources 1987, pp. 57, 58, 64).

During Mr. Bieber's testimony the issue of Japanese transplants using American labor is discussed. Mr. Bieber points out that the high value added portion of the car (engines, drive trains and transmissions) very often are produced in Japan and shipped to the U.S. transplants.[14] Many of those cars produced by the transplants have very little American input into them[15] (Howes 1991, pp. 113-132). Mr. Biebers testimony continued.

Mr. Bieber. "The American auto companies were very, very late in trying to get any share of the small car market, because they didn't, frankly, want to build them. The profit margin on the small cars is much, much narrower than it is on the big cars . . . but just as sure as the sun rises in the east and sets in the west, if you invite the Japanese or anyone else to come in and take over the small-car market-and that's what's been done—then you have to expect they are soon going to come after you in[sic] that higher, more expensive price market as well (United States, Congress, Senate, Subcommittee on Labor of the Committee on Labor and Human Resources 1987, p. 66).

GM's efforts to keep jobs in the United States, based on testimony of F. James McDonald, is difficult to see and are not substantiated by the reported facts. The concern about more, deeper market penetration by the Japanese has, indeed, become a reality.

The Japanese transplants are not only penetrating deeper into American small-car markets, but also are diversifying into the luxury, mid-size and sport car markets, a concern expressed by Senator Howard Metzenbaum and Owen Bieber in their testimony. Comparing the 1987 Japanese transplant car production in the United States with the Big Three production (GM, Ford, and Chrysler), these figures were 632,976 and 6,400,157 units, respectively. By 1992, the Japanese transplant total production accounted for 1,417,260 units. The share of production for the Big Three went down to 4,249,641 units (Wards Automotive Yearbook 1993, p. 17).

While General Motors continues to cede its small car (sub compact) market to the Japanese, the Japanese are making inroads into the larger U.S. car market with automobiles such as the Toyota Lexus, Nissan Infiniti and Mitsubishi's sporty 3000GT lines. General Motors is, in fact, producing some of its mid-size and sporty car lines outside the borders of the United States. The Pontiac Firebird; Chevrolet Camaro, Cavalier and Lumina; and the Buick Century and Regal, to name a few, are produced in Canada and Mexico for sale in the United States.[16] Hence, it has been argued that competition from Japanese affiliates operating in the United States may have provided a stimulus for United States automobile companies toward outward investment. The loss of domestic share may have encouraged United States producers to refocus more of their resources abroad in efforts to recover lost sales (UNCTAD 1994, p. 171).

General Motors imported about 314,175 cars into the United States from Canada in 1992, while in that same year, the firm exported 141,320 automobiles to Canada . Mexico's exports of General Motors cars came to nearly 80,000 units in 1992, while their domestic consumption was under 50,000 cars (Wards Automotive Yearbook 1993, p. 99 and 104).

Global automotive production data, together with the testimony of F. James McDonald, seems to indicate that the automobile industry and General Motors in particular are more interested in making a profit, particularly at the expense of American auto workers, than in the economic strength of the United States. This point is of little surprise to some. What is more surprising is that attempts, by the federal government, at regulating the auto industry (with such things as the CAFE standards or assistance in overseas market penetration to gain "competitiveness") has been met with a similar outcome of plant closings.

General Motors' restructuring is not, in some respects, about competition. In order to become more competitive you do not close plants but you make better products. Closing factories does not do anything to reduce the number of man-hours in vehicle production or to improve overall appearance and quality. But closing plants, in the short run, could and certainly may have raised their earnings per share for their stock holders.

General Motors efforts to build small cars overseas at a lower cost as well as enter into production relationships with competitors for the purpose of bringing these cars back into the U.S., is of little proof of excess capacity or a drop in consumer demand.[17] It seems that General Motors and other corporations, in some respects, are retreating from competition at the expense of their workforce and communities; a workforce which agreed to concession bargaining and communities that offered tax incentives in hopes that their plants would not be closed.

In the months following F. James McDonald's Senate Subcommittee appearance, the GM Norwood assembly facility was shutdown. The closing of the GM Norwood facility has had a devastating effect for the community say nothing for those 4,300 workers who lost their jobs. Norwood is a city of 26,000 residents and since the city is not diversified in its economic base, the plant accounted for some 40 percent of the jobs in the area at the time of the closing. The reliance on the plant for gainful employment has encourage many younger people to forgo college in search of making a living at the GM facility. Only 5 percent of the cites younger population have a four year college degree.

The ripple effect of the closing will have a drastic effect on area businesses and residents. The Norwood facility has made annul purchases of goods and services of over $70 million. Regional earnings may decrease by as much as $1.02 billion and the city has lost an estimate 29 percent of the city's budget due to the lost tax revenue. The public school system will lose 30 percent of its revenue (Wallace and Rothchild 1988, pp. 25-27).

When plants do close, similar to the GM Norwood plant, a variety of reasons can be expressed for the closure. Some reasons point to the hardships that corporations face in attempting to make profit. What types of disadvantages do corporations face in attempts to maintain production? and how legitimate are these claimed hardships?

THE SIGNIFICANCE OF PLANT CLOSINGS

A variety of reasons have been offered for plant closings. As expressed earlier in this paper, it is the hyper-mobility of capital in pursuit of greater profits that have contributed to plant closings in the United States. However, some researchers view plant closings as the result of the high wages paid to workers, high corporate taxes and too much government regulation. Still others offer the interesting argument that plant closings can be beneficial to the economy as well as workers. However, data on the consequences of plant closings do not support the claimed benefits of job losses.

Why Do Plants Close

The claim that wages have been rising, thus giving U.S. businesses a disadvantage in the global market, is in error. The real hourly wage rate (adjusted for inflation) for the working class (defined by the U.S. Census Bureau as "production and non-supervisory workers") was lower in 1991 than it was in 1979. Between 1979 and 1989 the average wage rate of the working class fell by .O7 percent per year (Mishel and Bernstein 1993, p. 194).[18]

Viewed from another vantage point, the Employment Cost Index (which measures wages, salaries and benefits paid to all civilian American workers) increased by 3.0 percent in the fourth quarter on 1994. That was the smallest increase since 1982, which was the year the United States Labor Department began reporting the figures (Uchitelle 1995, p. D1).

In terms of labor, U.S. manufacturing labor costs are lower than other industrialized nations. In 1993, total hourly labor costs of United States workers were $16.79. In Europe (on average), Japan and Germany hourly labor costs are reported to be $18.67, $19.20, $25.56 respectively (U.S. Department of Labor, USDL-94-26; Wallace and Rothchild 1988, p. 28). In terms of productivity or output per worker, U.S. workers produce 20 percent more each year than their Japanese counterparts and 25 percent more than those in Germany (Economist p. 4. 1994).

A common complaint of corporations is their growing share of taxes they are burdened with. This is not entirely the case. Corporations are paying fewer taxes and individuals' are making up the difference. During the 1950s, U.S. income taxes collected from corporations amounted to 39 percent of the total, while individuals share of income taxes were 61 percent. In the 1980s, the corporate share of income taxes collected amounted to 17 percent of the total, while the individuals' share made up the balance.

Another view of the issue makes the point more clear. In the 1980s the average annual taxes that corporations paid amounted to $67.5 billion. But, in that same decade, the average annual taxes that corporations did not pay amounted to over $92 billion. In fact, throughout the 1980s corporations actually avoided paying more taxes than throughout the 1950s, 1960s and 1970s combined (Barlett and Steele 1992, p. 41). In conclusion, the percent of corporate income paid out in tax in the 1990s will be lower than in the 1980s (Baker and Mishel 1995, p. 8).

Tax breaks have also saved corporations money. Corporations have the option of taking a Net Operating Loss (NOL) deduction. NOL's allow a firm to reduce the amount of current year taxes owed because of money lost the previous year. Throughout the 1980s, NOL deductions enabled corporations to escape paying more than $100 billion in income taxes (Barlett and Steele 1992, p. 41).

It is interesting to note that in 1981 the Reagan Administration passed the Recovery Tax Act, claiming it would allow business the opportunity to increase investment and create jobs by offering generous tax breaks. By 1982, while the total share of corporate taxes paid were in decline, so too was U.S. business investment in plants and equipment, by some 7 percent (Haas 1985, p. 15).

Not only are high wages and taxes claimed to burden the financial position of many corporations, but governmental regulation, too, has been cited as a reason for many corporations to close plants. Regulatory agencies, such as the Occupational Safety and Health Administration (OSHA) and the Environmental Protection Agency (EPA), have been established to enforce minimum safety standards for protecting workers and the environment from harmful industrial practices. Occupational injury is, in fact, a major concern for American workers.

Between six and eight million Americans are injured on the job every year, including 2.5 million who are disabled and 14,000 who are killed at work. One only has to mention the outrageous misconduct of the asbestos industry (and the thousands of Americans who have died or will die from asbestosis) to see the importance that regulation can play in saving American lives. If this type of regulation is a cost burden to corporations and one that should be done away with, should American workers be expected to choose between their jobs or their health?

Although corporations may complain about environmental and safety regulation, it is often overlooked that this type of regulation has created jobs. In the 1970s, just before the Reagan Administration began "defanging" OSHA and the EPA, over 677,000 new jobs had been created by pollution control legislation (Haas 1985, p. 17, Jodi 1998, p. 1).

Not all forms of regulation can be seen as burdensome on corporate profits; as was mentioned earlier, some regulation has encouraged corporations to do business offshore, and, as a result, contributed to plant closings in the United States. Amendments to the Internal Revenue Code have provided tax credits for American firms to relocate production offshore and transfer profits back to the United States, without paying taxes on those profits.

As previously mentioned, a vast number of pharmaceutical companies have closed down in the United States and have relocated to areas such as Puerto Rico. Associated with this type of industrial relocation is a loss of corporate income taxes paid to the Federal Government. Throughout the 1980s, companies escaped paying $14 billion in income taxes as a result of a tax credit. In fact, "congress [ends up] spending $60,000 of taxpayers' money to eliminate one job in the United States that pays $28,000 a year and to create one job in Puerto Rico that pays $12,000." (Barlett and Steele 1992, pp. 95 and 98).

Not only have some forms of regulation contributed to corporate profitability, but deregulation has also shown to benefit large corporations. The arguments for deregulation call attention to the removal of government restriction which would free up and open competition. Reducing the amount of regulation would spur the growth of new companies and existing ones would either become more efficient or dissolve; consumers, too, would benefit.

In actuality, deregulation has resulted in reduced competition, job losses and disadvantages for consumers. Because of deregulation, many trucking and airline companies closed down and left tens of thousands of workers jobless. Since the 1980s, more than 100 trucking companies have closed down and some 150,000 workers lost their jobs. In the airline industry, a dozen companies have either merged or gone out of business. More than 50,000 employees lost their jobs. After fierce competition that drove down prices initially, eventually only large corporations in both industries survived, which resulted in the escalation of travel and freight fares (Barlett and Steele 1992, pp. 106-109).

With arguments similar to those for deregulation, some industrial observers view plant closing as an means for eliminating inefficient operations and providing new economic opportunities. Schumpeter (1947) views the destruction of jobs and businesses as a normal process of the history of progress.

Mckenzie (1984) views the process of plant closings of unionized plants as allowing for the growth of smaller, more productive firms, which are better able to adapt to economic situations. As firms close, they release their resources to more productive firms which are able to offer consumers attractive prices (Mckenzie 1984, p. 85). Other researchers point to the lack of using advanced technology in industrial production as well as a lack of investment in research and development for the reasons behind deindustrialization (Perrucci 1988, p. 4).

There are a variety of claims that can be given for a firm to either permanently close down or relocate. While other issues such as transportation costs and trade may be associated with plant closings, Erickson (1990) found plant closings to be strongly associated with a firm's internal operating constraints. What does seem typical is that most often plant closings are seen by management as ways of improving the company's competitive and/or financial position. Sometimes plant closings accomplish this objective while other times they do not.

Issues of "creative destruction" or "the release of resources to more productive firms" after plant closings tend to be on a level of abstraction that is supported by only limited data. The responses by unions, local governments and the local business community of a firm's notification to cease operations seem less than rejoiceful.

Firms Reasons for Closure. When a plant does close, businesses can give a variety of reasons, and unions and local government officials and community leaders can give a variety of responses. Even though this being the case, some generalizations can be made. The closing firm often calls attention to falling rates of profit or a loss of profits due to increased competition or outdated manufacturing technologies that initiated the closing of the plant. Major concerns of the closing plant centers on the ability to keep productivity as high as possible up to the date of closure, avoiding public opprobrium in efforts to avoid legal action; and keeping the peace with all parties concerned to avoid tax penalties; and enlisting cooperation from local leaders in the sale of the facility.

Responses by Labor. Labors response to a plant closing can be more predictable. It is not uncommon for the rank and file workers as well as the union management, to downplay the reasons for the closing and to make an effort to postpone the closing. Very often, concession bargaining or give backs by the rank and file have occurred before notification of plant closing. A major concern of the union is to maintain its importance in the face of a loss of membership; maintain job security through the possibility of transfers or other means; maintain the income levels of its members; and assist in problems associated with unemployment and readjustment.

Governmental Responses. Local and state governments have been seen to offer incentives to the firm to remain open. These incentives may include tax breaks, special loans or assistance in manpower training. Failing that, efforts may be made to compensate workers for lost income and assist in their training or retraining, as well as to set in motion social service agencies that can ease the physical, emotional and social consequences of job loss.

Community Responses. In locations where plant closings have occurred, business community and the community at large have traditionally responded well after the fact. Responses have been somewhat varied, ranging from concerns about the loss of revenue and sales to the hope that the local economy will "pick up" once displaced workers are reemployed elsewhere. Other concerns revolve around the importance of maintaining a population and industrial base in the area, which is tied to maintaining a tax base. A loss in taxes can jeopardize the maintenance of roads, schools, public services, that can play an important role in attracting other industries (Gordus, Jarley, Ferman 1981, pp. 7-9).

One might expect that smaller communities would be more affected by a plant closing than a larger community, because of the lack of adequate social services protection for dislocated workers and economic dependence on the firm's workforce. This is not always the case. Smaller communities may offer strong kinship and friendship relations to assist in the adjustment of the dislocated worker. Also, in smaller communities that play host to large corporations, many workers may commute and therefore not reside in the community in which they are employed (Gordus, Jarley, Ferman 1981, p. 54).

Process of Plant Closings: Advance Notification

The process of a plant closing can take on as many forms as the reasons for a plant closing. A much debated topic has been the successfulness or unsuccessfulness of advance notification of plant closings. Stern (1969, pp. 21-28) has shown that advance notification can be beneficial to workers and communities. Folbre, Leighton and Roderick (1984) has argued that notification reduces the time displaced workers are on unemployment. The Folbre, Leighton and Roderick (1984) work was followed by Addison and Portugal (1987), their study reviewed the effects that advance notification had on the duration of unemployment. Their findings revealed that the duration of unemployment was significantly reduced for those workers who did not draw unemployment insurance. But, advance notice had less of an effect on length of unemployment for those workers receiving unemployment insurance. Others view plant closing legislation as an avenue to the possible prevention of the shutdown or limiting its effect (Rothstein 1986).

Not everyone sees the successfulness of advance notification. Lipsky (1979), has found that advance notification had little effect on duration of unemployment. Others see advanced notification as having little effect on the workforce since 1 out of every 10 workers actually leave their jobs before being dismissed (Flaim and Sehgal 1985, p. 7).

Still others see any form of restriction of shutdowns as counter to productivity and efficiency (McKenzie 1984 p. xxi). These arguments usually raise the issue that notification will cause the higher skilled workers to quit first which will jeopardize production over the shutdown period. Also, workers attitudes on the job may cause them to adversely effect productivity once their impending dismissal is known.

At present, the Worker Adjustment and Retraining Act requires employers (with 50 or more employees) to notify their workforce 60 days prior to a plant closing. While the debate on the successfulness of the act continues, some points are necessary to review. Little, if any, of the literature surrounding plant closing notification reveals that workers length of unemployment is increased because notification was given. As discussed, some of the literature reveals notification to help little, while other research points to lowering the length of unemployment for those workers who received advance notice. Since notification does not seem to hurt workers who may suffer as a result of a plant closing, advance notification is a positive step.

Although plant notification may, in some respects, benefit those workers who find employment after loosing their jobs, it does little for addressing the central issue. The central issue is, of course, jobs. Getting a job has more to do with the availability of jobs then much else. All the notification of closures along with education and experience does little if there is simply no work to do. If jobs are few or not available then advance notification turns into a competitive struggle, pitting worker against worker for the jobs that may be left. Advance notification does not create jobs or prevent jobs from going overseas. Advance notification does nothing at preventing U.S. deindustrialization.

Plant notification may indeed be a victory for working people but it should not deter any efforts at addressing the issues mentioned above. If capital has made profits which translates to closing plants (as testified in this book) then those profits should be shared with the communities and workers who paid the cost. Plant closing legislation should be aimed at the creation of gainful employment, the prevention of job loss and the satisfactory compensation of workers, families and communities who have struggled with a plant shutdown.

Consequences of Plant Closings

Schumpeter (1947) believes that plant closings are a form of "creative destruction," McKenzie (1984) points to the advantages that job loss can have:

> "Many people lose their jobs when plants are closed, but their loss does not necessarily mean that they are somehow worse off. Workers unemployed because their plants close are also beneficiaries of the competitive process (involving closings and openings) in other markets, which yields higher quality of goods at lower prices. Workers unemployed because of their firms' failures can sometimes find other jobs in expanding sectors of the economy-in those firms that are winning the competitive struggle. Furthermore, workers unemployed by plant closings are often compensated in advance for their expected loss in income when their plants do close. Where the

risk of plant closing is high, the supply of labor is often restricted (who would prefer to work where the loss of employment is highly probable or imminent?). As a result, in those risky jobs wages are comparatively high, with the wage differential providing a form of prepaid compensation for the risk of unemployment" (McKenzie 1984 p. 87).

The attractiveness of job loss for workers is certainly not shared by many other researchers. But, there is variability of the consequences a plant closing can have. Length of unemployment, nature of reemployment, access to alternative sources of income, and economic effects of closings by gender, race and age are but a few consequences that vary greatly in the degree they effect workers (Perrucci 1988, p. 69).

A plant closing during a recession may have an even more devastating impact in terms of re-employment. A view of some of the consequences of plant closings within certain industries can illustrate the growing problems that workers may face. These problems are best understood in relation to the aggregate data as well as case studies.

Unemployment and Income. Aggregate data on plant closings more fully explains the effect that plant closings can have and is having on the American workforce. Between 1957 and 1975, 833,000 workers were employed in industries such as apparel, textiles, shoes and rubber good. By 1975, 674,000 people no longer worked in those industries, mainly as a result of plant shutdowns. Fewer than 3 percent of that total made the transition to the high technology sector that has been claimed to replace the jobs of old mill-based smokestack industries. More than five times as many, or 16 percent, experienced downward mobility into service jobs in retail sales and fast foods. Many left the labor force while others relocated to seek employment (often unsuccessfully) in other areas (Bluestone 1988, p. 33).

In 1984 the U.S. Bureau of Labor Statistics gathered employment information on 2.5 million persons who had been employed at manufacturing plants for at least three years and had lost their jobs because of plant closings or workforce contractions between 1979 and

January of 1984.[19] Less than 60 percent of the displaced workers had found jobs as of January 1984. Approximately 25 percent were unemployed and looking for work. The rest had left the labor force (Zippay 1991. p. 9).

By the early 1990s the conditions of displaced workers had improved little.[20] Between 1987 and January 1992, a total of over 5.5 million workers (twenty years of age or older, with at least three years of tenure) lost their jobs due to a plant closing, slack work or abolishment of positions. Of this 5.5 million, less than 65 percent found employment. More than 22 percent were unemployed and 12 percent were not in the labor force. Over 52 percent of the job losses were a result of a plant shutdown or company move (Statistical Abstracts 1993, p. 412).

A 1995 New York Times poll[21] announced that in one-third of all households, a family member has lost a job and nearly 40 percent more knew a relative, friend or neighbor who was laid off. One in ten adults acknowledge that a lost job in the family has produced a major crisis in their lives. In the 1990's, for any two year period, an astounding one in 20 workers have lost their job (New York Times 3 March 1996, p. A1 and A26).

Additional economic costs result from the lower incomes of workers who found jobs. Nationally, among workers displaced from 1979 to 1983, some 45 percent who were employed full-time had taken pay reductions. Of that 45 percent, about 30 percent took pay reductions of one-fifth or more of their former earnings (Perrucci 1988, p. 73).

In efforts to further "unwrap" the effects job displacement can have on worker's earnings, the Congressional Budget Office (CBO) of the Congress of the United States examined the experiences of nearly 20 million workers displaced[22] during the 1980s. Their analyses was based on data collected from the Bureau of Labor Statistics in January of 1984, 1986, 1988, 1990 and 1992. CBO found that "one to three years after being displaced, half of the workers who lost jobs over the past decade either were not working or had new jobs with weekly earnings that were less than 80 percent of their old earnings" (Congressional Budget Office 1993, p. xii).

During the 1990s, the pay conditions of workers returning to work after being displaced was less than enchanting. During January of 1991 and December of 1992, some 2.8 million workers (who worked at their jobs three years or more), lost their jobs due to plant closings, slack work or abolishment of position. By February of 1994 less than 32 percent had full-time wage and salary jobs with earnings the same or higher than the ones they lost (Gardner 1995, p. 50). Presumably those workers experiencing higher paying employment represents upper managerial or professional people. In the 1990s, with the increase in the ratio of low paying service jobs to manufacturing employment, pay reductions should not be surprising.

A qualifying note on income loss. In further emphasizing the loss of income associated with worker displacement, case studies using aggregate data for all workers in all industries over a given time period have been used. Many case studies such as, de la Rica (1995) and Podgursky and Saim (1987), have shown only modest income losses of 10 percent or less. Unfortunately, many case studies measure the total loss of earnings as the difference between pre and post displacement earnings, as a result, serious underestimation's can result.

Jacobson et al. (1993) have successful argued that income loss after displacement is best represented by incorporating measures that 1) control for macroeconomic factors that cause changes in workers' earnings regardless of whether they are displaced, 2) account for earnings that would have occurred in the absence of job loss and 3) calculate earning declines relative to a point before the workers' separation (firms declining profits, as they approach shutdown, may have effected workers wages years before separation). Their study has shown that (adjusting for these factors), displaced workers earnings losses to be, on average, 25 percent per year (Jacobson et al. 1993, p. 691 and 697).

Other important factors to be considered when reviewing income loss is to adjust for diminishing benefits (i.e. paid sick days, lack or lowering of health benefits, paid days off) resulting from "give backs or "concession bargaining" that may have occurred before job loss. Many unionized manufacturing positions have had a very substantial benefits package. By not incorporating the loss of these benefits and merely reporting incomes overlooks other pertinent factors in determining ones "wages."

Industry specific[23] data further exacerbates unemployment and income loss. A survey of 220,000 steelworkers who lost their jobs because of plant closures and contractions between 1979 and 1983 found that 40 percent of them were still looking for work in 1984. Among those workers who found jobs, earnings had declined by an average of 40 percent (Flaim and Sehgal 1985, p. 3-16.).

Other case studies within the steel industry further supports the aggregate data. In 1984, some 6,400 questionnaires were mailed to Chicago steelworkers who lost their jobs in U.S. Steel Corporation's South Works plant in 1979. Of those who responded to the survey, 46 percent remained unemployed in 1983. Of those who found jobs, the average income dropped from $22,000 a year to $12,000 a year (Putterman 1985, p. 50).

Surveys of over 100 steelworkers displaced between 1983 and 1984 from the Shenango Valley in western Pennsylvania showed a trend similar to the one described above. Four years after the first plant closing, 35 percent still had not found jobs. Among the 65 percent who were working, the average wage was $6.50 an hour. This amounted to nearly half of the average wages formerly paid at the mill. Approximately one-third of their jobs offered no benefits; and almost two-thirds held service sector positions. The job position most frequently held was janitor, followed by delivery truck driver and security guard (Zippay 1991, pp. 45-47).

Perrucci (1988)[24] studied several effects of a closed RCA electronics plant in Monticello, Indiana, where 800 workers lost their jobs. The 1983/84 study of over 300 workers found 71 percent of the displaced workers were still unemployed eight months after the plant closed; 17 percent were re-employed full-time, and 12 percent part-time.

At the time of the study, Perrucci (1988, p. 74) found that many workers were either drawing unemployment compensation or receiving severance pay. As a result, the immediate loss of income was not as dramatic as reported in the steel industry. However, among those workers who were displaced and re-employed, either full or part-time, one year after the closing of the plant, the men earned 67 percent or their former weekly salaries; women were earning 59 percent.

Seitchik (1989) presents some interesting data in relation to earnings and family income resulting from labor displacement caused by plant closings. His main findings are as follows: 1) Increased equality [?] in earnings between both husband and wife provides "cushion" following spousal job displacement; 2) Permanency of a wife's employment may reduce a family's ability to replace the lost earnings of the male job loser. While the wife's salary may offset economic catastrophe, in turn there has been a loss of the traditional safety value afforded by the flexibility of a wife's earnings; 3) Now that more married women are working full time and year around, their job loss is a source of potential disruption to family income; 4) Lacking spousal earnings, the growing number of women who maintain families may be at considerable risk following job loss, thereby decreasing their labor force participation and increasing their use of public transfers. If these findings could be supported by other case studies and data, it would seem that programs intended to assist displaced workers are best designed around family earnings rather than individual needs.

It is quite possible for some victims of plant closings to suffer a loss of family wealth. Families at times may not only lose their current income but also their accumulated assets. These could range from total depletion of their savings to mortgage foreclosures. Families who fall victim to these hardships are left with no other alternative but to seek reliance on public welfare (Bluestone and Harrison 1989, p. 69).

In conjunction with unemployment and income loss, Perrucci (1988, p. 76) found that "perceived economic distress" (how workers perceive themselves to be experiencing financial hardships in relation to consumer goods) is sometimes detected. For example, displaced workers may fear not being able to supply their families with the types of food and shelter they were accustomed to. Many workers may be distressed for not being able to purchase household necessities or proper clothing .

Perceived economic distress has been supported by Hoffman, et al., (1991 p. 106)[25] who found "perceived financial hardship" among displaced auto workers. One conclusion of the study was that not being able to afford the basics i.e., mortgage payments, generated a worker's sense of financial discomfort, insecurity, or disaster more so than spousal employment or unemployment.

Re-employment/Relocation. The shift to low-wage jobs after a plant closing, as in the case of the steel industry, is not a unique example. A shift in employment patterns on a national scale adds to what was found in the steel industry studies. Between 1975 and 1985, there was a 25 percent increase in the number of part-time and temporary workers in the workforce. By 1985, about 29.5 million of the 107 million U.S. workers were temporary or part-time employees (Serrin 1986, p. 9).

A variety of factors have been found to influence labor market re-entry and relocation. Age, race and gender have all been found to influence ability to gain access to another job after termination (Congressional Budget Office 1993, pp. 17-25). Age has been found to be negatively related to re-employment. For example, employers may view older workers as less productive and a "poor investment" than younger ones. Since it is not unusual to find older workers who have lower educational attainment levels, this to could be a factor in re-employing older workers. When a plant does close, the workers with the most seniority (usually the mature workforce) are the last to go. As a result, the labor market in a particular area may be saturated by the workers who were previously laid off.

Older workers may find it more difficult to relocate than younger workers resulting from their family obligations of a house mortgage. Selling ones home may be difficult and warrant selling at a considerable loss which adds to workers financial hardships. Children may be attending school which could further influence their decision to move. Many older displaced workers have not been in the job market for a number of years and may feel inadequate in their efforts to look for work (Wallace and Rothchild 1988 p. 24). These reasons and a host of others may influence a older workers decision to stay in their given locality and "wait for things to get better."

Race and gender are other important issues. A workers' race may have a impact on finding re-employment given the higher rates of unemployment for nonwhites than whites. Nonwhites are especially hard hit because many are concentrated in central cities and regions were economic dislocation has been most pronounced, making re-employment more difficult. This is particularly true in industries such as steel, rubber and auto (Bluestone and Harrison 1987, p. 63). For example, in the 1980s, while 18 percent of the automobile industry workforce experienced layoffs, 32 percent of the industry's black workers were unemployed. While unemployment for U.S. teenagers was 21 percent, it was 28 percent for Latino youths and 50 percent for black teenagers (Haas 1986, p. 31).

Some studies indicate that discrimination against women, on the grounds of age, appears much earlier than against men, and that women receive lower pay for similar types of jobs. If a woman's job is considered a secondary income, then risking the primary income in the family would make little sense in terms of job relocation. Also, displaced female workers are twice as likely as men to remain unemployed for longer than a year, after a plant has closed. Research is needed to find a method to determine if women value family or community ties more than men. If so, they may choose to stay in a given locality. (Haas 1986, p. 32).

Re-entry into the labor market, influenced by age, race, and gender, may also be a function of the availability of jobs as well as the possession of transferable skills. The inter-relatedness of these issues and more come to bear on one's opportunity for re-employment and relocation (Gordus, Jarley, Ferman 1981, pp. 67-96).

In general, relocation decisions may be influenced by commitments and ties to a given locality. The cost of packing up and moving and leaving behind family and friends has to be weighed carefully regardless of age, gender or race.

Relocation opportunities can stem from company transfers, which are sometimes available as part of a plant shutdown. Some transfers may be negotiated within the collective bargaining agreement, or at the discretion of management. If transfer policies are available, there can be a wide variance in respect to the inducements and/or obstacles that the policies have for workers. Stern (1969 p. 23) showed how some transfer policies can be attractive to a company's workforce by offering a worker the option of returning to her/his home town and take severance pay if a relocation is not satisfactory. Lipsky (1979 p. 62) found seniority and a variety of other benefits favorable to a worker's decision to relocate.

While these studies help highlight what might be considered favorable transfer policy conditions, other researchers found obstacles in policies that gave workers the right to relocate. Dorcey (1967 pp.

178-182) found that the transfer policy implemented at a heavy equipment plant (Mack truck) was seen to purposely discourage worker mobility. Workers who wished to relocate were guaranteed only a job and little else. Issues of productivity standards at the new plant, incentive pay to relocate, as well as seniority issues, were to be decided upon after the workers were relocated.

Interplant transfer policies must cover a whole array of conditions to be favorable for worker relocation. If mobility of the workforce is indeed important to the firm closing a plant, and it may not always be, then maintaining the same or nearly the same conditions of employment in the new plant would seem to be a solid starting point. Relocation policies also should address the external costs of relocation to the worker. The availability of housing, cost of living in the new area, secondary role of a spouse's job in the family, children in school, etc., are all factors to be considered.

As may be evident, there are a number of issues affecting a dislocated worker in reference to relocation and re-entry into the job market. Company transfers certainly should not always signal some type of "happy ending" for the workers who lost there jobs.

Early Retirement.[26] If re-employment to similar incomes holds little prospect or if moving is next to impossible and company transfers do not exist, employees may be able to take a early retirement option. Throughout the 1990s, a greater share of businesses are offering early retirement inducement programs and a grater proportion of workers are taking early retirement and returning to work.

In 1992, Charles D. Spencer and Associates, Inc., conducted a study of 142 private employers and six public employers totaling 553,551 active employees. In 1990, early retirement incentive plans were offered by 7 of the 125 employers prompting 26.1 percent of the early retirements. In 1992, of the 125 employers, 20 offered early retirement inducements effecting 37.6 percent of the early retirements[27] (LaRock 1993, p. 10-12).

The escalating rise in the number of early retirements are, in part, due to workers choosing the early retirement option in attempts at avoiding mandatory layoffs and plant shutdowns (Herz 1995, p 16). Early retirement packages may not always meet the financial needs of the displaced worker. As a result, entry into the labor market, often in low paying jobs, could become necessary.

Early pensioners have indeed returned to work at increasing rates. From 1984 to 1993 the proportion of pensioners returning to work increased among all age groups under the age of 65. Increases were large among those age 50-54. The employment to population ratio increased for this age group from 64 percent in 1984 to 73 percent in 1993. For those early retirees between the ages of 55 to 61 their employment re-entry went up even more; from 37 percent in 1984 to just under 50 percent in 1993 (Herz 1995, p 13 and 14).

Many large corporations that negotiated job security clauses in return for concessions in the late 1980s, and are at present downsizing, have found early retirement options less costly than company transfers or holding workers in job banks (who will never return to employment). General Motors in particular will save nearly $1 billion in annual employment costs as many workers take the early retirement option.

Employees of smaller companies may have chosen the early retirement option fearing imminent termination of employers pension plans. Eligible employees may have been "convinced" to take early retirement "while they still have a chance" (LaRock 1993, p. 16 and 18).

Effects on Health and Family Relations. In addition to unemployment, income loss and re-employment adjustments, displaced workers may suffer from health and family problems associated with these factors. Job loss and unemployment have been associated with psychological problems such as increased depression, anomie, anger, and increased suspicion of others (Buss and Redburn 1983b p. 30).

The literature dealing with the relationship of job loss and mental health began, arguably, in the 1970's and 1980s. The literature in this area has been somewhat varied and contradictory.[28] Some studies show that on individual levels, unemployment can effect mental and physical health (Gore 1978; Dew, Bromet, and Schulberg 1987). Other studies showed similar and very detailed results concerning individual health and family problems in times of layoff (Cobb and Kasel 1977; Kasel and Cobb 1979).[29] Still other researchers point out how family and marriage life can be negatively affected (Liem and Liem 1988), while some argue that the effects on families and marriages are minimal (Thomas, McCabe and Berry 1980). Brenner (1973) shows unemployment causing mental health problems, while Catalano (1985) feels that unemployment uncovers rather than create social and psychiatric pathology.

Although physical and psychosocial problems may be uncovered as a result of job loss, Kates, Greiff and Hagen (1990) argue that those problems may be exacerbated as a result of job loss. They have also found that the accumulated findings of previous studies conclusively reveal that the loss of a job can lead to physical and psychosocial problems (Kates, Greiff and Hagen 1990, p. 79).

Archival research, surveys and case studies, collectively, provide a connection between job separation and individual pathology on both aggregate and individual levels. What is less firmly established is the relationships between these connections. Also, one problem that has been found is that it may be difficult to determine if an event, in this case job loss due to plant closing, was the catalyst for the individual's increased stress or if that stress preceded job separation. It is also possible that certain personal characteristics enable people to cope with different types of stresses in different ways. Simply stated, any number of reasons could exist to influence the relationship between mental health and job loss due to a plant shutdown. However, case studies can reveal some interesting data on the relationship between these issues.

Aiken, Ferman and Sheppard's (1968)[30] study of former autoworkers found that certain situational pressures (i.e. economic deprivation), are the links between labor market outcomes and behavioral and attitudinal states. Issues such as pre-displacement status and labor market outcomes were found to be necessary but not sufficient conditions to influence mental health. The important force was economic deprivation, i.e. the extent of resource depletion. It was found that older workers (characterized by low skill level and low educational attainment) experienced difficulty in finding and keeping jobs, high rates of unemployment and downward mobility, all of which were seen to cause high economic deprivation and high feelings of anomie. Younger workers with higher skill levels and higher educational attainment who had few months of unemployment and upward mobility were found to have low economic deprivation and low feelings of anomie.

The Aiken, Ferman and Sheppard's (1968) study clearly indicated that reduced status and reduced wages of succeeding jobs were related to high anomie scores, low satisfaction with life and reduced contract with family and friends. Former auto workers who returned to jobs with similar wages, benefits and status obtained higher mental health scores than those workers who found employment in lower status and less wage and benefit positions. Work, in and of itself, is not necessarily the answer to job displacement. Work that is downwardly mobile can be more destructive than no work at all (Gordus, Jarley, Ferman 1981, p. 140).

The study conducted by Perrucci (1988) came to findings somewhat similar to Aiken, Ferman and Sheppard (1968) in relation to economic hardships and mental health. The later found that displaced workers were not optimistic about their economic future. As a result of decreased wages, a re-employed person's well-being was generally no better than that of individuals still jobless. Perrucci (1988) concluded that unemployment from a plant closing had adverse impacts on individuals' psychological well-being. Moreover, the study indicated that to a significant extent, economic hardships and unemployment did indeed impact mental health.[31]

Perrucci also found that displaced workers reported significant degree of increases in smoking, headaches, and alcohol consumption, less significant findings in elevated blood pressure and respiratory and heart problems. In addition, increases in depression were also found. With reference to family relations, over 31 percent of the 324 respondents indicated worsened marital relations (Perrucci 1988, pp. 83-96).

Hoffman, et al., (1991) conducted a study of four closing and 12 non-closing General Motors plants located in Detroit and Flint Michigan, during the late 1980s. Their total number of respondents was over 1500 workers, of which 831 workers were from closing plants and 766 workers were from plants that would remain open. In exploring the effects of mental health differences across worker groups, Hoffman et. al., used the Hopkins Symptom Checklist. [32] Not only did their results show a significant increase in symptoms of poor mental health for those workers who were already laid off, but their findings showed important effects concerning race and education.

> "Results showed that being black and without a high school degree and being already laid off had a powerful negative effect on mental health. Those black workers who lacked a high school degree who were already laid off had extremely high levels of somatic symptoms, depression, and symptoms of anxiety" (Hoffman et al. 1991 p. 105).

Using some of the same data as Hoffman, et al., (1991), Broman, Hamilton and Hoffman (1990), in a very in-depth quasi-experimental design and using a variety of statistical measures, found that financial hardships produced by unemployment experience had powerful negative effects on the families of workers. Increases in family quarrels, insults and scramming as well as physical contact were a few of the problems mentioned.

One obvious point needs to be made when referencing the effects job loss can have on health and family relations. Simply stated, job loss usually means the loss of health insurance and very often little chance of purchasing health benefits from a private carrier. During 1981 and 1982 over 11 million unemployed workers and families lost their employer health benefits. Those who obtained insurance from a private carrier used 25 percent of their unemployment compensation (Wallace and Rothchild 1988, p. 23). The health insurance that was obtained through a private carrier may have been a lower coverage of health care than provided by the workers employer.

The loss of health benefits, in and of itself, can bring on added stress to workers and their families. When sickness or accidents do occur, the loss of medical coverage may translate to a absence of needed care.

Social Integration. Another consequence of being a displaced worker is that the loss of personal self esteem can influence one's social relationships and views on society. Being displaced may mean having others view you as downwardly mobile. A change in one's economic and social standing may cause others to view you as "different." The unemployment stigma of a displaced worker has also been found to condition workers into thinking that others may see them as, in part, responsible for their job loss. Also, the unemployed may believe that others view them as just sitting back and not really trying to look for other work (Kelvin and Jarrett 1985, p. 90; Kates, Greiff and Hagen 1990, p. 82).

Workers' reactions to their depersonalization may be informative in regards to issues of order, conflict and change. In efforts to probe more deeper into these feelings of demoralization questions such as these could be asked: To what degree do displaced workers accept their displaced status? How do they respond to their positions? How do they view the government and social institutions?

Displaced factory workers can be viewed as members of the "working class" and may represent a segment of society that stand the most to gain through a changed social order. Victims of a plant closing are members of a collective and their actions and responses may take place on a level other than individualized action (Perrucci 1988).

In researching some of the above mentioned issues, Perrucci (1988, p. 123) found that displaced workers can exhibit a high level of alienation and distrust of the groups and institutions that comprise the social fabric at both a local community and national level. Displaced workers can be suspicious of why their plants closed, incorporate feelings of being ignored by their local communities, see limited job opportunities in the future and may see a need for radical social change to help the less privileged.

Buss and Redburn (1983a) found displaced steel workers feeling a sense of dispair, loss of self esteem and not very optimistic about community efforts to assist them. Many steel workers felt ashamed of their loss of employment and despite efforts by community mental health organizations, many workers chose to suffer privately.

The closing of the General Motors components plant in Syracuse, New York has effected its workforce in similar ways as mentioned above. It is to the review of some of the particulars prior to the shutdown that follows.

NOTES

1. Quick disbursing loans closely monitored by either the World Bank or the IMF.

2. SALs bailed out many U.S. private banks which loaned money to the third world debtor countries which were unable to service their loans.

3. The increased poverty and social disruption of many host countries is duly recognized but its study is not thoroughly explored in this work

4. As of 1990 poverty level was set at $13,360 for family of four. see (Schwarz and Volgy 1992, p. 42).

5. The average AFDC benefit dropped 20 percent in real terms from 1979 to 1986 (see Currie 1990, p. 305).

6. Chrysler ranks about 11th on the world scale see Dicken 1992, p. 289.

7. To list the number of joint ventures and foreign subsidiary formation would be beyond the scope of this document. For a precise list consult Moodys Industrial Manual vol. 1, 1994 p. 1122.

8. Blusestone and Harrison (1982) estimates that a loss of 5,000 automobile jobs in certain industrial sectors would lead to a further 3,000 job losses in the auto industry and an additional 12,000 job losses in other related industries.

9. While General Motors slated the Norwood facility for closure and former General Motors Chairman F. James McDonald appeared before the Senate subcommittee hearings, the corporation was expanding its *Maquiladoras* plants.

10. Author contacted a Saturn dealership.

11. The NUMMI plant had 1992 production of Geo Prizms totaling 85,000. The Geo Metros are assembled in Ingersoll Ontario, Canada as well as Kosai, Japan. Canadian Output of the 1992 Geo Metro, for sale in the United States was 86,500 units. The Geo Metro made in Japan, for sale in the United States, had total 1992 sales of 20,414. The Geo Storm had total 1992 sales of 68,970 units. This vehicle is made in Fufisawa, Japan, and is sold in the United States. The Pontiac LeMans is made in Inchon, Korea and had a total 1992 sales in the United States of 19,499 units. See citation for this footnote.

12. Author contacted a Chevrolet dealership to obtain size of vehicles.

13. GM has around 25 plants in Mexico.

14. For example the NUMMI car Chevrolet Nova had the engine, drive train and transmission built in Japan.

15. It has been argued that Japanese transplants create thousands of new jobs. This is not the case and, in fact, the opposite is more likely to occur. When a foreign automobile company produces cars in the United States total demand for cars has not increased. The transplants "eat" into U.S. market share. The result is that jobs are at best "transferred" from a closed U.S. plant to a

transplant. In actuality, though, this is not even the case, jobs are not transferred (one job for one job). Many transplants are not unionized which reduces workers' power on the job. Also, high-value added parts shipped from home countries (as indicated in testimony transcripts in this document) to transplants reduce the need for American workers. This is further compounded by the fact that U.S. transplants import smaller component parts from other countries. In effect, transplants can be seen to not only not create jobs in the U.S. but also seen to reduce the number of jobs.

16. Some of these car lines are produced in several of these countries. Some are also produced for home markets.

17. One way to view consumer demand is by the number of motor vehicle registrations. Between 1983 and 1987 motor vehicle registrations in the United States have gone up each year. In fact, between 1987 and 1992 motor vehicle registrations have gone up each year with the exception of 1991 (Standard and Poors 1994, p. A81).

18. Other figures show that in 1993 average real wages (adjusted for inflation) were 9 percent below what they were in 1973 (Barnet and Cavanagh 1994, p. 293).

19. A total of 13.5 million workers 20 years and older were originally identified as losing their jobs due to plant closings, employers going out of business or layoffs form which they had not been recalled. Adjusting for seasonal employment and workers employed for less than three years, the total survey population for the study numbered 5.1 million workers displaced. Thus, 2.5 million displaced blue collar workers represents nearly half of the survey population studied (Flaim and Sehgal 1985, p.5).

20. Gardner (1995, p. 45) makes the point more clear. " ... the number of workers displaced during 1991 and 1992 was greater than the number who had lost jobs in the prior 2 years. In fact, the number displaced was even greater in the early 1990's than a decade earlier ... "

21. Based on telephone interviews in early December of 1995 with 1265 randomly computer selected adults. Statistically, in 19 out of 20 cases the results based on such samples will differ by no more than three percentage points in either direction from what would have been obtained by seeking out all American adults.

22. Defined here as people who reported having lost of left a job because of a plant closing, an employer going out of business, a layoff from which they

were not recalled or other similar reasons during five years preceding each survey.

23. As one might expect, worker displacement (broadly defined) throughout the 1980s varied significantly among industries and occupations. Workers in the goods producing industries (agriculture, mining, construction and manufacturing) suffered the greatest likely hood of permanent job loss. Also, as can be expected, blue collar workers (broadly defined) accounted for a majority of workers displaced throughout the 1980s and into early 1990s.

24. It would have been interesting if Perrucci's study could have been conducted after unemployment insurance ran out. Topics of interest might be: What effect does unemployment insurance have on workers' interests in finding a job as well as their perceptions of a plant closing in general? Do workers downplay the effects of a plant closing if unemployment insurance is available to them?

25. It is interesting to note that Hoffman, et al, found that although many workers were still eligible for full medical coverage after being laid-off, they still reported as not having enough money to afford the kind of medical care they or their family should have. This raises interesting questions in reference to workers perceptions of problems associated with losing one's job and actual or "real" problems.

26. Over the age of 50 and under age 65

27. These were incentive programs to induce workers to take the early retirement option. In 1990 of the 10,043 retired employees in the 125 companies reviewed, 74.9 percent took early retirement. In 1992 of the 13,246 retired employees 79.5 percent took early retirement.

28. For a in-depth review of the literature concerning job loss and mental health consult Kates, Greiff and Hagen (1990) chapters 3 and 4. The direction of their approach is from a medical point of view. Although they argue that the psychiatric literature contains few scientifically sound studies, these studies (referencing job loss and mental health) taken together (even though contradictory), should be viewed as pieces of a larger puzzle connecting job loss and mental health.

29. Cobb and Kasel (1977, 1979) is a classic plant closing study with a control and treatment group. Their evidence showed slight mental health affects but later analysis showed that workers who received little social support were effected, psychologically as well as physically, and in a number of ways (hypertension, high cholesterol, ulcers, respiratory diseases, etc.) by a plant closing. In addition, it was also found that the final number of respondents was only 100 workers in the plant closing and 74 in the comparison plans. These

figures have been found to have limited statistical power. See Hamilton, V. et al. 1990. "Hard Times and Vulnerable People: Initial Effects of Plant Closings on Autoworkers' Mental Health. *Journal of Health and Social Behavior* 31: 123-139.

30. Case study of 305 displaced autoworkers at a Packard plant in Detroit, Michigan.

31. Shortly after the closing of the General Motors Fremont plant in Fremont California in 1982 nine workers committed suicide. Around that same time period the closing of GMs South Gate plant in Los Angles led to six suicides see: Haas, Gilda. 1985. *Plant Closures: Myths, Realities and Responses.* Boston: South End Press (p.8).

32. Each respondent completed a booklet containing 33 items concerning problems and complaints which focused on issues of depression, somatization, obsession, anxiety and interpersonal sensitivity.

CHAPTER 3

A Plant Closing

THE AUTOMOBILE COMPONENTS PLANT AND ITS SHUTDOWN

The General Motors Syracuse Inland Fisher Guide plant, as well as its location, is a typical scenario of many industrialized northeastern cities. The following reviews: the area that the plant is located in; the history of the plant; the types of jobs performed by the workforce; and a brief discussion on union and management relations.

The City and County

The automobile components plant is located Syracuse, New York, a city once noted for its booming salt industry during the mid 1800's. The city has since moved toward a more varied economic base. In the 1950's and 1960's, the city's broad business and population base made it a frequent choice for test marketing new products. But, like many cites across the industrial northeast, Syracuse too has experienced a decline in population and manufacturing employment.

The population of the city now is just over 160,000. It has been experiencing a steady decline in population as far back as the 1950s where it once had a population of over 340,000. In accordance with its population decline, there has been a decrease in total housing units. From 1980 to 1990, the percent change in housing units was-2.3 percent.

Since the late 1970's a variety of manufacturing businesses in the city area have closed or relocated. As a result, between 1982 and 1987 there was a 13.8 percent loss of manufacturing employment. On average between 1980 and 1986, the city's unemployment rate has been

7.97 percent. In 1991, the city's unemployment rate was reported to be 6.9 percent of the civilian population (United States Bureau of Census, County and City Data Book 1994, pp. 785-795).

Employment in Syracuse has been maintained by some growth in the low paid service sector of wholesale and retail trade. The local government has attempted to attract businesses by allowing the recent construction of a new convention center, as well as offering tax abatement programs and financial assistance to new business ventures.

City planners have attempted to attract area residents by allowing the construction of a large mall near the downtown area as well as the development of a downtown section of the city to attract a "night life" population. The city has frequently sponsored a variety of concerts and festivals during the summer months. And, as of 1994, Money magazine has rated the city about midway between the 300 cities reviewed for best places to live in the United States.

Although the city has been spared some of the devastating shocks that some northeastern cities have faced, its economic future does not look promising. The county, in which the city and automobile components plant are located in, has also been experiencing deindustrialization.

Onondaga county has, up to the early 1980's, offered a variety of employment fields. Light and heavy industries, health and education, finance and insurance, and retail sales have made the county well diversified in employment. No manufacturing or service-related industry or firm, completely dominated the local economy. And, as a result, the county has been spared, unlike what many "company towns" have experienced, the devastating effects that a single plant shutdown can have.

The county, covering more than 750 square miles, had a population in 1994 of over 470,000. Although the population has increased by 10,000 people since 1980, its population today is nearly equal to what it was in 1970 (United States Bureau of Census, County and City Data Book 1994, pp. 380-390).

Like the city, the county has experienced industrial layoffs and plant closings. Starting in the early 1980s, several plant closings and layoffs in both light and heavy industry put thousands of workers out of jobs. Between 1982 and 1987, the number of workers employed in manufacturing declined by 11.8 percent. Taking a more broader perspective, the number of employees in the county involved in manufacturing totaled just over 49,000 in 1980. In 1992 the total number of manufacturing employees totaled just over 35,000. Between 1980 and 1992, manufacturing employment fell by more than 28 percent. It is most interesting to note that within the same time frame, retail trade in the county increased by nearly the same percent (United States Bureau of Census, County Business Patterns 1980, pp. 104; United States Bureau of Census, County Business Patterns 1992, pp. 205).

The industrial base of Onondaga county continues to erode. Some of the larger corporations in the area have scaled down operations and employment. The decline of the county's economic base, resulting from deindustrialization, has been "somewhat slowed" by low-paying service type occupations.[1] But even in the service sector, there have been retail store closings and personnel reductions. The announcement of the closing of the automobile components plant only added to the economic hardships of the city and county.

The economic impact of the Syracuse plant closing has had a negative effect on the area residences and community. Area newspapers reported that, for every worker laid-off from the plant, three workers in related fields would be out of jobs (Herald Journal 4 December 1992, p. A7). The loss of revenue from the plant will effect the community for several years. On a yearly basis, the components plant had spent nearly $83.4 million in salaries and purchases from local suppliers, $29 million locally on plant supplies alone.

Other areas of the community have also been affected. The plant was the school district's largest taxpayer where in the early 1990's it paid school taxes in excess of $205,000 per year. That figure is over 7 percent of the district's budget. The plant also paid over $195,000 in county taxes in 1992 (Abbott 1992, pp. A1 and A8).

Also affected, was the community's largest charity organization. The upstate New York plant was one of the area's largest contributors to the local chapter of the United Way. In the early 1990s, the average employee gift was $113 per year for a total of $181,000 (Brieaddy 1992, p. A8).

The Plant in a Historical Perspective

In the early 1990s, the General Motors Inland Fisher Guide plant was one of the corporate division's 25 plants worldwide. Of those, 13 were located in the United States (Herald American 21 December 1993, p. G6). Eight of the 25 plants, including the New York plant, manufactured trim products for cars[2] (Herald American 8 March 1992, p. A7).

The upstate plant manufactured interior and exterior plastic trim parts. Some of the products included interior door panels, arm rests and interior door and window molding. Exterior parts included bumper and bumper inserts, light fixtures and grills. Since many of these parts required painting, the plant also had a "paint line." These parts went on over twenty different makes and models of automobiles.

Although this particular plant was considered small (with only 850,000 square footage of factory space) compared to other component and assembly plants, it was the largest plastics plant in the corporation. In fact, it was the third largest injection molding facility in North America, based on the usage of 41 million pounds of plastic per year. Although plastic part fabrication has been the business of the plant for many years, it has not always been in plastics.

The history of the plant begins at the turn of the century with the manufacturing of bicycle gears. By the early 1920's, General Motors corporation purchased the plant, manufacturing turned from bicycle gears to automotive gears.[3] In the late 1930's the plant began producing automotive "hardware" such as die castings, chrome plated hub caps and headlights.

In the years leading up to World War II, the plant was converted from the production of automotive parts to machine guns and other war materiel. It was also during this time frame that the hourly workers joined the United Automobile Workers union.

After the war, the production of automobile hardware resumed and new machinery and product lines were introduced. Die casting machines were added and product lines such as hood ornaments, brass hubcaps, and stainless steel wheel disks were now being manufactured.

As business began growing, automotive parts production was again interrupted with the advent of the Korean War. Production then turned toward the manufacturing of stator blades for jet engines. After the Korean War, the plant was expanded in the area of plastics molding.

By the mid 1960s, die casting was being phased out and plastics became 50 percent of the plant's business. By 1973, the plant was entirely converted to plastics production. Over the next few years injection molding machines were installed and the corporation decide to expand the plant.

In the 1980s and early 1990s, the plant experimented with new concepts in quality programs, work reorganization schemes and focused on "high tech" plastic molding. In efforts to increase quality, the plant instituted a product weight control program known as Statistical Process Control.

Just-in-time warehousing was utilized in efforts to reduce time in intraplant shipments and storage. The plant also experimented with a team based manufacturing plan which was to incorporate more operator involvement and responsibility into the production process.

In efforts to become more competitive, the plant installed automated equipment in their warehouse and manufacturing processes. In the late 1980s, OPTICS (an optical system) was installed which permitted scanning product label bar codes as containers were moved into and out of the warehouse. To reduce some of the forklift truck traffic in the warehouse and on the factory floor, a Automated Guided Vehicle Systems (AGVS) was introduced.

Robotic part unloaders were attached to the injection molders in order to reduced manual effort and scrap. Also, the plant purchased more than 20 state-of-the-art injection molders with a price tag of nearly $500,000 per machine. By early 1992, the plant had 131 injection molders. Injection molding and subassembly of molded parts accounted for most of the hourly workforce employment (Memories 1993, p. 8-11).

Injection Molding and Other Job Classifications

Molding machines range in size from that of a car to a small bus. These machines melted a plastic mixture, injected the material into a die or mold cavity to form a specific part (such as a door panel or bumper) and then cooled the plastic. Once all operations to the parts were completed, they would then be shipped to a assembly plant.

Injection machine mold operators[4] (IMMOs) fabricated the plastic parts. They were responsible for removing parts from the machine, trimming any excess material and packing the parts in containers. Many of the machines molded right- and left-hand pieces. Some of the machines were fully automatic, and the IMMOs were paced by the speed of the machine.

Other machines were semi-automatic, which required an IMMO to reach in and remove the part from the die, spray the die with a solvent to prevent parts from sticking, and re-cycle the machine. If the re-cycle button was not pushed within a few seconds of the die opening, a light would flash notifying the supervisor that the operator was not making the required number of pieces. Many of the cycle times, on both the automatic and semi automatic molders made a part(s) every 20 to 45 seconds.

The other largest job classification was machine operator light or MOL. These workers performed subassembly on molded parts. The MOL's job was to perform another operation (other than trimming) on the plastic parts before they were shipped to an assembly plant. Such an operation might consist of gluing carpet on a door panel or applying a brace to the inside of a bumper. Since many of these jobs were located next to the IMMOs, the pace of the MOL was also set by the speed of the molding machine and its operator.

Job classifications associated with injection molding include maintenance-type functions for cleaning the machines as well as workers who were responsible for making sure that plastic was flowing to the machines in a given area.

Other employment[5] was found in the paint operations. The paint line was similar to what many people have come to envision as an assembly line. Parts that needed to be painted (once sprayed by hand but now more often by robotics) were hung on racks that carried them through paint booths and ovens. The paint line worker's job was to either attach a part to the rack or, after a part was painted, to remove it from the rack. Her/his job was, of course, paced by the speed of the line.

Union and Management Relations

Up to the early 1980s, union/management relations was considered adversarial. The union responded quite vehemently to any contract violations and there were a significant number of backlogged grievances.

The author's experience at the Syracuse plant, attests to the strained relationship between labor and management. Shop floor committee people[6] and supervisors would often exchange heated words when workers complained about contract violations. If management pushed workers to work harder, the union responded by having the workers "work to rule," in effect slowing down the work process. It was quite common for members of management to complain to union workers how difficult the plant chairman and president could be during times of local negotiations. In times of union elections, it was common for management to voice a positive opinion of any opposition that seemed to be "more cooperative" than the incumbent president and chairman.

By the mid 1980s, cooperation at the national and local level between labor and management began to be more serious. The corporation began to "strongly encourage" lower levels of management to be a "team player" with their local unions. At the Syracuse plant, a former plant president was considered to be a "reasonable man" by union officials. As a result, his actions were believed to influence many "old style" union officials toward attempting cooperation. Teams of both union and management personnel began working closely together in areas of total quality management, implementing such programs of Statistical Process Control. Although there were some failed attempts at cooperation[7] prior to the plant closing, cooperation was considered by both sides to be quite high (Interview 23 March 1993).

THE CLOSING

On December 3, 1992, General Motors corporation announced the shutdown of seven assembly and components plants affecting some 17,950 workers. That announcement also brought word that the corporation would cease operations at its Syracuse, New York components plant by the fourth quarter of 1993. In all, some 1250 workers would no longer be employed at the Syracuse plant. The announcement of the closing surprised area residents as well as many plant workers.

Management's Reasons for the Closing

In the news release, General Motors corporate headquarters cited the importance of reducing costs, improving productivity and continuing to provide outstanding quality to its customers. The reasons for closing the seven assembly and components plants in North America took into consideration the physical characteristics of the plant's size, age, condition, operating capacity and flexibility, and future investment requirements. Also cited were "tangible measurements" including product quality, workforce productivity, current and future market demand and customer satisfaction (News Release, Corporate, 12/3/92). The corporation believed that continued downsizing is necessary. Since 1990, the corporation has lost more than $12 billion (Post Standard 4 December 1992. p. p1).

The specific reasons for closing the Upstate New York plant dealt with the plant's inability to compete. The corporation cited the following reasons for the shutdown:

- The high costs at operating a 40 year old plant. For the plant to become competitive, the corporation would have to invest too much money.
- The interior and exterior plastic trim and moldings that the plant made, were not high profit, high technology components. The foundation of future business for the corporation will focus on high technology and high profit components.
- The shipping costs from the upstate location were too costly. The plant had to ship its products to midwestern assembly plants; this made shipping too costly for the corporation to absorb (Post Standard 4 December 1992, p. 12).

The upstate New York plant employees heard of their closing just hours before the official news broadcast. The in-plant management memorandum cited the reasons for closure to be the result of: the corporation losing nearly one-half of its U.S. market share; the company's inability to turn a profit since 1989, (it lost some $6 billion in North America alone during the first three quarters of 1992); and the burden of excess capacity and products that cannot compete in a global market (News Release, Local Management, 12/3/92)

Union's Response to Shutdown

Upon notification of the North American plant closings, UAW President Owen Bieber said "Let no one misunderstand, GM did not get into this predicament by putting workers and customers first. Rather, they put quick profits and Wall Street demands ahead of all else" (Post Standard 4 December 1992, p. 12).

A few days after the closing announcement, the UAW local issued a memorandum to its rank and file and community residents condemning the reasons for closing the plant. The local union stated that the plant:

- Was not an "old facility." The plant was built in 1953. In the mid 1970's there were major revisions to the building including an addition to the warehouse and other changes to assure compliance with environmental standards. The facility was further upgraded in the past ten years by a modern process which controlled the flow of plastic pellets to the molding machines; the construction of a training center; an automated vehicle transport system; and power house conversion from coal to gas.
- Was a "high tech" plant. Since 1986 plant equipment improvements included 22 new, state-of-the-art molding machines; a variety of robotics and machinery to assist production; and the investment of millions of dollars, by the corporation and state, to retrain the employees.
- Was expected to lose $2 million, but a number of other plants in the division are expected to lose a great deal more. In fact, a majority of facilities within the corporate system had lost money over the past ten years. The local plant was expected to break even or show a profit in 1993.
- Is very competitive, since, for years, members of the union and management have been working together on successful cost cutting measures. These measures included, more of a cooperative approach to manufacturing (i.e. teams), as well as, concession bargaining in the form of "give backs" which

included reduced break times and a reduction in the number of paid days off (News Release, UAW local, 12/9/92).

The local union did agree in the memorandum that the plant was burdened by its distance from assembly plants. After the union's initial response to the shutdown, many members of the union bargaining staff felt that politics between local plant management and corporate management were also to blame for the plant closing.

The General Motors Syracuse plant was a former division of Fisher Body. The plant was later acquired by General Motors Inland Division and remained such up to the closing. It is believed by some union members that management of the Inland division, having stronger political ties with other long standing Inland plants, opted to close the Syracuse plant as opposed to other plants in the division. Some union members have mentioned that inter division rivalry between Fisher Body and Inland has aided the decision to close the plant instead of other Inland plants. One worker mentioned:

> "The plant could have sent almost all of its employees [to one of the other plants in New York state] but, being a Inland Fisher Guide plant, management wanted to take care of its Inland plants first . . . General Motors showed a total lack of caring for their people in a disgusting manner."

Local and State Government Responses

Local and state politicians, upon notification of the closing, pledged to help the upstate plant gain competitiveness, but government leaders believed that the decision to close the plant was final. The vice-president of economic development at the local Chamber of Commerce saw the decision to close the plant as a strategy for the corporation to outsource more of its products to remain competitive.

A state assemblyman maintained that, months earlier, corporate officials ignored his offer to get state and local aid to keep the plant open. The assemblyman found the companies attitude "surprising" since in 1987, the corporation asked for and received over $1 million from the state for job training, including the building of a training center. (Post Standard 4 December 1992, p. 12). In fact, during the late 1980s, the corporation threatened to close the plant if it did not receive state funding (Herald Journal 19 November 1987, p. 2).

How Workers Responded to the Shutdown

Upon initial notification of the plant closing, most workers responded in shock and anger . Many workers and their families were shocked by the suddenness of the plant closing. Some mentioned that when the closing was announced, no information was given as to how the workers would be affected. Reasons for the closure ranged from blaming the corporation, the state politicians, the national economy and foreign competition.

A former production worker had the opinion that because of "bad management and a lack of foresight, problems developed and because of that I'm losing my job." He added that bad foresight came as the result of the corporation getting rid of certain car lines and "missing the boat on the minivan market." Other reasons he stated were that General Motors "dragged their feet" on new model lines and cars were overpriced, poorly designed, and too costly for repairs. He added the corporation is attempting to get rid of their component plants and transfer jobs out of union shops to nonunion shops and to areas outside the United States (Post Standard 25 December 1992, p. A10).

The former shop chairman said "They [General Motors] are bleeding us to death, and now we're going to take it on the chin for their inability to run their business. The corporation has really lost touch with what's going on out there." (Abbot 1992, p. A1).

A fork truck driver responded that the Syracuse Inland Fisher Guide plant could have remained open if the politicians in New York "went to bat for the workers. " He added that he was shocked at the decision to close the plant and stated:

> "Since 1965, the corporation had always threatened to close the plant, but this threat was seen by many workers as a way to get the workers to work harder. Although the plant might have been in a financially unstable position the workers did "tighten their belts" to become more competitive." (Interview 21 July 1993).

Other workers have responded to the closing and blamed failed labor/management cooperation programs, poor state of the national economy, foreign competition and American workers buying foreign cars as the reasons for the shutdown.

Most workers were concerned about where they would end up. Some workers did not like the idea of having to move out of the area and leave family and friends behind. Others saw the coming change in their life as a hardship and something to be feared. All wondered what the financial ramifications would be.

Not all the hourly employees responded in anger and fear at the closing. A former salaried worker who turned hourly several years before the announcement to close the plant, felt very thankful that he had a job as long as he did and in some ways felt sympathetic to the corporations decision to close the plant. He expressed the opinion that the corporation was in a bind and that it had to shut plants down to gain competitiveness. He mentioned that although he did not agree with all the decisions made by both the union and management since he had been employed, the union and corporation did all they could do to have the plant remain open (Interview 28 July 1993).

Other workers saw the closing as an opportunity for a "new beginning." Some workers expressed the opinion that moving to a new location would give their parents the option of moving out of the upstate area and live some place "new." One truck driver was optimistic at moving to the "bible belt" area of the United States, in efforts to carry on her religious beliefs "more fully." One former mold operator mentioned, if he was relocated, how nice it would be to "get away from the wife and kids" and be on his own for awhile (Interview 12 October 1993).

What Happened to the Workers: Retirement and Relocation

The process of closing the plant occurred in stages between January and December of 1993. The hourly work force was offered early retirement, regular retirement or relocation rights. As the regular employees were either retired or relocated, the UAW and management agreed to hire temporary workers until the plant was officially closed in December. During the time of shutdown, both the UAW and plant management "worked together" to make the process as smooth as possible.

An estimated 500 hourly workers took the corporate-wide early retirement package or regular retirement that was offered to them over the shutdown period.[8] The early retirement package was available to workers 50 to 61 years of age with a minimum of ten years seniority.[9] The package included pro-rated pensions with full benefits.[10] Also available to the early retirees was a "mutually satisfactory retirement agreement." The agreement waived the cap on the amount of money early retirees could make outside the plant.[11] Hourly employees 62 years of age or older would not only receive full pensions and benefits but also a $10,000 voucher toward the purchase of any U.S. made General Motors vehicle[12] and $3,000 in cash (Interview 23 March 1993).

The remaining workers, some 750, were either relocated to other plants[13] within the corporation or left the company. An estimated 325 workers were relocated under Document 28 of the corporate-UAW contract. Most of the workers relocated under this section of the agreement were allowed to move within a 150 mile radius. All Document 28 workers kept their seniority for purposes of retirement. But these workers forfeited their in-plant seniority (i.e. their earned seniority at the upstate New York plant). They received a new in-plant seniority of 1/7/85 at their new location, which could affect shift and job preferences. Also, these relocatees could be the first workers to be laid off in a economic downturn at their new location.

Over 225 workers were transferred under paragraph 96 of the national agreement. This meant that any jobs (i.e., molding machines) that were transferred from the closing plant to another location within the corporation must also be accompanied by the number of hourly workers needed to perform the jobs. Although the receiving plant could be located anywhere in the United States, the work force "following" the jobs were able to keep their in-plant seniority as well as their seniority for purposes of retirement.

An estimated 100 workers terminated their relationship with the corporation, thereby ending any in-plant seniority,[14] and were re-employed by the Saturn Company. Both the closing plant and Saturn entered into a special agreement to allow workers to transfer to Saturn. Many hourly workers, as well as local union representatives at the closing plant, found Saturn to be a better relocation option than the others. The Saturn company seemed to present a "mystique" to some of these workers, many of whom mentioned how nice a "change from the old way of doing things" would be.[15]

Of the estimated 100 or so remaining employees, a few quit after finding other employment in the area. Sixteen quit and were helped by the UAW in finding jobs with another automobile company in upstate New York. Most of the workers took a layoff and then were put on involuntary leave of absences. Some workers also enrolled for UAW-sponsored retraining. And a few remained on some type of disability.

The plant shutdown rights that the hourly workers received were judged by the UAW local as "the best closing agreement that any plant in the industry, if not the United States, has had." The local union president was quite enthusiastic that the entire work force would be able either to retire or would be offered a job at another location (Interview 23 September 1993).

Spokesperson for the UAW have said that retirement packages encourage workers to retire so the corporation can reduce the number of workers who are in the "jobs bank."[16] Under the terms of the national contract, the corporation must recall one worker on layoff for every two workers, over the age of 61, who retire. For each worker who retires between ages 50 and 61, the corporation must recall one worker on layoff (Post Standard 15 December 1992, p. A7).

Summary and Conclusions

The Corporation and Local Management. The reasons given by General Motors for closing the Syracuse plant and responses by the union and state and local government officials are typical of those reported earlier in this book. The corporations reasons for shutting down several plants, including the upstate New York plant, focused on falling profits, competition and outdated manufacturing technology.

Management at the Syracuse plant was very careful not to blame the workforce for the effect of its wages on falling rates of profit in order to help assure continued operation through the shutdown phase. This was a primary business concern. Provoking the workers into a strike, which some former employees mentioned they would have favored, is something a closing plant wants to avoid.

The Union. The union's responses (i.e., downplaying the reasons for closure; citing how the union was offering give-backs to help keep the plant open; and securing transfer options) are typical efforts in shutdown situations. The local union's earlier attempts at cooperative efforts with management in the mid 1980s, may have influenced its decision not to strike. It is not known if the option to strike would have prevented or delayed the plant from closing.

Interviews with several of the former workers at the plant and conversation with former work associates revealed some interesting facts. Some workers were willing to go on strike, and, at least in their opinion, a strike may have prevented the plant from closing. Also, some workers believed that one of the union's past presidents, who held office before the plant closing announcement was made, was more skeptical of cooperative programs between labor and management and would have chosen the strike option.

State and Local Government. State and local governments' assistance in keeping a plant open is not an uncommon practice. When the GM Syracuse closing was announced, politicians offered assistance to help prevent the shutdown, but the corporation declined. Once the shutdown was imminent, state and local officials made resources available to community groups and social service organizations to help dislocated workers.

It also is not uncommon for companies to threaten plant closings, to influence federal or state legislation. For example, in Congressional testimony, General Motors management threatened closure of its Norwood, Ohio, facility if certain fuel economy standards were not changed. They were changed, but the plant was closed anyway. As was reported earlier, in the late 1980s General Motors threatened to close the upstate New York plant if the corporation did not receive New York State monies for worker retraining. The monies were made available, yet the plant eventually closed. In fact, the training center that was built with state monies was eventually torn down.

The local newspapers in Syracuse, New York reported that residents were questioning the use of their tax money. Questions mounted, as to why the corporation was allowed take over $1 million of taxpayers' money, only to close the plant four years later.

It would seem reasonable that if funding is made available to assist companies in staying open, then legislation should be created to require plants to remain open (after receiving help). A violation could require repayment of the funding or subject the company to legal action.

Workers. When first notified of the shutdown, many workers were angry. Some blamed the corporation, some blamed politicians, and a few blamed the union for not doing more to fight the closure.

Initial investigation into the reasons workers felt the plant was being closed revealed that they shared no one cause. They did not know the reason for the plant closing and could only speculate. The lack of a shared cause for the closure may have suppressed any militant response against the shutdown.

During times of plant shutdowns it is not uncommon for workers to blame themselves for the closure (Perrucci 1988, p. 81). In the case of the upstate New York plant, there was no indication of workers blaming themselves. The blame was externalized. This should not be surprising; the workers had agreed to concession bargaining and did participate in cooperative efforts with management to remain more competitive.

Several months after the initial shutdown notification, and after workers were aware of their transfer and retirement options, some felt a bit more complacent toward the reasons for the shutdown. Local newspapers quoted one worker who said, "I will have happy memories about [the plant] ... I've got no anger, because General Motors is in a bind right now ... " (Post Standard 23 October 1993a, p. A4). Interviews conducted by the author found this response to be consistent with the feelings of other workers.

Complacency was not shared by all workers. The local papers reported that, of the hundred or so workers who did not retire or relocate, some blamed the union and the company for their financial hardships. A group of 30 to 40 workers alleged that the corporation and the union changed the contract rules of relocation. The corporation and the union agreed to increase the relocation hiring area from 50 to 150 miles. As a result, if workers refused work at another location within that area, they would be unable to collect 85 percent of their income for an estimated two years.[17]

These workers claimed that the corporation and union did not understand that some people did not want to move away from family and friends. Their position was that the primary responsibility of the UAW should be helping workers, not the corporation. [18]

The union president responded by saying "We are not going to be paying people to sit at home when there are other . . . facilities that need people. That's just draining the corporation" (Post Standard 23 October 1993b, p. 17). Other union officials remarked that the 50 mile radius was increased to give people the option to make the same amount of money as they were before the shutdown. The unions job is to keep people working, according to those officials.

Those few workers unwilling to move claimed that moving with the corporation was no guarantee of a job, because the plant to which workers relocated could shut down. One worker responded, "I don't want to be a GM gypsy . . . There was this guy . . . [who worked at the plant] who worked at 10 different General Motors facilities . . . He lost his family. He just has the corporation now. I want more than General Motors in my life" (Post Standard 23 October 1993b, p. 18).

The issues raised by these workers and the union's responses to them pose further interesting questions,[19] but the one that concerns us here is: What are the social effects of job loss and relocation, and how much of a hardship is moving away from family and friends.

Family counselors in the Upstate New York area rank the devastation of job loss as second only to the death of a spouse. Many workers may grieve openly while others suffer in silence and deny their emotions. The head of employee assistance programs for Child and Family Services for Onondaga county mentioned that "people are coming in for marital problems and relationship problems, but when we get to the root of the real issue, we're finding a layoff."

According to some Upstate New York psychologists, layoffs can trigger violent behavior, increase stress and tension, and increase the possibility that people who use drugs will come to depend on them more, as well as have adverse effects on relationships (Post Standard 24 December 1992, p. B1 and B2).

Interviews with workers who have relocated have mentioned what the loss of family and friends means to them. One production worker who was eligible for early retirement but refused for financial reasons said:

"I don't like living out of a apartment in [his relocated area] and coming home on weekends. It may be a strain on my marriage, I'm sure it will be. Hopefully there will be no divorce down the road. I feel emotionally strained because I had to move and leave my family. I've had sleepless nights [for the last seven months] since the closing. It's been a traumatic experience for me. I think 1993 was the worst time in my life." (Interview 5 August 1995).

Similar stress and strains were also seen on the families of other workers. Another worker mentioned:

"I would be sitting in the kitchen talking to my wife about maybe selling the house [move to his relocated area] maybe we should move. My daughter would get so excited she would walk, no run, right out of the house. She did not want to hear me talking about moving." (Interview 7 August 1995).

When asked how other workers were getting by, many mentioned that a number of their friends wives did not want to relocate with their husbands and leave family and friends behind. One worker in particular responded:

"One of my friends has a 15 year old daughter and his daughter ran away from home already at the prospect of moving ... now she [his wife] has to get a court order for her to move" (Interview 9 August 1995).

The closing of the General Motors Syracuse Inland Fisher Guide components plant in Upstate New York has brought a variety of hardships for many workers. In efforts to further explore the effects the plant closing has had on the workforce, as well as uncover the views many workers had on more broader issues (i.e. economy and society in general), interviews and questionnaires were administered.[20] Chapter 4 begins with a review of the methodology.

NOTES

1. I use the term "somewhat slowed" cautiously. A recent local newspaper reported that the average production worker at the components plant made $600 per week. A secretary in the upstate New York area makes an average of $290 per week. A restaurant worker averages $168 per week.

2. Of the eight trim plants mentioned, the corporation has either shut down or announced the shut down of six of them (which are located in the United States and Canada). The other two are located in Juarez and Matamoros, Mexico and are not slated for closure.

3. Although the plant has been through several name changes it has remained with the same corporation.

4. The following elaboration was drawn from the author's own personnel experience at the plant.

5. There were other "unskilled" job classifications such as stock persons and clerks. Also, within the hourly workforce, there were the "skilled" trades.

6. Union members also known as union stewards, committeemen etc.

7. During the mid 1980s a quality team program between labor and management was attempted at the local level. Members of both the union and management regretted its failed outcome citing the lack of incorporating all workers into the team process.

8. This figure represents nearly all the workers who were eligible for either early retirement or retirement. Of the 500 total, nearly 400 workers went on early retirement.

9. The package was extended to workers 48 years of age. The workers would go on unemployment insurance and subpay until age 50. At which time early retirement would begin.

10. On average an hourly employee with ten years seniority would be eligible for an estimated $600 per month plus benefits. The benefit package is estimated to be $500 to $600 per month. The majority of early retirees had close to 15 years seniority which would allow them to receive an estimated $1200 to $1600 per month plus benefits. The importance of the benefit package goes beyond the obvious. Some believe that employees are better able to negotiate for employment now that the new employer need not pay benefits.

11. Typically, a retiree had their pensions reduce if their annual wage exceed a certain limit.

12. This option was effective through March of 1993 and not through the entire phase down period of the plant.

13. Workers were assigned a specific plant to relocate too. Seniority, as well as other factors (i.e. job description at time of offer), played a role in determining which workers were assigned to which plant. Relocated workers received a transfer (moving) allowance which averaged about $1200. Workers who refused to relocate (or retire) were first laid off and then were put on involuntary leave of absence.

14. Pension is transferred from closing plant to Saturn

15. Interviews have revealed that some workers (an estimated 10) have requested a return to the New York area. These workers found Saturn to "not live up to the claims of cooperation and team work" between management and labor.

16. The jobs bank are pools of workers who have been laid off for long periods of time because of a lack of work. While in the jobs bank, workers receive full benefits and full pay for performing community service. Workers may also perform nonunion jobs at the plant where they were last employed.

17. During times of layoffs, auto workers would usually collect New York state unemployment benefits and subpay totaling 85 percent of their take-home pay. Interviews conducted in August of 1995 revealed that this group of workers had filed a class action lawsuit against the corporation and the union for allegedly violating the contract.

18. The author failed in an attempted to make further inquiry into this area.

19. Such as: Should relocation agreements incorporate provisions for moving away from family and friends, and, if so, how? Should those workers unwilling to relocate because of family and friends be allowed to stay behind with pay for several years or until they find gainful employment? If so, who should pay? Should the union be concerned about the corporation? These questions and others are certainly important in answering.

20. The Onondaga county library in Syracuse, New York supplied important newspaper clippings of the closing. These documents were valuable in understanding the dynamics of the shutdown as well as the feelings expressed by many of the former hourly employees at GM Syracuse.

CHAPTER 4

Research Results

METHODOLOGY

Data collection consisted of interviews that were conducted one year before the plant officially closed doors in December 1993. A small number of interviews were again conducted in August of 1995. Also, questionnaires were distributed in the fall and winter of 1995 to some 275 former Syracuse hourly employees. A review of the data collection techniques are as follows.

Fourteen hourly employees (including representatives of the local union) from the Upstate New York components plant were interviewed between January and December of 1993. This was a period of time after official notification of closure was given but while workers were still employed at the plant. During the earlier part of the interviewing phase, the early part of the year, many workers were still unsure of their options following the plant closing. In the ensuing months, workers decided on either relocation, early retirement, or termination.

During the last few months of 1993, some of the workers interviewed were in the process of moving to their relocation sites. Others already had relocated to different assembly and components plants but maintained residences in their former location. Some eligible workers opted for early retirement.

All the 14 interviews were conducted by the author and taped[1] with the consent of the interviewee(s). The interviews were conducted at several locations including restaurants, personal residents of workers, the authors residence, and the local UAW union hall and training center. Some of the interviews were conducted in a group setting.

The interviews were unstructured. No structured questions were asked of all interviewees. Although many workers were asked similar questions, most often the conversations were allowed to develop in the fashion with which the interviewee felt most comfortable. The atmosphere in which the dialog took place allowed for a variety of topics to be discussed as well as eliciting some of the "true" feelings of many of the workers. At times, the workers interviewed were chosen by the local union representatives; at other times, acquaintances of the author were interviewed. The interviewing process eventually led to a snowball type sampling of the workers, removed from the control of either the local union or acquaintances of the author.

Between January and August of 1995, two questionnaires were developed to ascertain more clearly the effects the plant closing has had the workforce.[2] One questionnaire dealt with the experiences shared by relocated workers. The other was conditioned around the experiences most often shared by former GM employees who took early retirement. The early retirement questionnaire was a bit more complex. It was broken down according to early retirees who were re-employed by other businesses, those who did not re-enter the job market, and those who were not re-employed but were looking for work. The first 44 questions were common to both questionnaires. This was done in order to compare and contrast experiences and views that both groups (relocated workers and early retirees) had in common.

The two questionnaires were pretested on nine workers in August 1995. The workers were randomly chosen but represented as nearly as possible the sample as a whole. Minor problems with the two instruments were found and corrected.

During the pretest, second interviews were conducted after workers were administered the survey. The nine subjects were quite frank in discussing their experiences either in relocation or early retirement. Some of the interviewees were accompanied by their spouses which added to the richness of the taped interviews. Issues concerning the effects the plant shutdown had on families were explored, as well as more general issues of work, society, and the state of the union.

The distribution of questionnaires began during the middle of October 1995 and continued through January 1996. Out of a total population of 550 relocated workers, 325 workers were relocated to two GM complexes (engine and parts plants) in New York State. Originally, of the 325 workers, 200 were randomly chosen and going to be distributed questionnaires at one of the work sites (Complex No. 1) but problems in distribution required distribution in another work site (Complex No. 2) some 80 miles away.

A relocated former GM Syracuse worker at Complex No. 1 was responsible for distributing the questionnaires inside one of the buildings. While doing so, this worker was confronted by members of the local union and prevented from distributing the questionnaires. Another relocated worker from the closed Syracuse plant was selected to continue the distribution at Complex No. 1. This worker, too, was confronted by local union members at Complex No. 1 and asked to leave the plant. A few days later, the worker attempted questionnaire distribution in another building. He was again confronted by local union members as well as members of management, then escorted out of the plant by security personnel and threatened with disciplinary action. No further attempts were made to distribute questionnaires at Complex No. 1. Only 24 of the 200 questionnaires were distributed.

At Complex No. 2 the distribution was handled differently. All 51 relocated GM Syracuse workers had received their questionnaire by mail. The names and addresses were unobtainable by the author, so a member of the local union (at Complex No. 2) hand-addressed each questionnaire.

Enclosed with each questionnaire was a cover letter (explaining the intent of the study and directions), a new $1 paper clipped to the cover letter (to increase the response rate), and a return self-addressed, hand-stamped post card as a reminder of the importance of returning the questionnaire as well as to allow the respondent to leave her or his name, address and phone number so further contacts could be made. Also, a self-addressed, hand-stamped return envelope was enclosed with the questionnaire.[3]

A combined total of 75 questionnaires were distributed to relocated GM Syracuse workers. Two were undeliverable by the United States post office and four were unusable. Of the 69 remaining questionnaires, 31 were returned and usable. This yielded a response rate of 45 percent.[4]

It should also be noted that the cities in which Complexes No. 1 and No. 2 were located in had standards of living similar to those of Syracuse, New York. Although the population of each of the cities differed from Syracuse, both cities had a varied industrial base and both had experienced some form of deindustrialization.

The distribution of questionnaires to early retirees was done by mail only. The author obtained a list of names and addresses of nearly 400 early retirees, those workers who took early retirement as a result of the shutdown.[5] Of that group, 200 were randomly chosen and mailed questionnaires on November 17, 1995.

Surprisingly, 198 of the early retirees had addresses in or around the city of the closed plant. Each questionnaire was hand stamped and enclosed with an attached cover letter, a $1 bill, and a self-addressed, hand-stamped, return envelope.[6]

On November 24, 1995, one week after mailing the 200 questionnaires, a second mailing took place. Each potential respondent received a post card as a reminder of the importance of returning the questionnaire. Also, each post card informed the potential respondent that if he or she did not receive a questionnaire, one would be mailed upon request (a local phone number was supplied on each post card). Of the 200 questionnaires mailed, 18 were determined to be undeliverable by the United States Postal Service two weeks after the mailing; 17 were mailed to employees who were not on early retirement (due to errors in the address listing); four respondents were deceased;[7] and five questionnaires were unusable. A total of 156 potential responses remained. Of that total, 88 were returned in usable order to the author. This yielded a response rate of over 56 percent.

The analysis of the data from each of the questionnaires was run through the software program Statistica® and SAS®. Significance testing was set at p= .100 or lower.

HOW WELL HAVE THEY FARED: EARLY RETIREES AND RELOCATEES

The effects of the Syracuse plant closing will be discussed in terms of some of the aggregate data mentioned earlier. In the first section the early retirees and relocatees will be compared to questions common to both surveys. Next, the early retirees and relocatees will be viewed in terms of unemployment, employment and income, mental health, perceived economic distress, physical health, family effects, and what is termed "social integration." Information in the first section may be elaborated on in the second. Also, some of the information obtained from the analysis of the survey will conclude with how it relates or does not relate to some of the aggregate data.

After a review of the economic, physical, social and psychological effects the Syracuse plant closing has had on its former workforce, discussions will follow relating to the experiences shared by each group of workers. A summary of research results, conclusions reached, and what has been learned from both groups of workers as well as some of the problems faced in researching the Syracuse shutdown end this section.

The Early Retirees and Relocatees

When comparing the early retirees to the relocatees some of the most interesting information uncovered was how the shutdown affected their mental and physical health as well as family life.

The early retirees and relocatees were asked three questions concerning their lack of enthusiasm for doing anything, feelings of loneliness, and feelings of being bored or having little interest in doing things. More than twice as many relocatees than early retirees reported experiencing each of these symptoms (See Table 1).[8]

MENTAL HEALTH

Table 1. Percentage of Early Retirees and Relocatees Responding "Very Often" to Mental Health Symptoms*

Mental Health Symptom	Early Retirees Responding "Very Often"	Relocatees Responding "Very Often"
Lack enthusiasm for doing anything	19%	42%
Feel lonely?	17%	42%
Feel bored or have little interest in doing things?	19%	39%

*A total of 88 early retirees and 31 relocatees responded to each of the Mental Health Symptoms. For complete table see Appendix F Table F-1.

A statistical difference in increased alcohol consumption (likely stemming from the shutdown) existed between the two groups. Nearly 39 percent of the 31 relocatees compared with about 14 percent of the 84 early retirees indicated experiencing increases in drinking (see Appendix F Table F-2).[9]

Changes in family relations were also found to differ between the two groups. Nearly two, and in some cases three times as many relocatees than early retirees reported worse relations with spouse, children, other family members and friends (see Table 2).[10]

FAMILY LIFE

Table 2. Percentage of Early Retirees and Relocatees Indicating Worse Relations with Family and Friends*

Worse Relations With	Early Retirees (n=)	Relocatees (n=)
Spouse	25% (72)	57% (28)
Children	10% (80)	38% (26)
Other Family Members	10% (88)	35% (31)
Friends	15% (88)	45% (29)
*For a complete tabulation of responses see Appendix F Tables F-3A, F-3B, F-3C.		

The dislocated workers were also asked to respond to specific questions concerning government policies and institutions and offices of the United States.[11] When asked if the government should limit the amount of money an individual is allowed to make in a year a statistical difference between the two groups was found. One hundred percent of all the relocatees compared to 90 percent of all the early retirees responded "no" to the question (see Appendix F Table F-4).[12]

Statistical significance between the two groups of workers was also found in relation to the degree of confidence they have in big business. Ten percent of the early retirees reported having "a lot of confidence" in big business compared with zero percent (none) of the relocatees (see Appendix F Table F-5).[13]

The former GM Syracuse workers were asked to respond to questions relating to the performance of their local union. Before there was any talk of closing the GM plant in Syracuse, how much did the union local help protect workers' rights? Thirty-two percent of the 31 relocatees felt the local union was "not much help" compared with 16 percent of the 88 early retirees (see Appendix F Table F-6).[14]

Also, the early retirees and relocatees were asked how satisfied or dissatisfied they were with most of the benefits negotiated in the plant closing contract. From the data previously reported one could predict that the relocatees would indicate more dissatisfaction with the plant closing contract then the early retirees. That is indeed what the data showed. About 58 percent of the 31 relocatees compared with 20 percent of the 88 early retirees acknowledge dissatisfaction with the closing agreement (see Appendix F Table F-7).[15]

Likewise, as is understandable, since the early retirees' incomes decreased and the relocatees' incomes increased after the shutdown,[16] a higher percentage of early retirees reported having to cut down on overall expenses and postpone anticipated purchases. About 88 percent of the early retirees compared with 73 percent of the relocatees indicated that it was necessary to cut down on expenses and postpone purchases (see Appendix F Table F-8).[17]

The relocatees were found to suffer more than the early retirees in terms of mental and physical health as well as the effects the closing has had on families and friends. The early retirees have faced different hardships.

The early retirees experienced financial hardships resulting from the closing of the GM Syracuse plant. Early retirees' current unemployment and underemployment have produced lower incomes than what was reported at pre-shutdown levels. These issues and many more will be reviewed next.

Unemployment

Two years after the closing of the Syracuse plant, 18 of the early retirees, or over 20 percent,[18] reported being currently unemployed or what was defined on the questionnaire as "looking for work." Another 22 workers, or 25 percent, reported either being withdrawn or retired from the labor force. Of this group, over 31 percent responded that it was still financially necessary for them to work (discouraged workers). In fact, over 72 percent of all workers reported that it was still financially necessary for them to work. Combining those "looking for work" as well as those defined as "discouraged" brings the number of currently unemployed to over 28 percent of the early retiree sample.

The workers who reported "looking for work" were also asked to respond to questions concerning when they thought they would find a job as well as what factors were the major cause of their not being able to find employment. Of the respondents, all (100 percent) reported that they really did not know when they would find a job.

In regard to reasons for the early retirees' inability to find work, the possible responses were lack of jobs, age, lack of skill, lack of education and illness. A overwhelming majority (56 percent) responded that a lack of jobs prevented them from finding employment. Age was the next highest category, with 39 percent of the early retirees citing it as a reason for not finding employment.

This point is somewhat interesting. The average age of the early retirees was 55 years.[19] Although this is certainly not "old," neither can it be considered a prime age to enter the workforce. It would certainly be understandable if most of these workers had reported that age was the factor in their inability to find work. They did not. One could speculate that these workers were more likely to blame the economic conditions of the times as opposed themselves for their inability find jobs.

Some of the early retirees were also asked to respond to the question, "Since the plant closed, what was your total length of unemployment?" Of the workers who responded,[20] four percent reported less than one month of unemployment, nearly 60 percent reported unemployment (on average) of nearly 13 months, and 36 percent reported unemployment of more than 2 years.

In reference to gender and unemployment/employment status (full time, part time, looking for work, withdrawn or retired from the labor) no statistically significant differences were found[21].

Of the 46 percent (or 6) of females who reported "withdrawn or retired from the labor force," only one female also reported that it was still financially necessary for her to work. This being the case raises the question of whether the income of the remaining women could or should be considered "secondary" income of the family as some literature states (see Haas 1986, p. 32).

For the secondary income argument to hold true, most of these women should have other income; for example, the income of a spouse. But, some of the females were never married and some were divorced. The data obtained in this study indicates that female incomes cannot be considered as "secondary" income to the household even though most were "withdrawn or retired from the labor force."

In reference to the spouses of early retirees, all the married respondents were asked to indicate either yes or no to the following questions; "When you are employed, does your spouse usually work?" and "When you are not employed, does your spouse usually work?" Taking into consideration the loss of income (reported later) and the high percentage of former employees looking for work one could have expected a large percentage of workers indicating their spouses have entered the workforce as a result of their own unemployment. This can be determined by the number of cases reporting a no-yes response to the above questions. But that was not the case. Only four workers, or less than six percent,[22] reported that when they do not work, their spouse usually does. Only four percent of the married workers responded that their spouses were currently looking for work.

Interviews, regarding the issue of spousal employment, have revealed that some of the male early retirees felt a responsibility to be the bread winners of the family and did not want their wives to work to support the family.

Unemployment, for the most part, pertains to the early retirees. The relocatees have experienced little unemployment. About 90 percent of the transferred workers reported not being laid-off since the Syracuse plant closed. Most of those reporting unemployment indicated the period to be less than one month. Presumably, this unemployment was the period of time after their termination at Syracuse and before beginning work at the other plant.

Similar to the early retirees, the spouses of transferred workers did not enter the workforce when their mates where unemployed or laid-off. The only other important fact that should be reported in reference to unemployment is that only 15 percent of the spouses of transferred workers had to give up their jobs in order for their husbands to relocate. This figure may seem to be a bit low, but many spouses did not relocate with their husbands.

The unemployment levels experienced by early retirees are supported by the aggregate data reported earlier. For example, of the

5.5 million workers who lost their jobs between 1987 and 1992, more than 22 percent were found to be unemployed (Statistical Abstracts 1993, p. 412). The study of the Syracuse workers reported that 20 percent of the workers were unemployed two years after the shutdown.

Employment

Approximately 22 percent (19) of all early retirees reported working full-time (defined as 35 hours a week or more). Another 24 percent (21 workers) reported that they were working part-time[23] (defined as less than 35 hours per week). Of the employed workers, most (or 88 percent) reported having one to two full-time jobs since the plant closed.[24]

There has been a wide variance reported as to how long these job holders have held their current employment positions. The breakdown is as follows: 5 percent held a job for less than one month; 5 percent averaged two months, 13 percent averaged 4.5 months; 10 percent averaged nine months; 15 percent averaged 15 months; 23 percent averaged 21 months; 23 percent averaged 2-1/2 years, and 5 percent have held their current positions for more than three years.

Of the current early retiree job holders, nearly 60 percent did not consider their jobs as permanent and most did not have another job lined up. A plurality of early retirees, some 40 percent, found their present hours and shift less convenient than they were at the General Motors plant in Syracuse. Approximately 40 percent, found their present work to be not as good as the work they did at the Syracuse automobile plant.

As can be concluded from what has been reported earlier, the job market in Syracuse, New York, is less than enchanting. This was confirmed by the experiences of the early retirees. For all respondents in this group, approximately 63 percent believe that finding employment in Syracuse (to support oneself/family) is very difficult and 33 percent believe that gaining access to a job in Syracuse is fairly difficult.

In the study of the GM-Syracuse plant closing, the 31 relocatees were all considered full-time workers and had held their positions since being transferred. Nearly one-quarter of the relocatees did not consider their job to be permanent and only one worker had another job lined up. Although the nearly 25 percent figure is not as high as reported for early retirees, it does indicate either a degree of pessimism for employment with General Motors or their preference for living in Syracuse. In fact, some 42 percent of the workers indicated that they looked for work in the Syracuse area before relocating.

Some 61 percent of relocatees believe that their present hours and shifts were less convenient then they were at General Motors in Syracuse. This figure is higher than that reported by early retirees who had job positions. But similar to the early retirees, 39 percent (the largest group) indicated that their present work was not as good as the work they did a GM Syracuse.

Workers were asked whether or not they believed their transfer was a good idea. The possible responses were a very good idea, good idea, good in some ways, a bad idea, a very bad idea or necessary. A plurality of workers, some 35 percent (or 11), responded that the move was necessary and 45 percent indicated that the reason for relocating was due to financial considerations.[25]

One of the most revealing figures in the study was that nearly 65 percent[26] or 20 of the 31 transferred workers indicated that their spouses and/or children (all of whom were household members at their former Syracuse location) were either unable or unwilling to move with them. The principal reason for a spouse to remain behind was due to employment. Some transferred workers indicated that their children were too small and required their mother's care. Others mentioned that their children stayed behind because of school.

It was also determined that, of the 20 transferred workers whose spouses and/or children remained in Syracuse, seven were commuting on a daily basis anywhere from 1-1/2 to 2-1/2 hours (one way) from Syracuse.

Relocated Syracuse workers have felt some of the same pressures as experienced by workers in other industries. The percentage of GM Syracuse workers whose spouses and children remained behind clearly makes the point. Although the hardships faced by relocatees will be discussed later, there certainly are costs involved in transferring to other locations.

Early retirees' shift to part-time employment is consistent with the national trend. And, as discussed earlier, there has been an increasing trend in the United States for workers to take an early retirement option and return to work. This was indeed the case with many of the early retiree Syracuse employees.

Income

Income loss for displaced workers is certainly not an unusual occurrence. Indeed, pre-and post-plant shutdown earnings of these forced early retirees at family and individual levels supports the supposition that income loss may follow job displacement. Also, the effects of income loss can be further underscored by reviewing the experiences of those currently employed early retirees.

A lowering of incomes was certainly not the case for the relocatees transferred to other General Motors facilities. In fact, those workers' wages increased well over pre-shutdown levels.

In 1992, one year before the plant shutdown, family incomes of the early retirees averaged around $53,200.[27] Family incomes earned in 1994 showed that 25 percent had incomes under $25,000. For those incomes that could be averaged, 75 percent had family incomes of $39,500[28]

Comparatively, the family incomes of the relocatees is different. Pre-shutdown earnings were estimated at $48,100.[29] Reported 1994 family incomes averaged $59,500.[30]

One year before the plant closed, the average individual income of the early retirees was estimated at $41,400.[31] Incomes earned in 1994 shows that nearly 75 percent of these early retirees had incomes of under $25,000.[32]

The individual incomes of the relocatees, one year before the plant closed, was also averaged at $41,400.[33] But, incomes earned in 1994 shows the average earnings to be an astounding $55,400.[34]

Of the early retirees, current full-time job holders showed wages losses. From incomes earned in 1994, six or 35 percent of the full-time job holders reported incomes of under $25,000. Of the incomes that could be averaged, 11, or 65 percent of the early retirees employed full-time reported 1994 incomes to be $39,300.[35]

The annual incomes for employed (both full and part-time) early retiree workers went down considerably more. Reported 1994 incomes for these workers show that 54 percent had earnings below $25,000. Of the retirees whose incomes could be averaged, 46 percent had an income of $36,600.[36] For those workers looking for work,[37] approximately 83 percent reported incomes of under $25,000.[38] One employed early retiree had this to say:

> "I now still work in my trade, I work for a non-union shop. I work twice as hard for less than half the pay, If it were not for my early retirement check, I could not live on the wages I make now ..."

Another mentioned:

> "I have submitted many resumes to other factories and have only been called once for a $5.00 an hour job ... for that amount of money, it wasn't worth it after taxes and the gas money I would have to spend each week. I'm still looking, and just getting by financially. I get a pension, but barely enough to get along on."

Substantial income losses for the employed early retirees leaves little doubt why approximately 88 percent of the early retirees reported that their current job pays "considerably less" than the job they had at GM Syracuse. In efforts to further understand the hardships that income loss may bring, some workers were asked to respond to the question, "What part of the income earned by other household members (other than your spouse) has been used for family expenses and maintenance?" Of the 22 workers that responded, 14 percent of the workers indicated half and 41 percent indicated some (defined as little on the questionnaire) of "other household members income" was being used for family expenses.[39]

In reference to the early retirees, gender has played a role. When income by sex is analyzed, 100 percent of the 11 female respondents indicted 1994 incomes to be less than $25,000. One the other hand, 71 percent of the 68 males respondents indicated 1994 incomes to be under $25,000 (see Appendix F Table F-9).[40]

The case of the relocatees is obviously different. The increase in their individual incomes (pre-to post-plant shutdown earnings) may be attributed to more than just a difference in pay scales or contract wage increases. In fact, workers complained of mandatory overtime requirements. One worker in particular complained that mandatory overtime "was not appreciated and was not worth it." During the interviewing process, other workers mentioned the strain that mandatory overtime has had on themselves and their families.

Early retirees, on the other hand, had income reductions considerably lower than those reported earlier in a study of national income loss due to plant closings. Gardner (1995) found that during January of 1991 and December of 1992, some 2.8 million workers (who had worked at their jobs three years or more), lost their jobs due to plant closings, slack work or abolishment of position. By February of 1994, less than 32 percent had full-time wage and salary jobs with earnings the same or higher than the ones they lost. The study of the General Motors early retirees revealed that of those that found full-time employment, only 11 percent had jobs that paid the same or more than the ones they lost.[41]

Mental Health

As was mentioned, the former workers at the closed General Motors Syracuse plant were asked to respond to three questions concerning how the closure affected their personal and social lives. The questions asked were: During the past month how often have you experienced a) lack of enthusiasm for doing anything; b) felt lonely, and c) felt bored or had little interest in doing things. Possible response categories ranged from "very often" to "somewhat often" to "not often or never."

What was found, other than the high percentage within each group indicating "very often" to each question, was how these two groups of workers (transferees and retirees) differed in responding to the above questions. As a percent within each group, more than twice as many relocatees then early retirees reported "very often" to each of the questions.[42]

Further analysis of each group sheds only some light as to the possible reasons for their responses. For the early retirees, analysis was run on each question separately for possible relation/correlation among marital status, employment status, gender and income. No relationship was found for each question concerning marital status, and employment status, however, correlation's were found for gender and income.

Thirty-three percent of the female respondents reported "very often" to feelings of loneliness, compared to 13 percent of the males (see Appendix F Table F-10).[43] Statistical significance was not found when lack of enthusiasm for doing anything or feelings of being bored was cross tabulated by sex. It cannot be ascertained from this study as to why a greater percent of female early retirees experienced a sense of loneliness. Female early retirees may have valued a closeness for workplace associates to a greater degree then their male counterparts. Being cut off from friends may have influenced their sense of feeling lonely.

Regression analysis performed on each of the three mental health questions did show a slight negative correlation with income,[44] however, statistical significance was found only for lack of enthusiasm. As income rose, the early retirees lack of enthusiasm went down, the correlation coefficient was found to be r=-.285.[45]

The case of the relocatees is quite different. Efforts were made to determine the effects several variables may have had on the mental health scores of the transferred workers. Since income rose for these workers and some complained of the stress and strains of overtime, could income be associated with the workers mental health scores? As incomes rose what was the effect on each of the mental health questions? Analysis showed that no correlation or association could be made.[46]

Further analysis was performed on questions related to marital status, as well as on those workers whose spouses remained in Syracuse, whose spouses relocated with them, and those workers who were commuting. No significant relation, correlation or association was found.

Another analysis of the data revealed interesting findings. The three questions concerning the effect of the closure on the workers' mental health were collapsed into a single dichotomized response variable representing "depression." Those workers who responded "very often" or "somewhat often" to all three questions were considered to be suffering some form of depression and received a "yes" response. Those workers who responded "not often or never" to any one or all of the three questions were considered not to suffer as severe a form of depression, if any at all, and received a response of "no."

Approximately 41 percent of the early retirees were found to suffer from some form of depression ("yes" depressed). In contrast, an astounding 68 percent of the relocatees reported being depressed.

Correspondingly, 59 percent of the early retirees were found to suffer from less severe forms of depression (or no depression), while approximately 32 percent of the relocatees reported little or no depression (see Table 3).[47]

DEPRESSION

Table 3. Percentage of Early Retirees and Relocatees Found to be Either "Yes" or "No" Depressed

Depressed	Early Retirees	Relocatees
Yes	41%	68%
No	59%	32%
% Total	100%	100%
(n=)	(88)	(31)

The single depression indicator of the relocatees was cross tabulated with workers' marital status, whether or not the spouse relocated or remained behind and with those workers who were commuting or lived alone. Also, income categories were combined in an effort to better analyze any relation with depression.[49] No significant correlation or association was found.

One correlation found was when relocatees' confidence in social institutions and offices was tabulated by the depression indicator. Relocatees were asked to indicate their level of confidence in six institutions and offices of the United States.[50] Relocatees reporting "hardly any confidence" in four of the six institutions and offices were classified as having no confidence in U.S. institutions and offices. The remaining relocatees were categorized as having some degree of confidence.[51] Of the 21 relocatees found to suffer from depression, 38 percent indicated having no confidence in social institutions and offices. Correspondingly, of the 10 relocated workers found not to be depressed, 0 percent (none) had reported no confidence in social institutions and offices (see Appendix F Table F-11).[52]

Earlier in this book it was reported that the literature on mental health scores and job loss appeared to be somewhat varied. Some literature indicated a relationship to income and anomie and self-esteem scores. As reported earlier, studies such as Aiken, Ferman and Sheppard (1968) and Perrucci (1988) indicated that reduced status and reduced wages of succeeding jobs or joblessness were related to high anomie scores and low satisfaction with life. Workers who found jobs with similar wages, benefits, and status obtained higher mental health scores than those whose employment offered lower status, wages and benefits, or who remained jobless.

The study of the General Motors workers reached different conclusions. Transferred workers, relocated to similar status and pay positions, reported greater problems with depression-related issues than the early retirees.

The relation between income and mental health seems to be more important within certain groups as opposed to between groups. Although no correlation or association was found to shed light on the reasons for the high depression scores of the relocatees, some points are in order.

Among relocated workers, regardless of whether they were commuting, spouses had or had not relocated with them, or they were not married and lived alone, all may have suffered differently as a result of their situations. Although any number of reasons may be responsible for the higher number of relocatees who reported being depressed, level of income had no bearing on these feelings.

Some relocated workers commented on the stress associated with relocating to another plant and the lack of making "ties" with current work associates. One worker said that, as a result of rivalry between UAW locals, workers in other plants are not very supportive and, a lot of times, even hostile towards displaced workers. Another relocated worker had this to say:

"Transferring is not a good thing to do to a workforce. Stress, Stress, Stress, Stress ... "

Further investigation of mental health issues facing displaced workers seems to be in order. It may be that each plant closing carries its own unique diversities, calling into question relocation as the best and only answer to plant closings. The circumstances accompanying relocation may be as important as the option to relocate. At least in the GM-Syracuse case, similar type jobs and wages were not enough to stave off feelings of depression.

Perceived Economic Distress

In contrast to actual income loss, displaced workers may perceive themselves as facing economic hardships. This perception may have an influence on their personal and social lives. Approximately 88 percent of the early retirees responded that they had suffered some financial hardships and as a result, had to cut down on overall expenses or postpone anticipated purchases.

Early retirees also were asked to respond to seven questions regarding their ability to either afford or not afford certain household and leisure items.[53] These question were different dimensions or categories of what was termed "perceived economic distress." Possible responses (to this created variable) ranged from each worker being able to afford all of the categories (all items of the seven questions), any combination thereof, to each worker being unable to afford any of the categories that defined "perceived economic distress. "

Analysis of the data showed that for those 18 people who reported "looking for work," 56 percent had reported not being able to afford five or more of the categories. For those 19 early retirees who were employed full-time, 21 percent had reported not being able to afford five or more of the categories. And, for those 21 workers who were part-time, 24 percent reported not being able to afford five or more of the categories (see Appendix F Table F-12).[54]

One of the categories or questions relevant to perceived economic distress was, "Do you have enough money for the kind of food you/your family should have." Approximately 15 percent of the 88 early retirees reported "no" to this question.[55]

Regression analysis was used in efforts to further explore perceived economic distress. Perceived economic distress was correlated with reported 1994 individual incomes of the early retirees. As incomes increased, workers' ability to afford more categories on the "perceived economic distress" indicator also increased. The product-moment correlation was found to be r=.445.[56]

Perceived economic distress was also cross-tabulated with the depression indicator. For those "unable to afford five or more categories," 75 percent were found to suffer some form of depression. In contrast, of the early retirees able to afford all items on the economic distress indicator, about 14 percent were found to suffer some form of depression (see Appendix F Table F-13).[57]

Looked at from another vantage point, of the 22 workers who were able to afford items in all of the categories of "perceived economic distress," more than 86 percent were found not to suffer from depression. In contrast, of the 28 workers who were unable to afford 5 or more categories under "perceived economic distress" 25 percent were "no" depressed.

Among early retirees, the correlation of "perceived economic distress" and depression supports the relation between income and depression.

In referencing the relocatees, the case was somewhat different. Relocatees were not asked to respond to questions indicating the degree to which they either can or cannot afford certain household and leisure items, although they were asked if they had suffered some financial hardships and, as a result, had to cut down on overall expenses or postpone anticipated purchases. Interestingly enough, 73 percent of the workers responded "yes" to this question. When the depression scores of the relocatees are cross tabulated with whether or not they had to cut down on expenses, no relation or correlation was found.[58]

It cannot be ascertained from the questionnaire just exactly what hardships and expenses were in question. It may indeed be that these relocatees responded the way they had, as a result of the cost associated with moving and/or commuting. Although these workers had received a moving allowance, problems in selling and buying a home or the costs associated with maintaining two separate dwellings (in their work area and the Syracuse area, as some workers indicated they were doing) may have been a factor.[59]

There is also the remote possibility that cutting down on overall expenses and postponing anticipated purchases were more of a "perception" and one not entirely based on a lack of financial resources. It should be remembered that the individual incomes of the transferred workers went up markedly.

Other researchers have reported similar findings. Hoffman, et al. (1991) found that not being to afford basics (i.e. mortgage payments) can generate financial discomfort and insecurity. They also found that, although many of the displaced autoworkers in their study were eligible for full medical coverage after being laid-off, they still reported not having enough money to afford the kind of medical care they and their families should have.

In some sense it is irrelevant if the relocated GM workers indicated that it was necessary for them to cut down on overall expenses and postpone anticipated purchases because of "real" problems or not. Those workers believe that they suffered financial hardships as a result of relocation. And it is the perception of problems that may have a strong influence on the way workers view themselves and react to their families, friends and society.

Physical Health

The author asked former General Motors-Syracuse employees if, as a result of their relocation or early retirement, had any of them experienced any of seven physical symptoms. One of the most striking findings was that a greater percentage of relocatees then early retirees reported experiencing each of the seven physical symptoms.

Approximately 42 percent of the relocatees responded that they have experienced headaches; 23 percent, a loss of appetite; 29 percent experienced gastrointestinal problems; 39 percent indicated that they were drinking more; 26 percent responded an increase in smoking; 26 percent had problems with high blood pressure; and an astounding 58 percent reported having problems sleeping.

In contrast, approximately 34 percent of the early retirees responded that they have experienced headaches; 18 percent, a loss of appetite; 27 percent experienced gastrointestinal problems; 14 percent indicated that they were drinking more; 17 percent responded an increase in smoking; 25 percent had problems with high blood pressure; and 44 percent reported having problems sleeping (see Table 4).[60]

PHYSICAL SYMPTOMS

Table 4. Percentage of Early Retirees and Relocatees indicating Physical Health Problems*

Physical Health Problems	Early Retirees	Relocatees
Headaches	34%	42%
Loss of appetite	18%	23%
Stomach trouble	27%	29%
Drinking more	14%	39%
Smoking more	17%	26%
High blood pressure	25%	26%
Trouble sleeping	44%	58%

*A total of 88 early retirees and 31 relocatees responded to each of the physical symptom questions. For a complete tabulation of responses see Appendix F Table F-14

Looking at some of the physical symptoms separately and relating them to the early retirees, other interesting correlation's were found. When "drinking" was cross-tabulated with the employment status, 33 percent of part-time employed early retirees indicated increases in drinking. For those who were "looking for work," 24 percent reported increases in "drinking." All (100%) of employed full-time early retirees reported no increases in drinking (see Appendix F Table F-15).[61]

The only other interesting correlation found was when problems in sleeping was cross-tabulated with employment status. Eighty-one percent of early retirees "looking for work" reported problems with sleeping. Compared with 50 percent of the full-time employed and 48 percent of part-time employed early retirees (see Appendix F Table F-16).[62]

For the relocatees, when each of the physical symptoms were analyzed against whether or not the workers commuted, whether their spouse remained behind or relocated, or against their income, no correlation or relationship was found.

To further understand the role that physical symptoms have played in the lives of the early retirees and relocatees, a single "Physical Symptoms" indicator (variable) was formed. Possible responses for each worker ranged in value from 1 (indicating the worker had experienced none of the seven physical symptoms) to 8 (indicating that the worker has experienced all seven physical symptoms).

The Physical Symptoms indicator was cross-tabulated with the sex, depression scores, employment status and perceived economic distress of early retirees. The most striking difference was found in relation to the depression indicator and perceived economic distress indicator. Of the 58 workers who were effected by up to two physical symptoms, 31 percent were found to suffer from depression. On the other hand, of the 28 workers who were effected by three or more of the physical symptoms, 61 percent were found to be depressed (see Table 5).[63]

DEPRESSION AND PHYSICAL SYMPTOMS

Table 5. Percentage of Early Retirees Indicating Feelings of Depression by Number of Reported Physical Health Problems

Depressed	Affected by 1 to 2 Physical Health Problems	Affected by 3 to 7 Physical Health Problems
Yes	31%	61%
No	69%	39%
% Total	100%	100%
(n=)	(58)	(28)

For the 22 early retirees who were able to afford all items on the perceived economic distress indicator, 100 percent were found to suffer up to only two physical symptoms. On the other hand, of the 27 respondents who were unable to afford five or more items on the economic indicator, nearly 60 percent were effected by three or more physical symptoms (see Table 6).[64]

Unfortunately, no statistically significant findings were found when the relocatees' "Physical Symptoms" indicator[65] was related to depression, whether or not the relocatees had cut down on overall expenses, income, commuting workers, workers who lived alone or spouses who remained behind or relocated.

PHYSICAL HEALTH AND ECONOMIC DISTRESS

Table 6. Percentage of Early Retirees Indicating Number of Physical Health Problems by Economic Distress (Ability Either to Afford or Not Afford Seven Household and Leisure Items)

Health Problems	Afford All Items	Not Able to Afford 1 to 4 Items	Not Able to Afford 5 to 7 Items
Affected by 0-2	100%	68%	40%
Affected by 3-7	0%	32%	60%
% Total	100%	100%	100%
(n=)	(22)	(37)	(27)

Statistical significance was found when the physical symptoms indicator was tabulated with whether or not the relocatees had confidence in social institutions and offices. Relocatees having "hardly any confidence" in four of the six institutions and offices were classified as having no confidence in social institutions and offices. Of the 17 workers found to suffer from zero to two physical symptoms 12 percent had no confidence in social institutions and offices of American society. On the other hand, of the 14 workers suffering from three or more (including all) of the physical symptoms, 43 percent were found to have no confidence in social institutions and offices (see Appendix F Table F-17).[66]

Literature concerning job loss has indicated a connection between job separation and individual pathology. Since the GM workers were not surveyed on this topic before and shortly following job displacement, causal connections are difficult to make. Among early retirees, low income seems to have been related to health problems, although higher income played no role with the relocatees who experienced physical symptoms. Here again, income seemed to be an issue within certain groups as opposed to between groups.

Family Effects

As noted earlier, former General Motors employees were asked to comment on any changes in family relations that resulted from their early retirement or relocation. It would seem to be understandable that if economic or psychological hardships followed job displacement, then significant changes in family relations would occur.

Although most of the early retirees reported no significant changes in relationships with spouses, children, other family members, and friends, interesting information was uncovered.

For all the categories mentioned above, the greatest changes for early retirees occurred for those who were married . Nearly 25 percent indicated worse relationships with spouses. Other responses were as follows: 10 percent reported worse relationships with children and other family members; and 15 percent reported worse relationships with friends.[67]

The situation for the relocatees was different. In percentages, nearly two and in some cases three, times as many relocatees than early retirees reported worse relations in all categories of relationships. Approximately 57 percent of the married relocatees reported worse relationships with spouses; 38 percent indicated worse relations with children; 35 percent experienced worse relations with other family members; and 45 percent reported worse relationships with friends.[68]

Financial hardships, similar to the GM early retirees, may have had negative effects on relationships with family and friends,[69] as some of the literature (for ex: Broman, Hamilton and Hoffman, 1990) points out. But, relocation (even with higher wages) had a far greater negative impact, regardless of whether the spouse relocated or remained behind, or if workers commute or live alone.

A greater percent of relocatees then early retirees reported negative relationships with family and friends. This fact, together with the greater percent of relocatees then early retirees affected by all of the physical symptoms and found to suffer more depression, begins to call into question the success of this particular relocation. Offering workers the same types of jobs and pay may not be enough to offset the negative effects of plant shutdowns. It would also seem plausible to question General Motors' intent for this particular relocation, and, perhaps corporate relocations in general. If relocation is hailed as a positive alternative to shutdowns, then the former GM-Syracuse relocated workers, it is hoped, should have reported fewer problems with; family and friends, physical symptoms, and depression then the early retirees.

Social Integration[70]

The early retirees and relocatees have experienced problems associated with the closing of the Syracuse plant. Some of the personal problems may be within the sphere of how others view the workers as "downwardly mobile." Indeed, workers may view themselves as downwardly mobile and may react to their perceived position. How workers perceive their situation may tell us much in reference to how they view order, conflict and change. Do these workers blame themselves? Do they perceive their situation as hopeless?, and a natural element of "just the way thing are?" Or do they react to their situation with anger, blaming, for example, institutions and offices that are supposedly on their side. Workers' reactions to their feelings can be informative in the way of whether or not they feel integrated into society.

Socially integrated workers may not see themselves as different and may just accept their situations with little reservation. On the other hand, workers not socially integrated may see themselves as different, distrust the "system," and are more likely to want social change.

The degree of social integration is defined here by the way in which workers respond to a variety of questions concerning the endorsement of governmental policies; why their plant closed; confidence in social institutions and offices; equality of opportunity for children of workers and executives; future employment opportunities; and the degree of shared interests between management and labor. It is to the investigation of these specific areas that are now reviewed.

Endorsement of Governmental Policy. Workers were asked six different questions as to whether they agree or disagree with government policies that would redistribute income or provide job programs. Workers who endorse government policy in these areas can be seen as less integrated into mainstream society and look toward social change.

A large percentage of both early retirees and relocatees (45 percent or more) were found to endorse four of the six policies calling for more government intervention. Workers agreed that the government should see that families have enough money to live on; increase taxes on big business; tax the rich in order to redistribute wealth; and not cut back in areas of health and education.

Responses to the remaining questions are as follows. Approximately 43 percent of the early retirees and 32 percent of the relocatees agreed that the government should end unemployment by offering a job to anyone who needs one. And, interestingly enough, 90 percent of the early retirees and 100 percent of the relocatees did not feel the government should limit the amount of money an individual can make in a year (see Tables 7 and 8).

RELOCATEES AND GOVERNMENT POLICY

Table 7. Percentage of Relocatees Endorsing Government Policy Intervention in U.S. Society

Government Policy	Agree	Dis-agree	Row Totals
The Government should end unemployment by offering a job to anyone who wants one.	32%	68%	100% (31)
The Government should see that every family has enough money to live on.	45%	55%	100% (31)
The Government should increase taxes on Big Business.	65%	35%	100% (31)
The Government should tax the rich in order to redistribute wealth.	48%	52%	100% (31)
The Government should limit the amount of money any individual is allowed to make in a year.	0%	100%	100% (31)
The size of Government should be reduced even if it means cutting back on services in areas such as health and education.	40%	60%	100% (31)

EARLY RETIREES AND GOVERNMENT POLICY

Table 8. Percentage of Early Retirees Endorsing Government Policy Intervention in U.S. Society

Government Policy	Agree	Dis-agree	Row Totals
The Government should end unemployment by offering a job to anyone who wants one.	43%	57%	100% (88)
The Government should see that every family has enough money to live on.	56%	44%	100% (88)
The Government should increase taxes on Big Business.	55%	45%	100% (88)
The Government should tax the rich in order to redistribute wealth.	56%	44%	100% (88)
The Government should limit the amount of money any individual is allowed to make in a year.	10%	90%	100% (88)
The size of Government should be reduced even if it means cutting back on services in areas such as health and education.	30%	70%	100% (88)

On this last point, it should be mentioned that during the pretest of the questionnaire, interviews indicated that workers believe people should be allowed to make as much money as they want, and that they should be taxed in order to redistribute the wealth. As a result, it could be argued that workers do see themselves as different. Historically, and as indicated in this book, it has been the case that the wealthy have strongly opposed governmental increases in personal income taxes and, in fact, have encouraged the "flat tax" over the "progressive" tax concept.

Why the Syracuse Plant Closed. Workers were asked three questions as to why the plant closed. Possible response categories were strongly agree, agree, disagree, strongly disagree and don't know. Strongly agree and agree were combined to form a response of agree. Strongly disagree and disagree were combined to form a response of disagree. The importance of the questions were to determine if the respondents did or did not have anti-management sentiments (management's decisions were profit-centered and anti-worker) as to the reasons for the closure. The workers can be seen as being more integrated by siding with management and believing that the closure was "just the way things were." Or the workers can see themselves as victims of a corporate struggle of "us against them." [71]

An analysis of the data on the former GM Syracuse workers showed that a majority of workers had anti-management sentiments. Over 69 percent of the early retirees and 71 percent of the relocatees disagreed with GM's claim that the plant was not making money because of foreign competition and that the corporation had little choice but to close the plant down. About 57 percent of the of the early retirees and 45 percent[72] of the relocatees agreed that the Syracuse plant was probably making money but not as much as GM wanted it to make. And a plurality of early retirees and relocatees (39 percent and 49 percent respectively) felt that GM was using the recession as an excuse to break the back of organized labor and get lower wages.

Confidence in Social Institutions and Offices. How much confidence do workers have in the social institutions and offices of American society? The displaced GM workers were asked to indicate their level of confidence or lack thereof in six institutions and offices.[73] The level of confidence for each item ranged from "a lot of confidence," and "some confidence," to "hardly any confidence." Workers with "a lot of confidence" in institutions and offices, that are alleged to serve their interests, will be more integrated into society than those with less confidence.

The percent of workers indicating "a lot of confidence" to these offices and institutions is startlingly low. About 13 percent of the early retirees and 10 percent of the relocatees reported having "a lot of confidence" in the President of the United States. The percentages for the remaining institutions and offices for both the early retirees and relocatees are respectively: 9 percent and 0 percent for big business; 8 percent and 12 percent for the Supreme Court of the United States; 5 percent and 3 percent for the Governor of New York; 5 percent and 0 percent for the United States Congress; and, 1 percent and 3 percent for the New York State legislature (see Table 9).

INSTITUTIONS AND OFFICES

Table 9. Percentage of Early Retirees and Relocatees Responding "A Lot of Confidence" to Institutions and Offices of the United States*

Institutions and Offices	Early Retirees Indicating "A Lot of Confidence"	Relocatees Indicating "A Lot of Confidence"
Big Business	9%	0%
Congress	5%	0%
Supreme Court	8%	12%
President of the United States	13%	10%
State Legislature	1%	3%
Governor of New York	5%	3%
*A total of 88 early retirees and 31 relocatees responded to each institution and office. A complete tabulation of responses is included in Appendix F Table F-18.		

A comparison with national poll data more clearly underscores how low the percentages of those workers expressing "a lot of confidence" in four of the six institutions and offices mentioned above are. A 1984 Lou Harris poll found: 42 percent of Americans expressing "a great deal of confidence" in the presidency; 19 percent in big business; 35 percent in the supreme court, and 28 percent in the congress of the United States.[74]

The data indicates that the early retirees and relocatees lack high levels of confidence in social institutions and offices throughout American society.

Equality of Opportunity for Children of Workers and Executives. Throughout this book it has been discussed that certain groups of individuals and institutions have been quite monetarily successful. Others have suffered as a result of economic dislocation. Do Syracuse workers believe that equality of opportunity is shared among their children and the children of the executive class? In attempts to uncover how workers think in terms of equal opportunity, we are, in effect, exploring the existence of what has been known as the "American Dream." Workers who believe that equality of opportunity exists (those who believe that the child of a factory worker has "about the same chance" as the child of a business executive to succeed in life) are more integrated into society than those who do not hold the belief.

The former Syracuse GM workers were asked if they think that the child of a factory worker has about the same chance to get ahead as the child of a business executive. Less than 20 percent of each group of workers indicated "about the same chance." In contrast, approximately 80 percent of each group of workers responded less of a chance.[75]

Future Employment Opportunities. What are the views on future job opportunities of forced early retirees. Optimistic views on future employment can tell us much in the way of how these workers view the strength of the economy. A healthy, growing economy offers more employment opportunities; a weak economy holds fewer opportunities. Workers who believe the economy is healthy and offers greater job opportunities may be more integrated into their society than workers who do not.

The 88 early retirees were asked, if they had to find another job right now, would they have a "very difficult time," "fairly difficult time," "fairly easy time," or a "very easy time." Sixty-three percent of the early retirees believed they would have a "very difficult" time finding another job and 33 percent indicated they would have a "fairly difficult" time.

As was reported earlier, the early retirees who were looking for work were asked when they thought they would be able to find a job. The possible responses were "in a few weeks," "a few months," or "really don't know." All (100 percent) of the 18 workers who were looking for work answered that they really did not know when they would be able to find a job.

Although the relocatees were not asked questions concerning future employment, nearly 25 percent did not consider their jobs as permanent. During the interviewing phase it was found that several years ago some workers from other closed plants had relocated to the Syracuse plant. The Syracuse closing represented the second plant closing for those workers. Many GM workers were fearful that their new work location may also close down and mentioned the problems associated with job security for all workers in the United States.

It is clear that the early retirees and, in many respects, the relocatees who do not see their jobs as permanent, do not see the economy as healthy. As a result, these workers do not seem to believe the lack of future employment opportunities is "just the way things are" and, in fact, may look forward to some type of change.

Shared Interest Between Labor and Management. The last dimension of social integration is the degree to which workers see mutual interests between labor and management. Workers were asked to respond to two questions. One question asked, simply enough, if workers believe that the interests of management and workers are basically opposed or are they the same. Response categories were either "basically opposed," "basically the same," "mixed," or "don't know."

The other question dealt with the issue of "cooperation programs and teamwork." Respondents were asked to indicate their opinion of cooperation programs and teamwork between labor and management. Possible responses were "a good idea," "a bad idea," "mixed," or "no opinion."

Assuming a relationship between social integration and labor/management relations, workers less integrated into the social system would see management interests diametrically opposed to their own and would distrust cooperative efforts. On the other hand, workers more integrated into the "social structure of accumulation," would see a mutuality of interest and welcome cooperative efforts.

The data supplied by the survey indicates something very interesting. In response to the question concerning the interests of management and labor, about 61 percent of the early retirees and 58 percent of the relocatees indicated "mixed; depends; some interests conflict, others don't." And, in response to cooperative efforts between labor and management, 53 percent of the of the early retirees and 65 percent of the relocatees indicated "mixed; can be good or bad."

From the data presented, one could argue that the responses tell us little in the way of workers being either more or less integrated into society. On the other hand, since the workers did not show opposition to shared interest in substantial numbers, it may be inferred that they are more integrated then not.

These responses, at first, seem to be somewhat unusual or contradictory, considering previous response to the other dimension of social integration. To gain a clearer understanding behind the meaning of the responses to "shared interests between labor and management," more elaboration is necessary.

A few years before the Syracuse plant closing, the local union and rank-and-file members embraced efforts to foster mutual interests and cooperative efforts with management. Interviews with local union leaders, rank-and-file members and management indicated that, rightfully or not, many workers believed that their cooperative efforts might save jobs and also increase workers' shop floor control. Union leaders and workers were careful about embracing cooperative efforts that would increase management control. Some efforts were seen as mutual, i.e. shop floor safety; other efforts were embraced that put workers in more control of their jobs, i.e. more say in the production process.

The workers clearly do not believe that the union "sold out" to management. Over 84 percent of the early retirees and 68 percent of the relocatees indicated that, before there was any talk of closing the Syracuse plant, the union was helpful in protecting workers' rights. In fact, some of the greatest resistance to "cooperation" came from management. Many supervisors at the plant felt a loss of control and made efforts to undermine cooperation programs.

An interview with one former Syracuse worker (closely aligned with the former union local) who relocated, indicated how some of the Syracuse workers viewed the meaning of "cooperation." During this interview the respondent mentioned tensions between relocated Syracuse workers and the local union at one of the receiving plants. When asked about the source of those tensions the worker responded:

> "Well, the local union and rank and file bought into this whole cooperation thing ... they are all on management side ... our cooperative efforts [at Syracuse] did not work that way."

In light of the elaboration on shared interest between labor and management, one can infer that the former GM Syracuse workers are not as integrated into society as their responses might indicate.

Summary of Social Integration

There seems to be little difference in the degree to which early retirees and relocatees responded to each of the different dimensions of social integration. The largest difference found was the degree to which the relocatees (68 percent) and early retirees (84 percent) felt the union was helpful at protecting their rights. The lower response of the relocatees may have been a result of their unhappiness with the plant closing even though the question was framed in "Before the plant closed . . . "

As a result, it can be determined that many of the former GM Syracuse workers did not see their situation as hopeless and a natural element of "just the way things are," and did not blame themselves. They look toward government policies that encourage change. They do not support the corporate practice of blaming foreign competition while profits of American corporations continue to rise. Former employees blame the institutions and offices that are supposed to be on their side as shown by their lack of having a lot of confidence in them.

Survey respondents are not optimistic about the economic future of the United States as posited by their pessimism regarding future employment opportunities. These workers see themselves as different because they believe that the opportunities for getting ahead are different for their children than for children of business executives. These workers were willing to work for the mutual interests of labor and management, but unwilling to be taken advantage of.

For a clearer understanding of the magnitude to which these workers lack social integration, their responses to the dimensions of social integration should have been compared to employed auto workers who were not relocated. Although it may be difficult to find employed U.S. auto workers and more difficult to find ones that have not been relocated, the author looks forward to further research and the task of comparison in the coming years.

The Early Retirees

Some very important information that was gained from the research but not yet discussed needs pointing out. The early retirees were questioned about when they began looking for work once they learned that their employment at the GM Syracuse plant would end. Of the 52 early retirees who indicated they had looked for work and did not already have employment, only 19 percent looked for work before the layoff and over 80 percent looked for work some time after their layoff.

It is not known why such a high percentage of workers waited to look for work. It may be that some wanted to take some time off before looking. It is also possible that some workers may have been unsure of their decision to take early retirement (as opposed to relocate) and, as a result, postponed the decision to look for work. Some 57 percent of all the early retirees indicated that, if they had to make the decision to not relocate over again, they either didn't know or would not have made the same decision. One early retiree had this to say:

> "I took early retirement, but if I had it to do over I would have relocated . . . I miss the people I worked with."

In light of the earlier reported aggregate data on advanced notification, it seems that further investigation into the reasons for delayed employment decisions is warranted. Simply reporting when workers begin looking for work after job displacement does not supply enough information to determine the success or shortcomings of advanced notification. The effectiveness of advanced notification may depend on a number of factors. If the early retirees were made aware of their decisions to take early retirement, then they may have started to look for work earlier. Some of the workers may have believed that they would be called back to work, or that the plant might just stay open. Rumors were circulating (at the time) that another company might buy the Syracuse plant.

Of the 83 questions to which early retirees were asked to respond, one seems most important. What was the major reason for workers deciding to stay in Syracuse? These early retirees had the opportunity to continue their employment with General Motors at other locations. Most acknowledged the financial necessity to continue employment and many took drastic reductions in income. These workers had to have been aware of the lack of employment opportunities in Syracuse since, on average, they have lived in Syracuse for 45 years.

An overwhelming majority of workers, some 56 percent, said they decided to stay in Syracuse because of family and friends.[76] Throughout the entire interviewing phase the central reoccurring factor in the decision making process for these workers (as for the relocatees as well) was the importance of family and friends. Syracuse was considered "home" and they wanted to stay. The importance of family and friends will be elaborated on in the discussion of relocatees, as well as in the summary and conclusions.

The Relocatees

The relocated workers were asked to respond to questions concerning living arrangements in their former Syracuse location and their current work location. Changed living arrangements certainly could have effected their personal, social, and economic situations.

Approximately 90 percent of the 31 workers either owned a home in the Syracuse area or were in the process of buying one, and lived with a spouse and/or other family members. At their present work locations, 23 percent owned a home or were in the process of buying; 16 percent were paying rent and living in a house; 39 percent were renting an apartment, and, as reported previously, 23 percent were commuting.

Relocatees' current living arrangements also have changed from those seen in Syracuse. About 16 percent reported that they now live with friends; 29 percent now live alone; 6 percent live with friends and family; and only 26 percent responded that they live with their spouse and/or other family members.[77]

The impact of family breakups understandably may have influenced relocatees' reporting of greater feelings of depression, more adverse physical symptoms, and worse relationships with spouses and family members then the early retirees.

Interviewed workers mentioned not only the stress and strains of no longer living with their spouses and/or families but also the fears of new living arrangements in their relocated areas. One worker said:

"It looks like I'm either going to have to live alone or with a friend(s) ... and that's something I haven't done since I left the service [military] 25 years ago ... now how do you think I feel about that?"

Just as devastating as the break up of the family is what relocated workers did with the homes they owned in Syracuse. An astounding 78 percent indicated that they still own their Syracuse residences.[78] The 24 workers who still owned their home exceeds the number of workers whose spouses or other family members remained in Syracuse. The costs associated with maintaining two dwellings may supply reasons as to why 73 percent of the relocatees indicated that they had to "generally cut down on overall expenses and postpone anticipated purchases."

As a result of these living arrangements it is understandable why so many relocated workers make routine visits back to the Syracuse area. Approximately 29 percent of all the workers make weekly visits and 23 percent make monthly visits.[79] Some workers have complained that they would like to go back to the Syracuse area more frequently to be with their families and friends, but mandatory overtime makes it impossible.

The Syracuse area is home for these relocated workers.[80] They had lived in the area for an average of 35 years, and all of their families and friends are in Syracuse.[81] When asked why, if they had several places to relocate, they chose the one they had, 68 percent indicated because it was close to Syracuse and none (0 percent) indicated because they wanted to live in their work area.

Research Results in Review: Summary and Conclusions

The Syracuse plant closing agreement negotiated by the United Automobile Workers and General Motors management can be seen, in some respects, as one of the best case scenarios if a plant closes down. All the former Syracuse workers were offered a job at other GM locations (with base pay and benefits the same) and nearly 100 percent of the eligible workers took the earlier retirement option. The Syracuse workers mentioned during interviews that they were quite aware of the fact that other plant closings in New York State and through the United States have offered workers far less. This being understood, many of these workers acknowledged that they have suffered as a result of the shutdown.

Approximately 28 percent of early retirees reported being unemployed at the time of the survey. Of those "looking for work" none knew when they would find employment. The 1994 incomes of the early retirees went down considerably from what they had reported one year before the plant closing. For those early retirees lucky enough to find jobs, the salaries were also lower than what they had been making before the shutdown. It was also determined that early retirees experienced a wide variance as to how long they held their new employment position.

The relocatees have suffered in different ways. Nearly 65 percent of the relocatees indicated that their spouses remained in Syracuse mainly for employment reasons. Some relocatees were found to be commuting daily from Syracuse to their relocated area (over four hours round trip). Relocation was not something to which the transferred workers looked forward too; over 40 percent had looked for work in Syracuse before relocating.

Survey results showed that relocatees may have suffered financial hardships as a result of maintaining two household dwellings. The adverse affects that relocation has had on the workers leaves little wonder as to why, as a percent, nearly three times as many relocated workers than early retirees were dissatisfied with the benefits negotiated in the plant closing contract.

A sizable portion of early retirees reported problems with feelings of depression, physical symptoms, and relationships with spouses. However, a far greater percent of relocatees indicated suffering more in these areas. It is interesting to point out that as a proportion within each group, a greater percent reported worse relationships with spouses, then other family members or friends.

The study also showed that just about equal percentages of both groups of workers can be seen as not socially integrated into society and not willing to accept the "natural inevitableness" of what has happened to them. These workers do not blame themselves for their situation but the economy, political leaders, and big business. They have been hurt by the closing of the Syracuse plant and look toward some degree of economic and or social change in the United States.

Some interesting conclusions can be reached from the findings of the Syracuse plant closing study. In the case of the early retirees, income was correlated with one element of depression (enthusiasm). As income rose, the early retirees lack of enthusiasm went down. Income was also correlated to the early retirees ability to afford certain household and leisure items on the "perceived economic distress" indicator. As income increased workers' ability to afford more items on the indicator also increased.

Perceived economic distress for the early retirees was correlated with the depression indicator. Workers unable to afford five or more household items suffered from more depression than those workers who were able to afford all household and leisure items. Also, those early retirees that were found to be depressed and who were unable to afford five or more household and leisure items, reported more physical health problems.

The spouses of early retirees were found to not re-enter the workforce even though family incomes went down. Also, even though a large percent of female early retirees saw themselves as "retired," the incomes of female early retirees cannot be considered secondary to family incomes.

Among relocatees, income was not found to be correlated with depression and physical symptoms. Rising incomes of the relocatees did not affect these scores either negatively or positively. For relocatees the greater problems with feelings of depression, more reported physical symptoms, and worse relations with family and friends, than were reported by early retirees may be due to broken family and community ties.

Relocatees confidence in social institutions was correlated with feelings of depression and physical health problems. Those relocatees found to suffer from depression and high levels of physical health problems were also found to have "hardly any confidence" in social institutions and offices.

What has been apparent throughout the reporting of this study of dislocated former GM workers has been the importance of family and friends. These workers consider Syracuse their home and they do not want to leave. Early retirees took that option because of wanting to be with families and friends. The relocatees choose their relocation site because it was close to Syracuse, where most of them preferred to live.

Some of the relocatees still have spouses and family members in Syracuse and were found to commute on a regular basis. Plant closing agreements or legislation that does not address the important issue of family, friends and community ties will fall short of any positive outcome.

Since a greater percent of relocatees, than the early retirees, suffered more feelings of depression, adverse physical symptoms and worse relations with family and friends, "Does capital want a mobile labor force?" Many of the relocatees acknowledged how "sloppy" their situation was handled by General Motors management. Some workers were contacted by phone and were forced to make a relocation decision on the spot. Some workers were not advised if they had more than one relocation option. Other workers did not know what would happen if they refused a option to relocate. The relocated workers had also reported that they were not happy with their new jobs compared to the ones they had a GM Syracuse, and many were not happy about their changed, in-plant seniority date.

On the other hand General Motors "encouraged" eligible workers to take early retirement. The age at which workers were allowed to take early retirement was lowered to incorporate a greater number of workers. And, the earnings ceiling on workers' yearly income was removed. It should also be remembered that the relocation option at Syracuse, even though problematic, was not gifted to the workers by GM management but fought for and won by the UAW.

In the larger context of the question; "Does capital want a mobile labor force? the answer seems to be "it depends." If it is to capital's advantage (for example, hiring migrant farm workers) then a mobile labor force may be seen as a good idea. On the other hand, one of the main points behind plant closings is to "get rid" of your workforce and, of course, that can't be done by relocating workers to other corporate facilities. One thing seems to be certain, if profits are important to capital and a mobile labor force represents a cost then it would seem that capital would want to entertain other ideas.

Research in Plant Closings

As important as it is to discuss the findings of the research on the Syracuse plant closing, it is equally important to discuss shortcomings of the study. One of the main shortcomings behind the research was the lack of names and addresses of the relocatees. Problems of anonymity prevented the author from gaining access to this information. Stronger arguments could have been made if larger sample sizes were obtained.

The study of the displaced GM workers should have been more comparative in nature. The conclusions drawn from this research could have benefited from the responses of employed (and not relocated) auto workers who have not experienced a plant shutdown. Also, the experiences of former GM workers who were bringing a law suit against the corporation and union for allegedly changing the contract may have added important information to the study. The reluctance of these workers to discuss their situation, resulting from the ongoing legal ramifications, made inquiry into this area impossible.

More information may have been extracted from the data if other statistical measures were utilized such as path analysis. Also, lacking interval scaling of the questions limited the use of some more elaborate statistics.

Although great care was taken in preparing the instruments, problems were found. Some questions were ambiguous and workers were unsure of how to answer. Other questions lacked possible responses experienced by the workers and workers wrote in their answers. A question concerning the respondents race was not asked. Somewhere in the pairing down of the instrument this question was removed.

One respondent in particular had this to say about the research:

"Syracuse was my second plant closing. I find it interesting that you worked five years with people whose plant was closed, but weren't concerned until it involved you. I doubt a college degree will help you get through to people that have not experienced it ... Your questions were from the assumption that I was from Syracuse and not one of the many other plants that were represented. I feel that your survey will suffer from tunnel vision, and that it leaves out the valuable insight of many workers that called Syracuse home for a short period of time."

Many questions that should have been asked were not. It would have been interesting to discover just how many GM Syracuse workers experienced more than one shutdown. About 12 percent of the relocated workers reported living in Syracuse for less than 10 years (relocation to Syracuse began within this time range). Many of those workers living in Syracuse less than 10 years may have experienced more than one shutdown.

Research such as this should be informative to others studying plant closings and their affects. Unfortunately or fortunately, many, including the author, have never experienced a plant closing. It may be the case that living an experience may add to the richness of reporting one.

The final chapter of this book places the closing of the GM Syracuse plant within the framework of the domestic economy and the larger international context of capital relocation.

NOTES

1. Numerous casual conversations with employees also were conducted but not taped.

2. Many of the questions (in whole or in part) were taken from the surveys administered by Perrucci (1988) and Lipsky (1979).

3. See Appendix D for questionnaire packet distributed to relocatees.

4. Of the returned questionnaires only males responded. It was determined that the total population of females at complex #2 was only three.

5. The early retirement option is normally not available.

6. See Appendix E for questionnaire packet mailed to early retirees.

7. The author was notified by phone of the deceased respondents.

8. Lack of enthusiasm, $z=2.45$ (Chi-square: 6.056, df=2, p=.048); Feel lonely, $z=2.57$ (Chi-square: 12.608, df=2. p=.002); Feel bored, $z=2.06$ (Chi-square: 4.946, df=2, p=.084). Statistical significance if $z\geq1.282$ @ p=.100

9. Chi-square: 8.179, df=1, p=.004

10. Worse relations with spouse, $z=3.00$ (Chi-square: 13.294, df=2. p=.001). Worse relations with children, $z=2.77$ (Chi-square: 18.767, df=2, p=.000). Worse relations with family, $z=2.73$ (Chi-square: 11.681, df=2, p=.003). Worse relations with friends, $z=3.61$ (Chi-square: 11.624, df=2, p=.003). Statistical significance if $z\geq1.282$ @ p=1.00.

11. Government policies and institutions and offices will be elaborated on later in the text.

12. Fishers exact test (one tail) p=.059

13. Chi-square: 6.325, df=2, p=.042.

14. Chi-square: 5.837, df=2, p=.054.

15. Chi-square: 15.368, df=1, p=.000.

16. Incomes to be discussed later in the text.

17. Fisher's exact test: p=.055 (one tail).

18. n=88

19. Average age of the relocatees was found to be 44 years.

20. A total of 47 workers responded to this question. Investigation into the wording of the question was found to be misleading for some workers who responded "more than two years" of unemployment. Analysis of responses to other questions as well as information supplied by the respondents indicated that some workers who had more than two years unemployment may not have responded. Also, workers who responded "more than two years" were ones who may have withdrawn or retired from the labor force. By factoring in only those workers who later reported currently working full-time, working part-time or looking for work an estimated three percent were unemployed for less than one month, 82 percent were unemployed an average of nearly 12 months and 15 percent were unemployed for more than two years (n=30).

21. No statistically significant difference was found showing women experiencing longer periods of unemployment. About an equal percent of men and women reported that they were currently looking for work.

22. n=68

23. As was mentioned, an estimated 20 percent (or 18) were looking for work; 25 percent (or 22) were withdrawn or retired and about nine percent (or eight) of the workers reported being ill or otherwise incapacitated.

24. Of the 68 married early retiree workers, 41 percent had a spouse with full-time employment and 19 percent reported part-time working mates. Also, 18 percent reported their spouses to be ill or otherwise incapacitated and 18 percent reported their spouses as not looking for work and four percent reported that their spouses were looking for work.

25. Other responses to "reason for relocating" were: to reach full retirement age or maintain health benefits.

26. Approximately 25 percent (or eight) of the relocated workers indicated their spouse or other household members moved to their relocated

areas. Approximately 10 percent (or three) indicated they lived alone in Syracuse.

27.   Incomes earned in 1992. Incomes were defined as "wages and other income sources before state and federal withholding taxes." Also, the $53,200 figure includes five employees who reported family incomes of over $75,000, n=68 with five workers not reporting family incomes.

28.   Figure includes two workers who reported family incomes of over $75,000, n=65 with five workers not reporting incomes that should have. In 1992 dollars, $39,500 is estimated at $38,770. This figure was obtained by dividing 1994 purchasing power of the dollar (.797) by the 1992 purchasing power of the dollar (.812) and then multiplying it by 1994 income.

29.   Income earned in 1992. Presumably the differences in family incomes can be attributed to higher earnings of the spouse of early retirees compared to the spouse of the relocatees. Family incomes of the relocatees includes one worker who reported an income in excess of $75,000. Total n=24 with two workers not reporting incomes.

30.   n=22. This figure includes 5 workers who had incomes of over $75,000. Also, there were three workers that should have reported family incomes but did not. In 1992 dollars, $59,500 is estimated at $58,400.

31.   Income earned in 1992, n=82 with six workers not reporting individual incomes.

32.   The remaining workers (25 percent) had average incomes of $36,000. In 1992 dollars, this figure is estimated to be $35,335, n=82 with six workers not reporting individual incomes.

33.   Incomes earned in 1992, n=29 with two workers not reporting incomes.

34.   Includes three workers who reported incomes over $75,000. Total n=28, with three workers not reporting incomes. In 1992 dollars, $55,400 is estimated to be $54,375.

35.   In 1992 dollars this figure is estimated to be $38,575.

36.   n=37. In 1992 dollars, $36,600 is estimated at $35,923.

37.   n=18

38.   As can be expected, 96 percent of workers that stated they were ill or otherwise incapacitated, or withdrawn or retired for the labor force, had incomes below $25,000.

39.   Only one worker who was suppose to respond did not.

40.   Fishers exact: p=.031 (one tail) .

41.   n=17

42.   As seen in table 1

43. Chi-square: 6.724, df=2, p=.035.

44. Regressions on incomes had n=82; all other analysis had no missing data (n=88).

45. p=.010. For the remaining mental health questions, analysis is as follows. As income rose, the sense of feeling lonely and the feeling of being bored went down. Respectively, correlation coefficients were found to be; r=-.117 (p=.296) and r=-.173 (p=.120).

46. Regressions are as follows. As incomes went up, lack of enthusiasm went down (r=-.045; p=.820). As income went up, sense of feeling lonely went down (r=-.067; p=.734). But, as income went up, feeling bored or having little interest in doing things also went up,(r=.096; p=.626).

47. z value was found to be 2.755. For statistical significance at p=.100, z≥1.282(one tail test).

48. Pearsons Chi-square; 1.933, df=1, p=.164.

49. This was done to increase the expected cell values for Chi-square analysis

50. Further elaboration on "Confidence in Social Institutions and Offices" will be taken up under the heading Social Integration. For list of institutions and offices see appendix D questions 16-21.

51. Eight relocatees were found to have "no confidence" in U.S. institutions and offices. Twenty-three were found to have some level of confidence in U.S. institutions and offices.

52. Fisher exact; (one-tailed), p=.026; (two-tailed), p=.032. In reference to the relocatees, the only other significant finding was when social institutions and offices was run against physical health (to be reported later). Also, no correlation or associations was found concerning early retirees and social institutions and offices.

53. See Appendix E questions 49-55.

54. Pearsons Chi-square: 8.065, df=4, p= .089. The perceived economic distress indicator was collapsed into 3 categories to raise expected cell values for this analysis.

55. For one of the finest plant closing agreements in the country, this figure seems a bit disenchanting

56. p=.000

57. Pearsons Chi-square: 21.599, df= 2, p= .000; G=-.730

58. Fisher exact test: p=.453 (one tail).

59. More on the purchase and sale of a home will be discussed later.

60. Missing data was not over 10 percent on any of the items for both sets of workers. Chi-squares/z values were run, but no statistical difference was found when relating each of the symptoms with both groups of workers

61. Pearsons Chi-square: 7.056, df= 2, p= .029.

62. Chi-square: 4.958, df=2, p=.084.

63. Pearsons Chi-square: 6.892, df=1, p=.009.

64. Pearsons Chi-square: 19.388, df=2, p=.000; Gamma= .770.

65. The categories of the physical symptoms indicator were collapsed in efforts to increase the expected cell values for Chi-square analysis. Still, no relation was found.

66. Fisher exact: (one-tailed), p=.060; (two-tailed), p=.097.

67. It is somewhat interesting to point out that 20 percent of all females indicated better relationships with friends, compared with seven percent of all males.

68. As seen in table 2.

69. Retiree analysis of relations with family and friends by financial hardship variables (i.e. perceived economic distress) was not possible due to low expected cell values. Analysis between relations with family and friends by whether or not the relocatees had to cut down on overall expenses or postpone anticipated purchases suffered the same problem.

70. This section, in whole or in part, was taken from Perrucci 1988, pp. 97-106).

71. The workers were asked four questions as to the reasons for closing the plant. One question applied to anti-union sentiments, not anti management sentiments, and was not used.

72. Percentages less than 50 (in this case a plurality) is a result of DK (don't know) responses to questions.

73. Workers were asked to respond to questions on a total of seven institutions and offices. Labor unions were the other institution polled. The displaced workers were members of the UAW and, as a result, their level of confidence can be expected to be higher than the other institutions and offices reviewed, and, in fact, it was. Thirty-one percent of the early retirees and 19 percent of the relocatees responded that they have "a lot of confidence" in labor unions. The low percentage of workers indicating "a lot of confidence" may obviously be the result of the closing of the Syracuse plant.

74. As seen in Perrucci 1988, p. 106.

75. Response of "less of a chance" was determined by those who indicated "somewhat less of a chance" plus those who indicated "much less of

a chance." DK (don't know) response was less than 3 percent, n=88 for early retirees and n=31 for relocatees.

76. Other responses were: job opportunity for self (3 percent), job opportunity for spouse (10 percent), education or retraining for self (1 percent), financial considerations (11 percent) and other (18 percent). n=88.

77. 23 percent commute.

78. The breakdown is as follows: 13 percent or 4 of the workers sold their homes; 23 percent or seven tried to sell but did not; 55 percent or 17 did not try to sell; 10 percent or three did not own a home. n=31.

79. As reported, those that commute, of course, make daily visits (23 percent), 6 percent indicated they do not return to Syracuse and 13 percent indicated an "other" time frame.

80. An estimated 74 percent prefer to live in Syracuse, 10 percent their relocated area and 13 percent had no preference (n=30)

81. Over 90 percent indicated that their families and friends remain in Syracuse, n=31.

CHAPTER 5

The Plant Closing in a Broader Perspective

CONCLUSION

This book began with a general overview of capital relocation and the many and varied reasons for its occurrence. Transnational corporations in general and General Motors in particular have used a variety of methods to either protect or enhance profits. Currently, the continued expansion abroad and production alliances with competitors, coupled with the downsizing of existing manufacturing operations in the United States, are the arsenal of weapons used by capital in its search for profits.

State policy can be seen as encouraging capital flight and domestic decay. Tax laws and trade policies encourage capital relocation which, in effect, contributes to manufacturing employment decline. In response to domestic decay some politicians encourage a "hard right turn" by attempting to link democracy with capitalism. Speaker of the House Newt Gingrich's "Contract with America" is no better example. When the House of Representatives passed the balanced budget plan (part of the Contract with America) in November of 1995, Gingrich said it was, " . . . the first blueprint to give our children lower interest rates, lower taxes and more freedom and more prosperity" (New York Times 8 March 1996, p. A22). Included in his tract is the idea that democratic principles of life, liberty and the pursuit of happiness are linked with the ideology of competition and the pursuit of profits. The message for Americans is that trust in the process of accumulation, expansion and reproduction of capital safeguards democracy through prosperity.

This new round of capital accumulation, reproduction and expansion achieved through the migration of U.S. manufacturing capital overseas, corporate production alliances with compititors and downsizing U.S. manufacturing operations, aided by state policy, has produced a systematic disinvestment of the nation's basic productive capacity known as deindustrialization, which has ushered in a variety of hardships for millions of Americans. Democratic principles are in conflict with capitalism as more and more American workers work for less and are left shell-shocked from an capitalist economy in which corporate profit is reaching historic highs.

The actions of General Motors in its search for profits and the consequences for its workers is typical of the scenarios created by many manufacturing firms. General Motors has continued to expand abroad, and recently announced that it would invest one billion dollars in China. GMs continued co-production relationships with former competitors such as Toyota, as well as GM's downsizing of U.S. operations, complements GMs strategy for increasing profits. The decline of U.S. manufacturing investment, typified by the operations of General Motors, has meant scores of layoffs (now euphemistically called "workforce imbalance corrections") and plant closing all across the United States.

The closing of the General Motors Syracuse plant exemplifies the outcome of the corporations' pursuit of profits in the 1990s. While General Motors closed many of its unionized plastics fabrication plants, including the one in Syracuse, its Mexican plastics fabrication facilities went untouched.

Management at the Syracuse plant outsourced some of its plastics manufacturing not only to low-wage and non-union job shops in the United States, but further diversified by buying component parts from German suppliers. The Syracuse plant also moved some of its plastics fabrication to other GM facilities in Spain and Mexico which then shipped fabricated parts back to Syracuse.

While the General Motors corporation in general and the Syracuse plant in particular were preaching the importance of buying American-made products, the Syracuse plant modernized its injection molding equipment by purchasing German-made machines. United States made "state-of-the-art" injection molders were not purchased.

A few years before the official notification of the shutdown of the Syracuse plant, local management threatened the State of New York with the possibility that the Syracuse plant would be closed if certain monies and tax incentives were not made available to help boost profitability. The monies were made available, but the plant still closed. GM and local Syracuse management cited the loss of profits as a reason for closing the plant even though the corporation, shortly thereafter, experienced record breaking profits.

State and federal intervention to assist plants in remaining open is not an unusual occurrence in many industrial settings. The GM-Norwood (Ohio) facility (as discussed in this book) received assistance, but the plant still closed. Also, citing the loss of profit as the reason for closing plants, is a typical explanation given by management.

The outcome of the corporate quest for profit has been detrimental to the U.S. domestic economy and American workers. As firms no longer invest in U.S. capital equipment and infrastructure, manufacturing employment declines through numerous plant closings. Plant closings have produced unemployment, underemployment, relocation and early retirement for hundreds of thousands of workers in many industrial settings. As a result, dislocated workers often experience mental and physical symptoms and family related problems.

Former workers at the closed General Motors Syracuse plant have paid significant personal and social costs, even though the plant shutdown can be considered a "best case" scenario of what happens when plants do close. The Syracuse workers were offered early retirement and relocation resulting from negotiation efforts of the United Automobile Workers. Options such as these have not always been part of shutdown packages; often workers are simply "involuntarily separated."

A growing trend in the 1990s has been the increase in the number of early retirement pensioners. The escalation of early retirements is, in part, because of workers opting for early retirement to avoid mandatory layoffs, plant shutdowns or relocation. The national trend shows that early retirees are looking for work in increasing numbers because of the lack of adequate early retirement income. Many of the early retirees in the Syracuse plant closing study re-enter the workforce in low-paying positions. This is indeed consistent with the experiences of early retirees in other industries who were lucky enough to find employment.

When plants do close, workers may have the option to relocate within the same company. Transfer options, to similar jobs and income (or higher income) may not always signal a "happy ending" for workers facing plant closings. Relocated Syracuse workers indicated greater mental and physical health problems and worse relations with family members then the early retirees. As a result, the GM Syracuse relocation option calls into question the "genuine" commitment to corporate relocation in general. On the other hand, if relocation is to be a solution to plant closings then the Syracuse case study should be helpful in understanding the many and varied negative effects relocation may have on workers.

The data presented in this book provide convincing testimony to the negative effects that the plant closing has had on former Syracuse workers in terms of adverse mental and physical symptoms and detrimental effects on family relations. This too is consistent with the findings of other case studies on other workers in other industries who have fallen victim to plant shutdowns.

The former GM Syracuse workers echo the voices of many workers across the United States in developing a diminished degree of trust in the national economy. A 1995 national opinion poll, referencing the state of the union, was conducted by the New York Times.[1] The poll compared the responses of Americans "hard hit by layoffs"[2] with those who were not. The survey found that a greater percent of Americans "hard hit" by layoffs: feel economically insecure about their future; place "a lot" of blame on the economic system of the United States for the loss of jobs; believe that the government should step in and do something about layoffs and job loss; feel that Congress and the President can do something about layoffs and job loss; place the blame of job loss on big business, and believe that layoffs and a loss of jobs will be a permanent problem in the United States.

The former GM Syracuse workers as well as workers across the country who have felt the misery of layoffs and job loss cannot be viewed as accepting the "inevitable[ness] of it all." These workers are angry and do not blame themselves, are critical of big business, and look toward government intervention. They are less socially integrated than those not "hard it by a layoff" into trusting an economic system that should be working for them also.

Growing tensions about job security for American workers continues to escalate. During the first week of March 1996, the UAW at two General Motors brake plants in Dayton, Ohio, went out on strike, idling more than 124,000 workers nationwide. The strike at these two plants shut down 90 percent of General Motors North American operations. It was estimated that GM will lose pretax earnings of $47 million per day. The two reasons for the strike were General Motors insistence on brake component outsourcing (similar to GM's outsourcing of anti-lock brake systems to Robert Bosh G.m.b.H., an independent Germany supplier) and mandatory overtime for its workforce.

While General Motors claims the need to remain competitive, and the importance of mandatory overtime, they continue to outsource more product and to furlough more workers. In February 1996, General Motors reported record breaking profits of $6.8 billion on sales of $168.83 billion (New York Times 13 March 1996, p. D19).

Global production, downsizing and rising corporate profits amid domestic decay, plant closings and underemployment, leads many Americans to now be suspect of a system that is supposed to benefit those who work, and help those who are unable to. The ensuing struggles between the growing wealth of some people and the loss of wealth and dignity for many others shapes the economic, social and political fabric of the United States. Many Americans and many more American workers stand ready for change; some are willing to act.

Researchers such Piore and Sabel (1984) claim that the present industrial performance of the United States results from the limits of the model of industrial development based on mass production. These researchers argue that if the U.S. is to move past its economic hardship, a turn toward more flexible forms of production is required. This flexibility of production uses present forms of technology and a skilled workforce. Economic change to prosperity is be made possible by furthering capitalist development.

Womack, Jones, and Roos (1991) claim that not only are new forms of production methods required, but labor/management relations must also be revised in efforts to move past U.S. decay. Labor and management relations should be more of a cooperative approach between workers and managers, with less need for contract rules and regulations. Drucker (1993) points to how "knowledge" housed within the corporate organization is the key commodity to major world transformations.

The authors who insist on a bright economic future for the U.S. by furthering a "free" market enterprise are either unwilling or unable to see the historical significance of the decline. History is not a random occurrence, and although history does not dictate the course of capital, it does offer possible trajectories for its future course. Phillips (1993) sees the decline of U.S. domestic manufacturing followed by the preoccupation of the internationalization of capital as not unique in history. Once dominant economic powers such as Holland and Britain experienced a crisis similar to what is happening to the United States .

The evidence thus far has not pointed to a "golden Age" for most Americans; however, some have prospered quite well indeed. As corporations pursue profits, roughly 50 percent more people, about three million, are affected by layoffs each year. Between the winter of 1991 and summer of 1995, corporate profits increased by $193.9 billion.[3] The present corporate disinvestment in the nation's productive capacity, coupled with social dislocation, does not support the continued belief that capitalist development, aided by TNCs, will come to benefit all.

A more plausible interpretation is that the United States is in the midst of both a decay and a transformation. This "restructuring crisis"[4] is leading toward a form of capital, profoundly more global and one currently at the expense of the domestic economy.

The explanation for this crisis of restructuring is grounded in the belief that although capital has historically been international, what has changed is that the internationalization of capital is no longer housed within national boundaries. The old adage, "What is good for General Motors is good for the country," had a degree of truth to the extent workers were employed, consumption was expanding and so, too, were GMs profits. At present, what seems to be more true is "What's good for General Motors is good for General Motors."

The expansion and scope of the international circuits of TNCs, no longer firmly rooted in national boundaries, benefits the corporations more than any national economy. Profitability is now contained within narrower limits, benefiting a number of corporations, import and export firms and a limited number of transnational actors, and the upper capitalist classes of specific nations.

Corporate rate of profit is the underlying determinant of the accumulation, reproduction and expansion of capital. While there are many avenues for increasing profits,[5] capital typically increases profits by restructuring three main relationships: capital-to-labor, capital-to-capital and capital-to-state. For example, capital can increase profits by lowering labor costs or increasing the intensity of labor, and/or by lowering production costs (replacing expensive labor with machines, replacing machines with inexpensive labor, or by replacing expensive labor with cheap labor). Capital-to-capital relationships can be affected by influencing foreign sellers and buyers to achieve favorable prices on exports and imports (e.g., through diplomatic and military pressures on the governments involved).

Capital-to-state relationships involve influencing the formulation of state policy that affects capital's profit base (e.g., legislation that provides for protective tariffs); pressures other countries (e.g., Japan) to "open the door" for trade; or calls for negotiated free trade agreements (e.g., NAFTA). Other capital-to-state relations may involve policies that guard against interference in the supply of labor; remove environmental restrictions; and lower or remove taxes on profits.

As capital expands in search of greater profits, the economic system may appear to be relatively stable, for a time, if the economic actors receive increasing gains. These economic actors include workers within a given economy, foreign buyers and sellers and the state. Profits are made possible by the power the capitalist class has over the economic actors it confronts. Confrontation with capital arises when one or all of the economic actors lose out.

When capital accumulation is threatened or more profit can be made elsewhere, capital puts its money to other uses. During the 1970s, the capitalist class successfully fought against challenges from the economic actors by expanding abroad (moving factories overseas and expanding existing ones, as well as making coproduction and outsourcing arrangements), and by seeking profits through financial investments. Capital also benefited by engineering the U.S. political machinery to fight on its side to reduce the corporate and personal upper income tax rates as well as to influence the IMF and World Bank for favorable policies to open up Third World economies to U.S. investment.

Petras and Vieux (1994) argue that the weakened bargaining power of labor in the 1980s which resulted from corporate attacks on labor and a political climate that encouraged these actions actually stimulated globalization as increased profits were now extracted from domestic labor. "In the workplace, labor unions increasingly trade work-rules for 'security,' wages and fringe benefits for 'jobs'-all of which facilitated greater accumulation of capital for export or conversion to new technologies, replacing labor. The net result was a 'flexible work force'—greater subjection of labor and greater autonomy and mobility of capital to relocate" (Petras and Vieux 1994, p. 2). Lower wages have, in effect, fueled TNCs to compete internationally, while millions of Americans dropped out of middle class ranks (Phillips 1993, p. 196).

Although the Petras and Vieux (1994) argument is not incorrect, it seems more accurate to state it was not the actions of labor unions that made possible the accumulation of capital for export or conversion to new technologies but economic pressures (such as competition combined with the corporate profit motive) that caused labor to acquiesce as well as facilitate the greater autonomy and mobility of capital to relocate.

In the 1990s capital is moving to further strengthen itself, increase profits and fuel the accumulation process. This is accomplished by a variety of measures similar to those seen in the 1980s such as increasing the amount of capital outflow from the United States by supporting policies such as the North American Free Trade Agreement, lobbying for further reductions in profit taxes, pushing for an end to the social safety net (i.e., capping welfare benefits) and downsizing operations in the United States in a more hurried fashion. The accumulation process currently is being accomplished, in part, through extracting further surplus from the domestic economy of the United States.

The present accumulation process will set in motion a round of confrontation. American workers, no longer receiving increasing gains, question the validity of the system. State policy, on the one hand clearly siding with capital, on the other hand, will see political and social unrest as more Americans slide down the economic ladder. Some political leaders vying for office may begin to voice concern, directly confronting capital or through furthering capitalist development through less restrictions on corporate activity. The path chosen will be to maintain the status quo, if possible by co-opting Americans into believing gains are at hand. Direct action by the state fearing social unrest such as that which was seen shortly after the Great Depression may well be the last resort.

If enough Americans continue the economic spiral downward, social unrest will escalate. Change will be brought about, eventually, through struggle. Struggle may lead to a challenge with capital. This will usher in a new round of capital formation. As capital attempts to re-gain control, in efforts to harness greater amounts of profit, one of the economic actors may again lose out (if increasing gains are not shared) and struggle will ensue. The cycle will begin again.

NOTES

1. Facts cited from series of articles in New York Times March 3-9, 1996.

2. Hard hit by a layoff means people who said they or someone in their households has been laid off at least once in the last 15 years and the layoff had caused a major crisis in their lives.

3. Bureau of Economic Analysis as seen in the New York Times 3 March 1996, p. 1.

4. Explanation in part from Ross and Trachte (1990) and Gordon, Weisskopf and Bowles (1983) (1987).

5. Capital can increase profits through the process of exchange as capital is redistributed among companies and through mergers, for example. The accumulation, reproduction and expansion of capital thesis was, in part, taken from Bowles, Gordon and Weisskopf (1990) and Ross and Tarchte (1990).

American Capitalism on a Global Basis since World War II

The years prior to World War II contributed to the global strengthening of the U.S. both during and shortly after the war. War mobilization bolstered the U.S. economy by increasing manufacturing production by 2-1/2 times. The war effort stimulated the growth of America's largest corporations through governmental contracts . Some $175 billion was awarded to 18,539 corporations between June 1940 and September 1944. Of this sum, $117 billion (or two-thirds) went to the largest 100 corporations. The top recipient was General Motors, which alone received some $13.8 billion or 8 percent of the defense contract value (Pursell 1972, pp. 151-171).

The defense contracting system further exacerbated the concentration and centralization of capital. Working capital for 802 corporations increased from $8.6 billion in 1939 to $14.1 billion in 1945. The global experience of war allowed the U.S. to define the character of the postwar international economic and political order. Shortly after the war the United States had three quarters of the world's invested capital and two-thirds of its industrial capacity (Horowitz 1971. p. 74; Perrucci 1988, p. 14). From 1949 to 1969, goods-producing jobs grew by more than 33 percent—from 15 million to about 20 million (Swinney and Metzgar 1987, 153).

The strength of the United States after World War II in part rested on the avenues by which reconstruction of a new world order proceeded. The economic, political and military strategies chosen by the United States forged a new world order to its own liking.

In July 1944 at Bretton Woods, New Hampshire, a meeting of industrial powers, under the leadership of the United States, established the creation of a international monetary order. The Bretton Woods agreements, as they became to be known, provided for the creation of the International Monetary Fund (IMF) and the International Bank of Reconstruction and Development (World Bank).

Through a multitude of regulations including the stabilization of exchange rates and long-term loan guarantees, the policies of the IMF and the World Bank encouraged private investment over governmental and deflationary polices in recipient countries. These policies brought severe economic hardships to host counties around the globe, and can be seen as serving the interests of monopoly capitalism (Hoskins 1982, p.5).

Another international economic institution that assisted in bolstering the image of the United States was the General Agreement on Tariffs and Trade (GATT). Formed in 1947, its purpose was to facilitate international trade by reducing state regulations that create barriers to trade. In the early years, GATT worked to free trade among the richest nations while propping up trade barriers to prevent the importation of goods from less developed nations.

Politically the United States adopted policies around the theme of containment that would support the continuation of capitalism among specific nations and ruling classes. One of the major post-World War II programs developed was the Marshall Plan. Initially the plan was claimed to be motivated by humanitarian reasons for Europe after the war. Its purpose was claimed to be the revival of the working economy that world permit conditions for free institutions to exist. The actual impact of the plan did not live up to the proposed claims. The capitalist classes in Europe were benefited at the expense of European working classes. Economic recovery meant repression of the working masses and reduced power of organized labor. Some $9 billion from the Marshall plan was channeled into key European countries, its dual effect was to subdue any socialist or communistic fervor while at the same time the funds were being used to buy U.S. exports (Targ 1986, p. 26; Du Boff 1989, p. 154).

In a similar structure to the Marshall Plan, President Harry Truman's Point Four Program offered economic and military assistance to some Third World countries. Initially the plan authorized use of some $35.4 million. This plan was hailed as a way to build up the infrastructure and offer these countries avenues by which to protect themselves. In reality the plan sought to create more stable, legitimate elites in these countries and militate against socialist regimes. U.S. weaponry and military technology ended up securing military dictatorships in some Third World countries (Targ 1986, p. 28).

Militarily, the United States laid the ground work for a extensive network of alliances, military bases and client-state relationships in order to maintain world stability to its own liking. The North American Treaty Organization of 1949 as well as several other military pacts positioned the United States around the globe as the world's policeman of capitalism (Du Boff 1989, p. 154).

The institutional structures that traveled the avenues of reconstruction created by the economic, political and military strategies were the Transnational Corporations (TNC). Formed in the period from the late 1940s and through the 1960s, TNC 's grew in both size and scope. Dicken (1992) clearly points this out:

- In 1950 only three of the 315 largest TNCs (both U.S. and non U.S.) had manufacturing subsidiaries in more than twenty countries. By 1975, 44 TNCs from the U.S. alone had such an extensive geographic spread.
- The activities of the TNCs grew faster than the world economy as a whole. During the 1960s the foreign output of TNCs was growing at twice the rate of world gross national product and 40 percent faster than world exports.
- Between 1946 and 1952 the average number of manufacturing subsidiaries formed each year was 50 percent greater than during the previous peak period of 1920 through 1929. After 1952 the growth rate was even more rapid (Dicken 1992, p .51).

The growth of U.S. transnational corporations assisted the United States in its magnitude of export capital. United States invested export capital rose from $12 billion in 1950 to almost $76 billion by 1970. During that time, profit margins from foreign investments were twice those of domestic operations (Du Boff 1989, p. 154).

In Latin America during the early 1960s, the U.S. accounted for roughly 70 percent of foreign investment.[1] United States investment in the Third World increased from $1.7 billion in 1950 to $5.3 billion in 1959, then to $21.6 billion in 1969. A similar scenario was repeated in Canada where U.S. firms dominated in nearly every major industry such as motor vehicles and parts, electrical equipment, rubber, pharmaceuticals, petroleum refineries, oil and gas, iron mining, and industrial chemicals, to name a few (Targ 1986, pp. 32-33).

In parallel with the growth of private investment and exports in the postwar era has been the emergence of international banking. The operations of Transnational Banks (TNBs) throughout the 1960s took the form of establishing branches and subsidiaries and offices for purposes of supporting the activities of transnational corporations. In 1960 about eight United States banks operated in 131 overseas branches with foreign assets of $3.5 billion. In 1967, 15 banks with 295 branches held $15 billion in assets. As of 1974 there were 129 banks with 737 branches and assets totaling about $155 billion[2]. Some 80 percent of the total foreign assets in the early 1970s originated in 19 of the largest U.S. commercial banks. Among the largest of these banks nearly half of their earnings originated abroad. While total domestic banking assets grew about 3-1/2 times between 1960 and 1974, overseas assets grew about 42 times (Targ 1986, p, 37).

NOTES

1   A debate exists on Transnational corporations (TNCs) being favorable or unfavorable to Third World development. Leff (1976) views TNCs as a powerful economic force in building the economies of less developed nations. Abbott (1978) remarks on the economic policy powers of less developed nations attempting to disrupt the lifestyles of the rich countries. Weintraub (1979) mentions the need for poorer countries to rely more on Official Development Assistance (ODA).

However, Petras (1983, 1986) has successfully argued the devastating impact that TNCs have had on many less developed countries. And, Streeten (1982) maintains that intergovernmental aid has allowed developed nations to meddle in the economic and political affairs of the less developed nations.

It is the position of the author that issues of sovereignty, technology transfer, finance capital and marketing techniques claimed to be beneficial to both TNCs and host countries provided little if any development to the countries in which TNCs operate.

Some foreign governments view TNCs and their subsidiaries as boosting their local economies through joint ownership ventures. Unfortunately, evidence indicates that joint ownership does not often take place. In 1967, of the 187 U. S. controlled TNCs reviewed, there were 1,924 foreign subsidiaries in Latin America. Of those subsidiaries, 1,195 were wholly owned (95 percent or more) by U.S. parent companies and 365 were majority owned.

Advanced technology is important to developing countries in securing a firm economic base. Technological innovation assists in the extraction of natural resources and certain industrial processes. TNCs have a vested interest in not transferring technology because it could increase potential competitors. Studies conducted by the United Nations and host countries indicate that there is a high percentage of foreign-owned patents which prevents host countries from using such technologies. The technologies that are bought by host countries are in many cases overpriced and outdated. TNCs have also placed restrictions on the use of technologies that increase a host country's export capacity of its own goods (Barnet 1974, p. 140; 163-165).

TNCs have claimed that they are major suppliers of financial capital to underdeveloped countries. Studies conducted for the United Nations found that between 1957 and 1965, TNCs financed 83 percent of their Latin American investment locally. This financial relationship drained local capital, which prevented host countries from supplying capital for their own investment purposes. Furthermore, between 1960 and 1968, TNCs took, on the average, 79 percent of their net profits out of Latin America (Barnet 1974, p. 153).

TNCs have claimed that marketing strategies can educate the populace of less developed countries by advertising beneficial products and have positive effects on values, tastes, and attitudes. However, marketing strategies have been shown to be counterproductive to economic growth and individual well-being in less developed countries. Advertising has stimulated consumption of foreign goods over locally produced goods and have emphasized products low in nutritional value (Vernon 1971, p. 185).

The spread of transnational corporations into less developed nations has had adverse effects on balance of payments, income distribution and the quality of life. TNCs show little sign of strengthening the balance of payments of Third World countries (Vernon 1971, p. 173). In fact, some evidence indicates that TNCs are contributing to balance of payment problems by increasing trade activity. TNCs increase in trading activity has reduced the price of certain goods, resulting in lower profits to less developed nations. Corporations' overseas trade with their own subsidiaries undervalue exports, which in turn reduces taxes paid to the less developed countries (Barnet 1974, p. 156).

Studies conducted by the United Nations as well as other international agencies leave little doubt that by the end of the 1960s, there was a rise in unemployment, greater income disparity and more poverty in less developed nations (Barnet 1974, p. 149, Vernon 1971, p. 184).

2.   The role played by TNBs has changed over time. Being a major force throughout the 1960s, in the 1970s and 1980s, TNBs in borrowing countries dwarfed financial inter mediation taking place through offices within deficit countries. The need for foreign bank branches also was lessened by information and communication technology. Today, international securities markets far outreach bank inter mediation as the prime medium for lending and burrowing international loan capital. Banks now play an important role as agents for facilitating direct lending and borrowing (UNCTC 1989, p. 103).

Author's Work Experience in Production Control

As a production control scheduler, the author was responsible for coordinating the manufacturing and shipping of molded plastic parts from 13 different vendors that were doing business for the GM Syracuse plant. These small, mostly nonunion, non-GM facilities (with the exception of the Logrono, Spain plant) were located throughout North America and shipped to assembly plants in the U.S., Canada and Mexico.

The author's duties were to gather data from a variety of sources on assembly plant requirements and to forecast production and shipping requirements for the vendors. It was the scheduler's job in part, to keep the assembly plants running *at any cost*.

The automobile industry perhaps requires more timely manufacturing coordination than any other industry on the globe. Delivery of thousands of parts, which may be produced virtually anywhere in the world, must be coordinated to reach one location at the proper time for a car to be assembled. The absence of a part could shut down an entire factory at an enormous factor.

The following scenarios were not exceptions to the rule. These events happened routinely in one form or another, to one degree or another and they exemplify the power, control and resources available to the corporation. In efforts to simplify matters, the following will be told in the first-person narrative

Traditionally, new cars come out during the Fall of each year. During the Spring and Summer of each year, new production model requirements, along with all the paperwork, starts flowing into all the

GM plants. Late in the summer of 1985, I noticed that a 1986 color appeared on the paper work as a 1985 color. What this meant was that a 1986 model year car, a Cadillac, was going to be painted with a 1985-designated color. This, of course, was an impossible situation and I immediately contacted the appropriate individual whose responsibility was to fix problems such as this one. I was told to ignore the error and pretend that the 1985 color was really a 1986 color. I mentioned to him that I could not pretend because the computer system, which he was supposed to know about, will not let me input 1985 color codes into 1986 model year paperwork and that I would appreciate it if someone would tell me what was going on. After pausing a few seconds, he finally agreed to tell me what was happening.

In 1985, the federal government raised the total miles per gallon requirement for the GM fleet of 1986 model year cars. In essence, the government said that, in 1986, all the vehicles sold would have to average a higher mile per gallon (mpg) than the year before or fines would be imposed. This did not make GM happy because the company makes more money selling large cars that burn more gas than small cars. GM decided to sell a line of 1986 Cadillacs, but call them 1985.5, in efforts to circumvent the higher 1986 mpg requirements. GM told the government that if they were not allowed to do this, they would close plants and lay off workers because the company was not able to meet the 1986 mpg requirements and was unwilling to pay the fines. GM won and was allowed to sell 1985.5 Cadillacs for six months into 1986.

GM dealt with its shipment problems in a somewhat different fashion then with its fuel economy standards. Shipment problems for the GM Syracuse plant, as well as for its vendors, occurred daily. On several occasions, jet aircraft ended up circling vendors' business locations because of the lack of a paved runway and/or jet fuel. On one occasion, GM contacted a private company and requested 24-hour availability of a jet for two weeks. The retainer cost was $200 a day just to have the plane available. Once another scheduler in the office had to contact the Michigan Highway Patrol to search for a truck that had not reached the assembly plant on schedule. Eventually the truck and the driver were found at a motel.

On another occasion, the manager of materials and production control, at the Syracuse plant, had two trucks, each loaded with the same parts, leave the plant at the same time. The parts were to eventually end up at the same vendor destination. One truck headed directly to the vendor about 30 miles away and the other to the airport where parts were to be loaded on a plane headed toward the same vendor's city. I questioned the manager as to why he was sending the parts to the same location by two different modes of transportation. He said that the parts had to be at the vendor's plant as soon as possible and that he did not know which transportation mode would be quicker. When I asked who won the race, he said the truck shipment was faster (by 10 min.) because the plane wasted time taxing on the runway.

On another occasion, GM used a helicopter to track down a tractor-trailer that was in route to a assembly plant but was not going to arrive soon enough. After instructing the truck to pull off the road (via CB radio), the helicopter landed in a field, the pilot removed the needed number of parts from the truck, and the truck and helicopter both continued their journey to the plant. I personally had conversations with co-workers at a Michigan assembly plant and was informed that the plant was receiving a number of shipments via helicopter and that 27 such shipments had already occurred. I was told that GM had created a temporary helicopter pad in the parking lot and that shipments were expected to occur for the entire day.

Crisis Theory

Crisis theory sees capitalism as generating obstacles to the reproduction of the system[1]. These obstacles are viewed as contradictions within capitalist production because they emerge from the process of capital accumulation. In understanding these contradictions a distinction must be made between the interest of the individual capitalist and the interest of the capitalist class. What the individual capitalist is compelled to do by the forces of production may have "unintended" consequences for the interest of the capitalist class in general. The cumulative effects of capital's strategies (the pursuits by individual firms) produces crisis (Ross and Trachte 1990, p. 29).

The concept that has been most often used to explain crisis theory is Marx's theory of the tendency of the falling rate of profit (O'Connor 1987, pp. 7-9). The falling rate of profit is presented in the form of a paradox.

"The more capitalism develops, the more the average rate of profit for capital declines. Falling profit rates result in a surplus of capital because the increasing mass of capital accumulated ... finds fewer and fewer possibilities for investment with a adequate return. There follows a decline in productive investment, which leads to a decline in employment and to a concomitant reduction of wages paid by capital. As wages decline, demand shrinks in a parallel way, provoking a crisis in the selling of the already stocked commodities. Thus, a crisis of overproduction occurs because even the restricted productive capacity cannot be absorbed by the existing solvent demand since demand in turn has been reduced by falling investments. The inability to realize its commodities induces capital to halt production, increasing unemployment and depressing markets. Because capitalism is organized on a world scale the crisis spreads throughout many nations in a highly interconnected spiraling process . . . The economy can only be restarted when mass unemployment allows very low wages, when the bankruptcy of many firms has devaluated fixed capital, creating demand for new means of production, and when the state intervenes or there is a sudden event that increases substantially the outlets for profitable capital investment" (Castells 1980, p. 16).

Within Marx's theory are three explanations for the occurrence. The first version of the falling rate of profit sees the growth of working class strength (unionization and militancy) creating impediments to capital accumulation. Workers' resistance to exploitation leads to a rise in the cost of labor, thus creating impediments to capitalist profits. As capital attempts to squeeze more from the workers, the workers react to the increasing rate of exploitation. Working class struggle explains periodic business cycles, transitions to new stages of capitalism and structural decline.

A second view of the causes of a falling rate of profit has as its central proposition the thesis that capitalists are compelled to continually revolutionize the productive forces. Firms develop labor saving technologies in response to competition from other firms and from factors that limit the rate of exploitation. Competition requires firms to lower production costs, and one way to accomplish this is to reduce the price of labor. This action presents two problems; first, the wage paid to labor cannot be lowered past the level physically necessary to reproduce the labor force for any length of time, and second, workers do resist domination. The answer to the dilemma is for capitalists to use labor saving technologies. The use of labor saving technologies, however, produces its own set of contradictions. The ultimate source of profits is living labor. If workers are not compensated for their labor then products will not be purchased which will result in a fall of profits.

The third version of crisis theory, which Marxists call realization problems, locates decline of profit in the sphere of circulation as opposed to production. Hence, the threat of profitability stems from the problems associated with difficulties in selling the commodities. Under consumption occurs as firms compete. This competition depresses the wage bill and eventually depresses the effective demand for commodities. Workers are then unable to pay for commodities. If alternative sources of demand are not found (i.e. in foreign markets) crisis ensues (Ross and Trachte 1990, pp. 31-35).

Several researchers studying crisis theory have used the preceding three frameworks to explain U.S. economic decline. Castells (1980) shows the importance of workers' resistance to exploitation as a structural barrier to capitalist production. Wright (1978) shows how labor saving technologies have aided the contradictions of capital. And Baran and Sweezy (1966) locate the effects of economic decline in the sphere of circulation and describe how the threat of profitability stems from the problems of selling the commodities at profitable prices.[2]

This rough overview of crisis theory was meant only to supply rudimentary building blocks to some of the ways U.S. decline could take shape. No one theoretical school of thought supplies all the answers, each has its own strengths as well as its own weaknesses. In fact, it is more likely that all three trains of thought in some combination, during specific times and within certain industries, offer the clearest explanation of economic decline.

NOTE

1   There are four trains of though in modern crisis theory: 1) Bourgeois economists (market theorist) see the disintegration of the capitalist economy at the level of exchange of market relationships. 2) neo-orthodox (traditional) Marxists (value theorists) see the disintegration of the capitalist economy at the level of production and circulation of capital and capital accumulation. 3) neo-Marxist (social theorists) see the disintegration of the capitalist system at the level of social disintegration. 4) Post Marxists (social-psychological theorists) see disintegration in the framework of personality (O'Connor 1987, p. 2).

Widely accepted by the Marxists and even some of the bourgeois economists (Keynesians), is Marx's theory on the falling rate of profit as a cause for crisis.

2. Castells, Manuell. 1980. "The Economic Crisis and American Society." Princeton: Princeton University Press.; Wright, Erik, Olin. 1978.

Class, Crisis and the State. London, England: New Left Books.; Baran, Paul and Paul Sweezy. 1966. *Monopoly Capital.* New York: Monthly Review Press.

Questionnaire Packet Mailed to Relocatees

R I D
(01-03)

General Survey
BACKGROUND INFORMATION

1. What was your age on your last birthday? _____ years old (04-05)

2. What is your sex? 1) ☐ Male 2) ☐ Female (06)

3. How many years did you complete in school? (PLEASE CIRCLE ONE)

<u>1 2 3 4 5 6 7 8</u>   <u>9 10 11 12</u>   <u>13 14 15 16</u>
  Grade School   High School   College (07-08)

4. How many years have you lived in Syracuse or its surrounding area?
_____ years (09-10)

5. Since the plant closing, how many times have you been unemployed or laid off for a month or more? (11)

1) ☐ Never (SKIP TO QUESTION 7) 2) ☐ Once   3) ☐ 2-3 times   4) ☐ More than 3 times

6. Since the plant closed, what was your total length of time unemployed? (12)

1) ☐ Less than 1 month   2) ☐ 1 month but less than 3 months

3) ☐ 3 months but less than 6 months   4) ☐ 6 months but less than 9 months

5) ☐ 9 months but less than 1 year   6) ☐ 1 year but less than 1-1/2 years

7) ☐ 1-1/2 years but less than 2 years   8) ☐ More than 2 years

7. Relocation/termination may or may not result in financial hardships. As a result of relocating/terminating, have you had to generally cut down on overall expenses or postpone anticipated purchases?   1) Yes ☐   2) No ☐ (13)

Here is a list of statements about the government. Put an "X" in the agree box if you agree with the statement; put an "X" in the disagree box if you disagree with the statement.

Statement	Agree	Disagree	
8. The government should end unemployment by offering a job to anyone who wants one.	☐	☐	(14)
9. The government should see that every family has enough money to live on.	☐	☐	(15)
10. The government should increase taxes on big business.	☐	☐	(16)
11. The government should tax the rich heavily in order to redistribute wealth.	☐	☐	(17)
12. The government should limit the amount of money any individual is allowed to make in a year.	☐	☐	(18)
13. The size of government should be reduced even if it means cutting back on government services in areas such as health and education.	☐	☐	(19)

14. Do you think that the interests of management and workers are basically opposed or are they the same? (20)

1) ☐ Basically opposed   2) ☐ Basically the same

3) ☐ Mixed; depends; some interests conflict, others don't   4) ☐ Don't know

---

Here is a list of institutions and offices in our society. **Please indicate the amount of confidence you have in that institution or office. For <u>each one</u>, put an "X" in the box to show whether you now have a lot of confidence in it, some confidence, or hardly any confidence at all.**

Institution	Lot of Confidence	Some Confidence	Hardly any Confidence	
15. Labor unions	☐	☐	☐	(21)
16. Big business	☐	☐	☐	(22)
17. Congress	☐	☐	☐	(23)
18. The Supreme Court	☐	☐	☐	(24)
19. The President of the United States	☐	☐	☐	(25)
20. State legislature	☐	☐	☐	(26)
21. Governor of New York	☐	☐	☐	(27)

---

22. **Do you think that the child of a factory worker has about the same chance to get ahead as the child of a business executive?** (28)

1) ☐ About the same chance   2) ☐ Somewhat less chance

3) ☐ Much less chance   4) ☐ Don't know

Do you agree or disagree with the following statements about why GM closed the Syracuse plant? (Circle a number for each statement.)

23. The GM plant was not making a profit because of foreign competition. Management had little choice but to close down.

Strongly agree	Agree	Disagree	Strongly disagree	Don't know	
1	2	3	4	5	(29)

24. The Syracuse plant was probably making money, but not as much as GM wanted it to make.

Strongly agree	Agree	Disagree	Strongly disagree	Don't know	
1	2	3	4	5	(30)

25. GM would have kept the plant open if the union had agreed to large cuts in wages and benefits.

Strongly agree	Agree	Disagree	Strongly disagree	Don't know	
1	2	3	4	5	(31)

26. GM was using the excuse of the recession to break the back of organized labor and get lower wages.

Strongly agree	Agree	Disagree	Strongly disagree	Don't know	
1	2	3	4	5	(32)

27. Do you think it's fair if a child of a business executive has better chance at getting ahead than a child of a factory worker?

1) ☐ Yes   2) ☐ No   3) ☐ Don't know   (33)

28. What is your opinion of "cooperation programs" and "teamwork" between labor and management?

1) ☐ A good idea   2) ☐ A bad idea   3) ☐ Mixed; can be good or bad   4) ☐ No opinion   (34)

UNION ACTIVITIES

29. Before there was any talk of closing the GM plant in Syracuse, how much did the union local help protect workers' rights?

1) ☐ A big help to workers   2) ☐ Some help to workers   4) ☐ Not much help   (35)

30. How satisfied or dissatisfied were you with most of the benefits negotiated in the plant closing contract?

1) ☐ Very satisfied   2) ☐ Satisfied   3) ☐ Dissatisfied   4) ☐ Very Dissatisfied   (36)

FAMILY LIFE AND HEALTH

Relocation/termination may or may not result in stress and/or in problems with spouses, children, family, and friends. How has relocation/termination affected your relationships? (Place an "X" in one box in *each* row.)

31. Relationships with spouse	1) ☐ Better	2) ☐ No change	3) ☐ Worse	4) ☐ Not married	(37)
32. Relationships with children	1) ☐ Better	2) ☐ No change	3) ☐ Worse	4) ☐ No children	(38)
33. Relationships with family	1) ☐ Better	2) ☐ No change	3) ☐ Worse	4) ☐ No family	(39)
34. Relationships with friends	1) ☐ Better	2) ☐ No change	3) ☐ Worse	4) ☐ No friends	(40)

Stress in relocation/termination may or may not result in physical symptoms. Please place an "X" in the appropriate box to indicate your experience with the symptoms listed below.

Symptoms	Yes	No	Don't Know	
35. Headaches	☐	☐	☐	(41)
36. Loss of appetite	☐	☐	☐	(42)
37. Stomach trouble	☐	☐	☐	(43)
38. Drinking more	☐	☐	☐	(44)
39. Smoking more	☐	☐	☐	(45)
40. High blood pressure	☐	☐	☐	(46)
41. Trouble sleeping	☐	☐	☐	(47)

Stress related to relocation or termination may or may not affect an individual's personal and social life. During the past month, how often have you experienced each of these symptoms? Place an "X" in the box that best describes your experience.

Symptom	Very often	Somewhat often	Not often or never	
42. Lack enthusiasm for doing anything?	☐	☐	☐	(48)
43. Feel lonely?	☐	☐	☐	(49)
44. Feel bored or have little interest in doing things?	☐	☐	☐	(50)

45. **Have any household members, at your former Syracuse location, either been unable or unwilling to move with you to your present work location?**

   1) ☐ Yes; some or all stayed behind (GO TO QUESTION 46-49)

   2) ☐ No; all moved with me (SKIP TO QUESTION 51)

   3) ☐ I lived alone in Syracuse (SKIP TO QUESTION 52)   (51)

Please indicate which of these household members remained in the Syracuse area because they were unable or unwilling to relocate with you.

Household Member	Remained in Syracuse Yes	No	Does Not Apply	
46. Spouse	☐	☐	☐	(52)
47. Children	☐	☐	☐	(53)
48. Parents	☐	☐	☐	(54)
49. Other relatives	☐	☐	☐	(55)

50. **If any household member stayed at your Syracuse location, in a few words, please list the person (i.e., spouse, mother, father, brother, sister, son, daughter) and give the reason why each one stayed.**   (56-69)

Household Member	Reason for Staying
_____	_____
_____	_____
_____	_____
_____	_____
_____	_____
_____	_____

51. Did anyone in your household move to your new work location with you and then decide to return to your Syracuse location?

    1) ☐ Yes   2) ☐ No   (70)

52. Would you say that most of your friends and relatives are *now* in your present work location, or are most of them in Syracuse or elsewhere?   (71)

    1) ☐ Most are in Syracuse or elsewhere   2) ☐ Most are in my present work location

    3) ☐ About an equal number of my friends and relatives live in both places

53. Did you make any effort to look for work in the Syracuse area before moving?   (72)

    1) ☐ Yes, actively   2) ☐ Yes, but not actively   3) ☐ No

54. What was your reason to relocate (ANSWER ONLY ONE)?   (73)

    1) ☐ Financial   2) ☐ Just needed to put time in for full retirement   3) ☐ Health Benefits

    4) ☐ Other (Specify) _____

55. If you had several places to relocate to why did you choose this one (MARK ONLY ONE)?   (74)

    1) ☐ Wanted to live here   2) ☐ Liked the job at this location   3) ☐ Close to Syracuse

    4) ☐ Did not like other locations   5) ☐ No other choice of location

    6) ☐ Other

56. In order to relocate, did your spouse have to give up a job in your old location?   (75)

    1) ☐ Yes   2) ☐ No   3) ☐ Not married

57. In your Syracuse location, did you own or did you rent?   (76)

    1) ☐ Owned a house, or was in the process of buying a house

    2) ☐ Paid rent and lived in a house

    3) ☐ Paid rent and lived in an apartment

    4) ☐ Lived with relatives or friends; paid no housing costs

58. In your Syracuse location, did you: (77)

    1) ☐ Live with friends

    2) ☐ Live with spouse and/or family

    3) ☐ Live alone

    4) ☐ Live with friends and family

59. At your present work location, do you own or do you rent?   (78)

    1) ☐ Own a house, or am in the process of buying a house

    2) ☐ Pay rent and live in a house

    3) ☐ Pay rent and live in an apartment

    4) ☐ Live with relatives or friends; pay no rent

60. At your present work location, do you: (79)

1) ☐ Live with friends

2) ☐ Live with spouse and/or family

3) ☐ Live alone

4) ☐ Live with friends and family

61. At your Syracuse location, what did you do with your house? (80)

1) ☐ Sold

2) ☐ Tried to sell, but did not sell

3) ☐ Did not try to sell

4) ☐ Did not own a house

62. How do you like the area where you now work? (81)

1) ☐ I like the area   2) ☐ I don't like the area

3) ☐ Mixed; sometimes I like it, sometimes I don't 4) ☐ No opinion

63. Do you prefer to live in your present work area or in the Syracuse area? (82)

1) ☐ Prefer to live in my work area   2) ☐ Prefer to live in Syracuse

3) ☐ No preference; I like each location about equally

64. Do you find your present hours and shifts more convenient or less convenient than they were at GM Syracuse? (83)

1) ☐ More convenient now   2) ☐ Less convenient now   3) ☐ About the same

65. How often have you returned to the Syracuse area since moving? (84)

1) ☐ Not at all   2) ☐ Daily   3) ☐ Weekly   4) ☐ Monthly

5) ☐ Other (specify) _____

66. All things considered, was the move a good idea? (85)

1) ☐ Very good idea   2) ☐ Good idea   3) ☐ Good in some ways, not in others

4) ☐ Bad idea   5) ☐ Very bad idea   6) ☐ Necessary

67. Do you consider your current job permanent? (86)

1) ☐ Yes (SKIP TO QUESTION 69) 2) ☐ No (GO TO QUESTION 68)

68. If not, are you looking for another job?   1) ☐ Yes   2) ☐ No (87)

69. How do you like your work at your current location compared to the work you did at GM-Syracuse? (88)

1) ☐ Much better now   2) ☐ Better now 3) ☐ About the same 4) ☐ Not as good now

5) ☐ Much worse now

70. What is your marital status?   1) ☐ Never Married (SKIP TO QUESTION 77)   (89)

2) ☐ Widowed (SKIP TO QUESTION 77)

3) ☐ Divorced, Separated (SKIP TO QUESTION 77)

4) ☐ Married (GO TO QUESTION 71)

HOUSEHOLD AND FAMILY

71. **IF MARRIED: What is the current occupational status of your spouse?**   (90)

1) ☐ Working full time (35 hrs per wk or more) (SKIP TO QUESTION 73)

2) ☐ Working part time (less than 35 hrs per wk) (SKIP TO QUESTION 73)

3) ☐ Looking for work (GO TO QUESTION 72)

4) ☐ Ill or otherwise incapacitated (SKIP TO QUESTION 73)

5) ☐ Not looking for work (SKIP TO QUESTION 73)

72. **How long has your spouse been looking for work?**   (91)

1) ☐ 1 to 2 wks 2) ☐ 3 to 4 wks   3) ☐ 5 to 6 wks   4) ☐ 7 to 10 wks

5) ☐ Over 10 wks

73. **When you are employed, does your spouse usually work?**   (92)

1) ☐ Yes   2) ☐ No

74. **When you are not employed, does your spouse usually work?**

1) ☐ Yes   2) ☐ No   (93)

WAGE INFORMATION

We both know how sensitive questions about income can be. You are, of course, free not to answer the following income questions. However, your cooperation with these questions will provide very valuable information to our effort to understand how plant closings affect production workers like yourself. Remember, also, that your responses are ANONYMOUS and will never be linked in any report with your name, address, or other identifier.

75. **One year before the plant closed, what was your *total family* income (wages and other income sources for you and your spouse) before state and federal withholding taxes?**   (94-95)

1) ☐ Under $25,000   2) ☐ $25,000 - $29,999   3) ☐ $30,000 - $34,999   4) ☐ $35,000 - $39,999

5) ☐ $40,000 - $44,999   6) ☐ $45,000 - $49,999   7) ☐ $50,000 - $54,999   8) ☐ $55,000 - $59,999

9) ☐ $60,000 - $64,999   10) ☐ $65,000 - $69,999   11) ☐ $70,000 - $74,999 12) ☐ Over $75,000

76. **Last year, what was your *total family* income (wages and other income sources for you and your spouse) before state and federal withholding taxes?**   (96-97)

1) ☐ Under $25,000   2) ☐ $25,000 - $29,999   3) ☐ $30,000 - $34,999   4) ☐ $35,000 - $39,999

5) ☐ $40,000 - $44,999   6) ☐ $45,000 - $49,999   7) ☐ $50,000 - $54,999   8) ☐ $55,000 - $59,999

9) ☐ $60,000 - $64,999   10) ☐ $65,000 - $69,999   11) ☐ $70,000 - $74,999 12) ☐ Over $75,000

77. One year before the plant closed, what was your *individual* annual income (wages and other income sources) before state and federal withholding taxes?   (98-99)

1) ☐ Under $25,000   2) ☐ $25,000 - $29,999   3) ☐ $30,000 - $34,999   4) ☐ $35,000 - $39,999

5) ☐ $40,000 - $44,999   6) ☐ $45,000 - $49,999   7) ☐ $50,000 - $54,999   8) ☐ $55,000 - $59,999

9) ☐ $60,000 - $64,999   10) ☐ $65,000 - $69,999   11) ☐ $70,000 - $74,999   12) ☐ Over $75,000

78. Last year, what was your *individual* annual income (wages and other income sources) before state and federal withholding taxes?   (100-101)

1) ☐ Under $25,000   2) ☐ $25,000 - $29,999   3) ☐ $30,000 - $34,999   4) ☐ $35,000 - $39,999

5) ☐ $40,000 - $44,999   6) ☐ $45,000 - $49,999   7) ☐ $50,000 - $54,999   8) ☐ $55,000 - $59,999

9) ☐ $60,000 - $64,999   10) ☐ $65,000 - $69,999   11) ☐ $70,000 - $74,999   12) ☐ Over $75,000

CONCLUDING REMARKS

Thank you for responding to this questionnaire. The information you have provided will be valuable input to this study of the effects of plant relocation on American workers.

Questionnaire Packet Mailed to Early Retirees

R I D
(01-03)

General Survey
BACKGROUND INFORMATION

1. **What was your age on your last birthday?** _____ years old   (04-05)

2. **What is your sex?** 1) ☐ Male   2) ☐ Female   (06)

3. **How many years did you complete in school? (PLEASE CIRCLE ONE)**

     1 2 3 4 5 6 7 8   9 10 11 12   13 14 15 16
       Grade School   High School   College   (07-08)

4. **How many years have you lived in Syracuse or its surrounding area?**
   _____ years (09-10)

5. **Since the plant closing, how many times have you been unemployed or laid off for a month or more?**   (11)

   1) ☐ Never (SKIP TO QUESTION 7)   2) ☐ Once   3) ☐ 2-3 times   4) ☐ More than 3 times

6. **Since the plant closed, what was your total length of time unemployed?**   (12)

   1) ☐ Less than 1 month   2) ☐ 1 month but less than 3 months

   3) ☐ 3 months but less than 6 months   4) ☐ 6 months but less than 9 months

   5) ☐ 9 months but less than 1 year   6) ☐ 1 year but less than 1-1/2 years

   7) ☐ 1-1/2 years but less than 2 years   8) ☐ More than 2 years

7. **Relocation/termination may or may not result in financial hardships. As a result of relocating/terminating, have you had to generally cut down on overall expenses or postpone anticipated purchases?**   1) Yes ☐   2) No ☐   (13)

Here is a list of statements about the government. Put an "X" in the agree box if you agree with the statement; put an "X" in the disagree box if you disagree with the statement.

Statement	Agree	Disagree	
8. The government should end unemployment by offering a job to anyone who wants one.	☐	☐	(14)
9. The government should see that every family has enough money to live on.	☐	☐	(15)
10. The government should increase taxes on big business.	☐	☐	(16)
11. The government should tax the rich heavily in order to redistribute wealth.	☐	☐	(17)
12. The government should limit the amount of money any individual is allowed to make in a year.	☐	☐	(18)
13. The size of government should be reduced even if it means cutting back on government services in areas such as health and education.	☐	☐	(19)

14. Do you think that the interests of management and workers are basically opposed or are they the same? (20)

   1) ☐ Basically opposed   2) ☐ Basically the same

   3) ☐ Mixed; depends; some interests conflict, others don't   4) ☐ Don't know

Here is a list of institutions and offices in our society. Please indicate the amount of confidence you have in that institution or office. For **each one**, put an "X" in the box to show whether you now have a lot of confidence in it, some confidence, or hardly any confidence at all.

Institution	Lot of Confidence	Some Confidence	Hardly any Confidence	
15. Labor unions	☐	☐	☐	(21)
16. Big business	☐	☐	☐	(22)
17. Congress	☐	☐	☐	(23)
18. The Supreme Court	☐	☐	☐	(24)
19. The President of the United States	☐	☐	☐	(25)
20. State legislature	☐	☐	☐	(26)
21. Governor of New York	☐	☐	☐	(27)

22. Do you think that the child of a factory worker has about the same chance to get ahead as the child of a business executive? (28)

   1) ☐ About the same chance   2) ☐ Somewhat less chance

   3) ☐ Much less chance   4) ☐ Don't know

Do you agree or disagree with the following statements about why GM closed the Syracuse plant? (Circle a number for each statement.)

23. The GM plant was not making a profit because of foreign competition. Management had little choice but to close down.

Strongly agree	Agree	Disagree	Strongly disagree	Don't know	
1	2	3	4	5	(29)

24. The Syracuse plant was probably making money, but not as much as GM wanted it to make.

Strongly agree	Agree	Disagree	Strongly disagree	Don't know	
1	2	3	4	5	(30)

25. GM would have kept the plant open if the union had agreed to large cuts in wages and benefits.

Strongly agree	Agree	Disagree	Strongly disagree	Don't know	
1	2	3	4	5	(31)

26. GM was using the excuse of the recession to break the back of organized labor and get lower wages.

Strongly agree	Agree	Disagree	Strongly disagree	Don't know	
1	2	3	4	5	(32)

27. Do you think it's fair if a child of a business executive has better chance at getting ahead than a child of a factory worker?

1) ☐ Yes   2) ☐ No   3) ☐ Don't know   (33)

28. What is your opinion of "cooperation programs" and "teamwork" between labor and management?

1) ☐ A good idea   2) ☐ A bad idea   3) ☐ Mixed; can be good or bad   4) ☐ No opinion   (34)

UNION ACTIVITIES

29. Before there was any talk of closing the GM plant in Syracuse, how much did the union local help protect workers' rights?

1) ☐ A big help to workers   2) ☐ Some help to workers   4) ☐ Not much help   (35)

30. How satisfied or dissatisfied were you with most of the benefits negotiated in the plant closing contract?

1) ☐ Very satisfied   2) ☐ Satisfied   3) ☐ Dissatisfied   4) ☐ Very Dissatisfied   (36)

FAMILY LIFE AND HEALTH

Relocation/termination may or may not result in stress and/or in problems with spouses, children, family, and friends. How has relocation/termination affected your relationships? (Place an "X" in one box in *each* row.)

31. Relationships with spouse	1) ☐ Better	2) ☐ No change	3) ☐ Worse	4) ☐ Not married (37)
32. Relationships with children	1) ☐ Better	2) ☐ No change	3) ☐ Worse	4) ☐ No children (38)
33. Relationships with family	1) ☐ Better	2) ☐ No change	3) ☐ Worse	4) ☐ No family (39)
34. Relationships with friends	1) ☐ Better	2) ☐ No change	3) ☐ Worse	4) ☐ No friends (40)

Stress in relocation/termination may or may not result in physical symptoms. Please place an "X" in the appropriate box to indicate your experience with the symptoms listed below.

Symptoms	Yes	No	Don't Know	
35. Headaches	☐	☐	☐	(41)
36. Loss of appetite	☐	☐	☐	(42)
37. Stomach trouble	☐	☐	☐	(43)
38. Drinking more	☐	☐	☐	(44)
39. Smoking more	☐	☐	☐	(45)
40. High blood pressure	☐	☐	☐	(46)
41. Trouble sleeping	☐	☐	☐	(47)

Stress related to relocation or termination may or may not affect an individual's personal and social life. During the past month, how often have you experienced each of these symptoms? Place an "X" in the box that best describes your experience.

Symptom	Very often	Somewhat often	Not often or never	
42. Lack enthusiasm for doing anything?	☐	☐	☐	(48)
43. Feel lonely?	☐	☐	☐	(49)
44. Feel bored or have little interest in doing things?	☐	☐	☐	(50)

45. Have you had any full-time jobs (35 hours a week or more) since you left GM-Syracuse?
   1) ☐ No (SKIP TO QUESTION 47)   2) ☐ Yes (GO TO QUESTION 46)   (51)

   46. IF YES, how many jobs have you had?
     1) ☐ One 2) ☐ Two 3) ☐ Three 4) ☐ Four 5) ☐ Five (52)

47. Can you tell me the major reason for deciding to stay in the Syracuse area?
   (CHECK ONLY ONE)   (53)
    1) ☐ Family and friends 2) ☐ Job opportunity for self 3) ☐ Job opportunity for spouse
    4) ☐ Education or retraining for self 5) ☐ Financial considerations 6) ☐ Other

48. If you had to make the decision to not relocate over again, do you believe you would make the same decision?   (54)
    1) ☐ Would have made the same decision 2) ☐ Would not have made the same decision
    3) ☐ Don't know

Here are some questions regarding your current financial situation. Please read each and indicate your answer with a check in the "Yes" or "No" box. Thank you.

Financial Situation	Yes	No	
49. Are you able to afford a home suitable for yourself/your family?	☐	☐	(55)
50. Are you able to afford furniture or household equipment that needs to be replaced?	☐	☐	(56)
51. Are you able to afford the kind of car you need?	☐	☐	(57)
52. Do you have enough money for the kind of food you/your family should have?	☐	☐	(58)
53. Do you have enough money for the kind of clothing you/your family wants?	☐	☐	(59)
54. Do you have enough money for the kind of leisure activities you/your family wants?	☐	☐	(60)
55. Do you have a great deal of difficulty paying your bills?	☐	☐	(61)

56. **When did you begin to look for work after you learned you would be laid off from GM-Syracuse?** (62)

1) ☐ Before the layoff   2) ☐ Immediately after the layoff   3) ☐ 1-2 weeks after the layoff

4) ☐ One month after the layoff   5) ☐ More than one month after the layoff

6) ☐ Did not look for work   7)☐ Already had other employment (SKIP TO QUESTION 58)

57. **In your search for work since leaving GM-Syracuse, can you tell me how many job offers you have had?** (63)

1) ☐ None   2) ☐ 1 to 2 3) ☐ 3 to 5 4) ☐ 6 to 10   5) ☐ more than 10

6) ☐ Did not look for work

58. **As a result of retirement/termination, have you had to move to a less expensive place to live?**
1) ☐ Yes   2) ☐ No (64)

59. **Do you receive early retirement benefits?**   1) ☐ Yes   2) ☐ No   (65)

60. **Did you receive a termination allowance or severance pay when you left GM-Syracuse?** (66)

1) ☐ Yes   2) ☐ No

61. **If you received some type of termination allowance, severance pay or early retirement is it still financially necessary for you to work?** (67)

1) ☐ Yes   2) ☐ No

3) ☐ Received no termination allowance, severance pay or early retirement

62. **Do you believe finding a job to support yourself/yourself and family in the Syracuse area is:** (68)

1) ☐ Very difficult   2) ☐ Fairly difficult   3) ☐ Fairly easy   4) ☐ Very easy

63. **Are there any other members of your household who work outside the home? (other than your spouse)** (69)

1) ☐ Yes (GO TO QUESTION 64)   2) ☐ No (SKIP TO QUESTION 65)

64. **IF YES, what part of the income earned by the other household members (other than your spouse) has been used for family expenses and maintenance?** (70)

1) ☐ All   2) ☐ Most   3) ☐ Half   4) ☐ Little 5) ☐ None

65. **At present are you: (PLEASE ANSWER ONLY ONE)** (71)
1) ☐ Working full time (35 hours a week or more)?
2) ☐ Working part time (less than 35 hours per week)?
3) ☐ Looking for work?
4) ☐ Ill or otherwise incapacitated?
5) ☐ Withdrawn or retired from the labor force?
6) ☐ Laid off?
7) ☐ Involuntary leave of absence?

66. **What is your marital status?**   1)☐ Never married (SKIP TO QUESTION 73)   (72)

                                             2)☐ Widowed (SKIP TO QUESTION 73)

                                             3)☐ Divorced, Separated (SKIP TO QUESTION 73)

                                             4)☐ Married (GO TO QUESTION 67)

HOUSEHOLD AND FAMILY

67. IF MARRIED: What is the current occupational status of your spouse? (73)

1) ☐ Working full time (35 hrs per wk or more) (SKIP TO QUESTION 69)

2) ☐ Working part time (less than 35 hrs per week) (SKIP TO QUESTION 69)

3) ☐ Looking for work (GO TO QUESTION 68)

4) ☐ Ill or otherwise incapacitated (SKIP TO QUESTION 69)

5) ☐ Not looking for work (SKIP TO QUESTION 69)

68. How long has your spouse been looking for work? (74)

1) ☐ 1 to 2 wks   2) ☐ 3 to 4 wks   3) ☐ 5 to 6 wks   4) ☐ 7 to 10 wks   5) ☐ over 10 wks

6) ☐ Spouse not looking for work

69. When you are employed, does your spouse usually work? (75)

1) ☐ Yes   2) ☐ No

70. When you are not employed, does your spouse usually work? (76)

1) ☐ Yes   2) ☐ No

WAGE INFORMATION

We both know how sensitive questions about income can be. You are, of course, free not to answer the following income questions. However, your cooperation with these questions will provide very valuable information to our effort to understand how plant closings affect production workers like yourself. Remember, also, that your responses are ANONYMOUS and will never be linked in any report with your name, address, or other identifier.

71. One year before the plant closed, what was your *total family* income (wages and other income sources for you and your spouse) before state and federal withholding taxes? (77-78)

1) ☐ Under $25,000   2) ☐ $25,000 - $29,999   3) ☐ $30,000 - $34,999   4) ☐ $35,000 - $39,999

5) ☐ $40,000 - $44,999   6) ☐ $45,000 - $49,999   7) ☐ $50,000 - $54,999   8) ☐ $55,000 - $59,999

9) ☐ $60,000 - $64,999   10) ☐ $65,000 - $69,999   11) ☐ $70,000 - $74,999   12) ☐ Over $75,000

72. Last year, what was your *total family* income (wages and other income sources for you and your spouse) before state and federal withholding taxes? (79-80)

1) ☐ Under $25,000   2) ☐ $25,000 - $29,999   3) ☐ $30,000 - $34,999   4) ☐ $35,000 - $39,999

5) ☐ $40,000 - $44,999   6) ☐ $45,000 - $49,999   7) ☐ $50,000 - $54,999   8) ☐ $55,000 - $59,999

9) ☐ $60,000 - $64,999   10) ☐ $65,000 - $69,999   11) ☐ $70,000 - $74,999   12) ☐ Over $75,000

73. One year before the plant closed, what was your *individual* annual income (wages and other income sources) before state and federal withholding taxes? (81-82)

1) ☐ Under $25,000   2) ☐ $25,000 - $29,999   3) ☐ $30,000 - $34,999   4) ☐ $35,000 - $39,999

5) ☐ $40,000 - $44,999   6) ☐ $45,000 - $49,999   7) ☐ $50,000 - $54,999   8) ☐ $55,000 - $59,999

9) ☐ $60,000 - $64,999   10) ☐ $65,000 - $69,999   11) ☐ $70,000 - $74,999   12) ☐ Over $75,000

74. Last year, what was your *individual* annual income (wages and other income sources) before state and federal withholding taxes? (83-84)

1) ☐ Under $25,000   2) ☐ $25,000 - $29,999   3) ☐ $30,000 - $34,999   4) ☐ $35,000 - $39,999

5) ☐ $40,000 - $44,999   6) ☐ $45,000 - $49,999   7) ☐ $50,000 - $54,999   8) ☐ $55,000 - $59,999

9) ☐ $60,000 - $64,999   10) ☐ $65,000 - $69,999   11) ☐ $70,000 - $74,999   12) ☐ Over $75,000

STOP

IF YOU HAVE WITHDRAWN OR RETIRED FROM THE LABOR FORCE AND ARE NO LONGER LOOKING FOR WORK GO TO LAST PAGE AND READ CONCLUDING REMARKS

IF WORKING PLEASE ANSWER QUESTIONS 75-81; IF NOT WORKING AND LOOKING FOR WORK GO TO QUESTION 82.

---

75. How long have you had your current job? (85)

1) ☐ Less than 1 month   2) ☐ 1 month but less than 3 months

3) ☐ 3 months but less than 6 months   4) ☐ 6 months but less than 1 year

5) ☐ 1 year but less than 1-1/2 years   6) ☐ 1-1/2 years but less than 2 years

7) ☐ Two years but less than 3 years   8) ☐ 3 years or more

76. Do you consider your current job permanent? (86)

1) ☐ Yes (SKIP TO QUESTION 78)   2) ☐ No (GO TO QUESTION 77)

77. IF NOT, have you another job lined up?   1) ☐ Yes   2) ☐ No   (87)

78. Do you find your present hours and shifts more convenient or less convenient than they were at GM Syracuse? (88)

1) ☐ More convenient now   2) ☐ Less convenient now   3) ☐ About the same

79. How do you like your work compared to the work you did before at GM-Syracuse? (89)

1) ☐ Much better now   2) ☐ Better now 3) ☐ About the same 4) ☐ Not as good now

5) ☐ Much worse now

80. In your current job, how does your weekly straight time pay compare with your weekly straight time pay at GM Syracuse? (90)

1) ☐ About the same 2) ☐ Considerably more   3) ☐ More 4) ☐ Less   5) ☐ Considerably less

81. Do you believe if you had to find another job right now that you would have a: (91)

1) ☐ Very difficult time? 2) ☐ Fairly difficult time? 3) ☐ Fairly easy time? 4) ☐ Very easy time?

STOP
If you answered Questions 75-81, go to Concluding Remarks.

82. Do you think you will be able to find a job: (92)

1) ☐ In a few weeks?　　2) ☐ Within the next month?　　3) ☐ Really do not know?

83. Which of the following factors do you think is the major cause of your not being able to find work at this time? (ANSWER ONLY ONE.) (93)

1) ☐ Lack of jobs　2) ☐ Age　3) ☐ Lack of skill　4) ☐ Lack of education　5) ☐ Illness

CONCLUDING REMARKS

Thank you for responding to this questionnaire. The information you have provided will be valuable input to this study of the effects of plant closings on American workers.

Research Summary Tables

MENTAL HEALTH

Table F-1. Percentage of Early Retirees and Relocatees Indicating Mental Health Symptoms*

Mental Health Symptom	Early Retirees			Relocatees		
	Very Often	Some-what Often	Not Often or Never	Very Often	Somewhat Often	Not Often or Never
Lack enthusiasm for doing anything	19%	41%	40%	42%	29%	29%
Feel lonely?	17%	30%	53%	42%	40%	18%
Feel bored or have little interest in doing things?	19%	41%	40%	39%	35%	26%
*A total of 88 early retirees and 31 relocatees responded to each of the questions related to Mental Health Symptoms.						

DISLOCATED WORKERS

Table F-2. Percentage of Relocatees and Early Retirees Indicating Increases in Drinking

Drinking	Relocatees	Early Retirees
Yes	39%	14%
No	61%	86%
Total	100%	100%
(n=)	(31)	(84)

FAMILY LIFE

Table F-3A. Percentage of Early Retirees and Relocatees Indicating Worse Relations with Family and Friends*

Worse Relations With	Early Retirees (n=)	Relocatees (n=)
Spouse	25% (72)	57% (28)
Children	10% (80)	38% (26)
Other Family Members	10% (88)	35% (31)
Friends	15% (88)	45% (29)
*Percent equals 100 by adding responses in each type of relations (i.e., spouse).		

FAMILY LIFE

Table F-3B. Percentage of Early Retirees and Relocatees Indicating No Change In Relations with Family and Friends*

No Change In Relations With	Early Retirees (n=)	Relocatees (n=)
Spouse	65% (72)	25% (2s8)
Children	76% (80)	31% (26)
Other Family Members	81% (88)	52% (31)
Friends	76% (88)	52% (29)
*Percent equals 100 by adding responses in each type of relations (i.e., spouse).		

FAMILY LIFE

Table F-3C. Percentage of Early Retirees and Relocatees Indicating Better Relations with Family and Friends*

Better Relations With	Early Retirees (n=)	Relocatees (n=)
Spouse	10% (72)	18% (28)
Children	14% (80)	31% (26)
Other Family Members	9% (88)	13% (31)
Friends	9% (88)	3% (29)
*Percent equals 100 by adding responses in each type of relations (i.e., spouse).		

DISLOCATED WORKERS

Table F-4. Percentage of Relocatees and Early Retirees Indicating Either "Yes" or "No" to the Government Limiting the Amount of Money An Individual Is Allowed to Make In a Year

Should Government Limit Amount of Money an Individual Is Allowed to Make	Relocatees	Early Retirees
Yes	0%	10%
No	100%	90%
Total	100%	100%
(n=)	(31)	(88)

DISLOCATED WORKERS

Table F-5. Percentage of Early Retirees and Relocatees Indicating Degrees of Confidence in Big Business

Confidence in Big Business	Early Retirees	Relocatees
a Lot of Confidence	9%	0%
Some Confidence	39%	61%
Hardly Any Confidence	52%	39%
Total	100%	100%
(n=)	(88)	(31)

DISLOCATED WORKERS

Table F-6. Percentage of Relocatees and Early Retirees Responding to How Much the Union Local Helped Protect Workers' Rights

Union Local Helpful	Relocatees	Early Retirees
A Big Help	16%	35%
Some Help	52%	49%
Not Much Help	32%	16%
Total	100%	100%
(n=)	(31)	(88)

DISLOCATED WORKERS

Table F-7. Percentage of Relocatees and Early Retirees Either Satisfied or Dissatisfied with the Benefits of the Plant Closing Contract

Benefits of Plant Closing Contract	Relocatees	Early Retirees
Satisfied	42%	80%
Dissatisfied	58%	20%
Total	100%	100%
(n=)	(31)	(88)

DISLOCATED WORKERS

Table F-8. Percentage of Early Retirees and Relocatees Reported Having to Cut Down on Overall Expenses and Postpone Anticipated Purchases

Cut Expenditures	Early Retirees	Relocatees
Yes	88%	73%
No	12%	27%
Total	100%	100%
(n=)	(85)	(30)

EARLY RETIREES

Table F-9. Income by Sex

Income	Male	Female
Under $25,000	71%	100%
Over $25,000	29%	0%
Total	100%	100%
(n=)	(68)	(11)

EARLY RETIREES

Table F-10. Feelings of Loneliness by Sex

Feelings of Loneliness	Male	Female
Very Often	13%	33%
Somewhat Often	36%	7%
Not Often or Never	51%	60%
Total	100%	100%
(n=)	(70)	(15)

RELOCATEES

Table F-11. Confidence in Social Institutions and Offices of U.S. by Depressed Workers

Confidence in Social Institutions and Offices	Depressed Yes	Depressed No
No Confidence	38%	0%
Some Degree of Confidence	62%	100%
Total	100%	100%
(n=)	(21)	(10)

EARLY RETIREES

Table F-12. Economic Distress (Ability to Afford or Not Afford Household and Leisure Items) by Employment Status

Economic Distress	Employed Full Time	Employed Part Time	Looking for Work
Afford all 7 categories	32%	33%	6%
Not able to afford 1 to 4 categories	47%	43%	39%
Not able to afford 5 or more categories	21%	24%	56%
Total (n=)	100% (19)	100% (21)	100% (18)

EARLY RETIREES

Table F-13. Depression Related to Economic Distress (Ability to Afford or Not Afford Household and Leisure Items)

Depressed	Can Afford All 7 Categories	Not Able to Afford 1 to 4 Categories	Not Able to Afford 5 or More Categories
Yes	14%	32%	75%
No	86%	68%	25%
Total (n=)	100% (22)	100% (38)	100% (28)

PHYSICAL SYMPTOMS

Table F-14. Percentage of Early Retirees and Relocatees Indicating Physical Health Problems*

	Early Retirees			Relocatees		
Physical Health Problems	Yes	No	DK	Yes	No	DK
Headaches	34%	61%	2%	42%	55%	3%
Loss of appetite	18%	73%	7%	23%	71%	6%
Stomach trouble	27%	67%	3%	29%	65%	6%
Drinking more	14%	82%	2%	39%	61%	0%
Smoking more	17%	78%	2%	26%	69%	6%
High blood pressure	25%	69%	3%	26%	68%	10%
Trouble sleeping	44%	51%	2%	58%	39%	3%

*Percentages may not equal 100 due to rounding and missing data.

EARLY RETIREES

Table F-15. Increases in Drinking by Employment Status

Drinking	Employed Full Time	Employed Part Time	Looking for Work
Yes	0%	33%	24%
No	100%	67%	76%
Total	100%	100%	100%
(n=)	(18)	(21)	(17)

EARLY RETIREES

Table F-16. Sleeping Problems Related to Employment Status

Sleeping Problems	Employed Full Time	Employed Part Time	Looking for Work
Yes	50%	48%	81%
No	50%	52%	19%
Total	100%	100%	100%
(n=)	(18)	(21)	(16)

EARLY RETIREES

Table F-17. Confidence in Social Institutions and Offices of U.S. Related to Physical Symptoms

Confidence in Social Institutions and Offices	Affected by 0 to 2 Physical Symptoms	Affected by 3 or All Physical Symptoms
No Confidence	12%	43%
Some Degree of Confidence	88%	57%
Total	100%	100%
(n=)	(17)	(14)

INSTITUTIONS AND OFFICES

Table F-18. Percentage of Early Retirees and Relocatees Indicating Confidence in Institutions and Offices of the United States*

Institutions and Offices	Confidence Among Early Retirees			Confidence Among Relocatees		
	A Lot	Some	Hardly Any	A Lot	Some	Hardly Any
Big Business	9%	39%	52%	0%	61%	39%
Congress	5%	33%	63%	0%	61%	39%
Supreme Court	8%	55%	38%	12%	71%	16%
President of the United States	13%	60%	27%	10%	65%	26%
State Legislature	1%	49%	50%	3%	61%	35%
Governor of New York	5%	45%	50%	3%	52%	45%

*A total of 88 early retirees and 31 relocatees responded to each institution and office. Percentages may not equal 100 due to rounding.

Bibliography

Abbott, George. 1978. "The New International Economic Order-What Went Wrong." *Co-existence* v. 15, April.

Abbott, Lilian. 1992. "Plant Closings will Ripple Throughout the Community." *Post Standard* 4 December.

Addison, John and Pedro Portugal. 1987. "The Effect of Advance Notification of Plant Closings on Unemployment." *Industrial and Labor Relationa Review* 41 (1): 3-16.

Aiken, Michael, Louis Ferman and Harold Sheppard. 1968. *Economic Failure, Alienation and Extremism.* Ann Arbor: University of Michigan Press.

Automotive News. 1994. "1994 Market Data Source Book." New York: Crain Communications, May 25.

Arrighi, Giovanni. 1978. "Towards a Theory of Capitalist Crisis." *New Left Review* 111: 3-24, September/October.

Baker, Dean and Lawrence Mishel. 1995. "Profits Up, Wages Down: Worker Losses Yield Big Gains for Business." A Briefing Paper from the Economic Policy Institute, Washington DC.

Baldwin, Marc. 1987. "Disastrous Job Losses in Michigan." *Dissent* Spring: 151-152.

Barlett, Donald and James Steele. 1992. *America: What Went Wrong.* Kansas City: Andrews and McMeel, Press Syndicated Company.

Barnet, Richard and John Cavanagh. 1994. *Global Dreams: Imperial Corporations and the New World Order.* New York: Simon and Schuster.

Barnet, Richard. 1974. *Global Reach: The Power of the Multinational Corporation.* New York: Simon & Schuster.

Bell, Daniel. 1976. *The Coming of Post-Industrial Society.* New York: Basic Books.

Bello, Walden and Shea Cunninghan and Bill Rau. 1993. *Dark Victory: The United States, Structural Adjustment and Global Poverty.* London: Pluto Press.

Bellon, Bertrand and Jorge Niosi. 1988. *The Decline of the American Economy.* Montreal: Black Rose Books.

Bennet, James. 1995. "G.M.'s Profits a Record in Quarter and Year." *New York Times* 1 February.

Bensman, David and Roberta Lynch. 1989. *Rusted Dreams.* Berkeley: University of Calafornia Press.

Berman, Jay. 1993. "Occupational Entrants in 1990-91." *Occupational Outlook Quarterly* 37 (1): 12-23.

Blade, D. 1987. *Goods and Services in OECD Economies.* Paris: OECD.

Blim, Michael. 1992. "The Emerging Global Factory and Anthropology." *Anthropology and the Global Factory,* New York: Bergin and Garvey.

Bluestone, Barry and Bennett Harrison. 1989. "Jobs, Income, and Health." Pp. 61-73 in *Deindustrialization and Plant Closure,* edited by Paul Staudohar and Holly Brown. Berkeley: Lexington Books.

Bluestone, Barry. 1988. "Deindustrialization and Unemployment in America." *Review of Black Political Economy* 17 (2): 29-44.

Bluestone, Barry and Bennet Harrison. 1982. *The Deindustrialization of America: Plant Closings, Community Abandonment and the Dismantling of Basic Industry.* New York: Basic Books.

Branson, William. 1984. "The Myth of Deindustrialization," Pp. 177-190 in *Plant Cosings: Public or Private Choices,* edited by Richard B. McKenzie. Washington: CATO Institute.

Brett, E.A., Martin Honeywell, Robert Carty, Robert Nickson and James Winston. 1983. *The Poverty Brokers: The IMF and Latin America.* London: Latin American Bureau.

Brieaddy, Frank. 1992. "Workers Gave Generously to Local Charities" *Post Standard* 4 December.

Britton, Stephen. 1990. "The Role of Services in Production." *Progress in Human Geography* 14: 529-546.

Broad, Dave. 1990. "Fordism and Imperialism." in *Monthly Review* 41 (10): 53-58.

Buss, Terry and F. Redburn. 1983a. *Shutdown at Youngstown: Public Policy for Mass Unemployment.* Albany: State University of New York Press.

Buss, Terry and F. Redburn. 1983b. *Mass Unemployment: Plant Closings and Community Mental Health.* Mevely Hills: Sage Publications.

Camp, Scott. 1995. *Workers Response to Plant Closings: Steelworkers in Johnstown and Youngstown.* New York: Garland Publishing.

Castells, Manuel. 1980. *The Economic Crisis and American Society.* Princeton: Princeton University Press.

Catalano, R., D. Dooley and R. Jackson. 1985. "Economic Antecedents of Help-Seeking: Reformulation of Time-Test Series." *Journal of Health and Social Behavior* 26: 141-152.

Cohen, Stephen and John Zysman. 1987. *Manufacturing Matters: The Myth of the Post-Industrial Economy.* New York: Basic Books.

Congressional Budget Office. 1993. "Displaced Workrs: Trends in the 1980s and Implications for the Future." *A CBO Study.* February. Washington DC: United States Government Printing Office.

Currie, Elliott. 1990. "Heavy with Human Tears: Free Market Policy, Inequality and Social Provision in the United States." in Ian Taylor ed. *The Social Effects of Free Market Polices,* New York: St. Martins Press.

Di La Rica, Sara. 1995. "Evidence of Preseparation Earnings Losses in the Displaced Worker Survey." *Jounal of Human Resources* 30 (3): 610-621.

DeLorean, John and Patrick Wright. 1980. "How Moral Men Make Immoral Decisions-A Look Inside GM." Pp. 31-42 in *The Big Business Reader,* edited by Mark Green and Robert Massie. New York: Pilgrim Press.

Dew, M. A., E. Bromet and H. Schulberg. 1987. "A Comparative Analysis of Two Community Stressors' Long-term Mental Health Effects." *American Journal of Community Psychology* 15: 167-184.

Dicken, Peter. 1992. *Global Shift.* New York: The Guilford Press.

Dorsey, John. 1967. "The Mack Case: A Study in Unemployment" in *Studies in the Economics of Income Maintenance,* edited by Otto Eckstein. Washington: Brookings Institute. As seen in Gordus, Jeanne and Paul Jarley and Louis Ferman. 1981. *Plant Cosings and Economic Disloation.* Kalamazoo: W.E. UpJohn Institute.

Drucker, Peter. 1994. *Post-Capitalist Society.* New York: HarperCollins.

Du Boff, Richard. 1989. *Accumulation and Power.* New York: M.E. Sharpe.

Economist. 1994. April 2.

Edsall, Thomas and Mary Edsall. 1992. *Chain Reaction.* New York: WW Norton and Company.

Elson, D. 1988. "Transnational Corporations in the New International Division of Labor: A Critique of 'Cheap Labor' Hypotheses" *Manchester Papers on Development 4*: 352-376.

Erickson, Jon Karl. 1990. *Factors Contributing to Plant Closings in the United States, 1969-1975.* (Dissertation) New Brunswick: Rutgers University.

Evans, Peter and Gary Gereffi. 1981. "Transnational Corporations, Dependent Development, and State Policy in the Semiperiphery." *Latin American Research Review* 6 (no. 1): 33-45.

Faux, Jeff. 1993. "The Crumbling Case for NAFTA: A Look at the Realities" *Dissent* 40: Summer.

Fitch, Robert. 1993. *The Political Economy of New York: Space, Class and Power, 1958-1992.* (Dissertation) Binghamton University, State University of New York.

Flaim, Paul and Ellen Sehgal. 1985. "Displaced Workers of 1979-83: How Well Have They Fared" *Monthly Labor Review* 108 (no.) 6: 3-16, June.

Folbre, Nancy and Julia Leighton and Melissa Roderick. 1984. "Plant Closings and Their Regulation in Maine, 1971-1982." *Industrial and Labor Relations Review* 37 (2): 185-196.

Frobel, Folker and Jurgen Heinrichs, and Otto Kreye. 1980. *The New International Division of labor.* Cambridge: Cambridge University Press.

Frobel, Folker and Jurgen Heinrichs and Otto Kreye. 1977. "The Tendency Towards a New International Division of labor." *Review* 1: 73-88, Summer.

Gardner, Jennifer. 1995. "Worker Displacement: A Decade of Change." *Monthly labor Review* 118 (no.) 4: 45-57.

General Electric Annual Report. 1993. Audited by K.P.M.C. Peat Marwick.

General Motors Press release dated Thursday, December 3, 1992. General Motors Corporation, General Motors Building, Detroit MI, 48202. 1992.

Gershuny, J. and I.D. Miles. 1983. *The Service Economy. The Tansformation of Employment in Industrial Societies.* New York: Praeger.

Gibbs, Murray. 1985. "Continuing the International Debate on Services." *Journal of World Trade law* 19: 199-218.

Gordon, David and Thomas Weisskopf and Samuel Bowles. 1983. *Beyond the Waste Land.* Garden City: Anchor Press/Doubleday.

Gordon, David and Thomas Weisskopf and Samuel Bowles. 1987. "Power, Accumulation and Crisis: The Rise and Demise of the Postwar Social Structure of Accumulation." in *The Imperiled Economy.* New York: The Union for Radical Political Economics.

Gordus, Jeanne and Paul Jarley and Louis Ferman. 1981. *Plant Cosings and Economic Disloation.* Kalamazoo: W.E. UpJohn Institute.

Gore, S. 1978. "The Effects of Social Support in Moderating the Health Consequences of Unemployment." *Journal of Health and Social Behavior* 19: 157-165.

Grunwald, Joseph and Kenneth Flamm. 1985. *The Global Factor: Foreign Assembly in International Trade.* Washington, DC: Brookings Institute.

Harrison, Bennett. 1987. "Cold Bath or Restructuring? An Expansion of the Weisskopf, Bowles, Gordon Framework." *Science and Society* 51(no. 1): 23-56, Spring.

Harrison, Bennett and Barry Bluestone. 1988. *The Great U-Turn: Corporate Restructuring and the Polarizing of America.* New York: Basic Books.

Hass, Gilda. 1985. *Plant Closures: Myths, Realities, and Responsibilities.* Detroit: South End Press.

Herald American. 21 December 1993. "Up to 850 Workers Have Agreed to Retire of Transfer to Another GM Plant."

Herald American. 8 March 1992. "Two GM Plants to Close."

Herald Journal. 4 December 1992. "Rescission Takes Heavy Toll."

Herald Journal. 19 November 1987. "GM Considers Closing its Salina Plant."

Herz, Diane. 1995. "Work After Early Retirement: An Increasing Trend Among Men." *Monthly Labor Review* 118 (4): 13-20.

Hill, Richard, C. 1989. "Divisions of Labor in Global Manufacturing: The Case of the Automobile Industry." in *Instability and Change in the World Economy,* edited by Arthur MacEwan and William Tabb. New York: Monthly Review Press.

Hill, Richard, C. 1982. "Transnational Capitalism and Urban Crises: The Case of the Auto Industry and Detroit." paper presented at The Society of the Study of Social Problems, Toronto, Canada.

Hoffman, Kurt and Raphael Kaplinsky. 1988. *Driving Force: The Global Restructuring of Technology, Labour, and Investment in the Automobile and Components Industries.* Boulder: Westview Press.

Hoffman, William et al. 1991. "Initial Impact of Plant Closings on Automobile Workers and Their Families." *The Journal of Contemporary Human Services* February.

Holmes, John. 1986. "The Organization and Locational Structure of Production Subcontracting" in *Production, Work, Territory: The Geographical Anatomy of Industrial Capitalism.* edited by Allen J. Scott and Michael Storper. Boston: Allen & Unwin.

Horowitz, David. 1971. *The Free World Colossus.* New York: Hill and Wang.

Hoskins, Linus. 1982. *The New International Economic Order*. New York: University Press of America.

Howes, Candace. 1993. "Constructing Comparitive Disadvantage: Lessons from the U.S. Auto Industry." Pp. 45-89 in *Trading Industries, Trading Regions*, edited by Helzi Noponen, Julie Graham and Ann R. Markusen. New York: Guilford Press.

Howes, Candace. 1991. "The Benefits of Youth: The Role of Japanese Fringe Benefit Policies in the Restructuring of the U. S. Motor Vehicle Industry." *International Contrabution to Labour Studies* 1: pp. 113-132.

Interview. 9 August 1995.

Interview. 7 August 1995.

Interview. 5 August 1995.

Interview. 12 October 1993.

Interview. 23 September 1993.

Interview. 28 July 1993.

Interview. 21 July 1993.

Interview. 23 March 1993.

Jacobson, Louis, et al. 1993. "Earnings Losses of Displaced Workers." *American Economic Review* 83 (4): 685-709.

Jenkins, Rhys. 1984. "Divisions Over the International Division of Labor" *Capital and Class* 4: 28-57, Summer.

Jeszeck, Charles. 1993. "Decline of Tire Manufacturing in Akron." Pp. 18-44 in *Grand Designs: The Impact of Corporate Strategies on Workers, Unions, and Communities*, edited by Charles Craypo and Bruce Nissen. Itaca: ILR Press.

Kates, Nick, Barrie Greiff and Duane Hagen. 1990. *The Psychosocial Impact of Job Loss*. Washington DC: American Psychiatric Press Inc.

Kelvin, Peter and Joanna Jarrett. 1985. *Unemployment: Its Social Psychological Effects*. Cambridge, England: Cambridge University Press.

Keochlin, Timothy and Mehrene Larudee. 1992 "The High Cost of NAFTA." *Challenge* September/October.

LaRock, Seymour. 1993. "Neither Federal 'Carrot' Nor 'Stick' Alters Early Retirement Patterns, 1979-1992." *Employee Benefit Plan Review* July: 10-16.

Lawrence, Robert. 1984. *Can America Compete?* Washington. D.C.: Brookings Institute.

Leary, Elly. 1994. "Testimony Before the Rich/Dunlop Commision January 5, 1994." *Monthly Review* October: 27-31.

Leff, Nathaniel. 1976. "The New Economic Order—Bad Economics, Worse Politics." *Foreign Policy* No. 24, Fall.

Liem, R. and J. Liem. 1988. "Psychological Effects of Unemployment on Workers and their families." *Journal of Social Issues* 44(4): 87-105.

Lipietz, Alain. 1986. "New Tendencies in the International Division of Labor: Regimes of Accumulation and Modes of Regulation." in *Production, Work, Territory*. Boston: Allen & Unwin.

Lipsky, David. 1979. *The Labor Market Experience of Workers Displaced and Relocated by Plant Shutdowns: The General Foods Case*. New York: Garland Press Inc.

McKenzie, Richard. 1984. *Fugitive Industry: The Economics and Politics of Deindustrialization*. San Francisco: Pacific Institue for Public Policy Research.

Mckenzie, Richard. 1979. *Restrictions on Business Mobility*. Washington, DC: American Enterprise Institute.

Mishel, Lawrence and Jared Bernstein. 1993. *The State of Working America*. Armonk: M.E. Sharpe.

Memories. 1993. *General Motors: Syracuse, New York Plant 1993-1923* Syracuse: Jostens Publishing.

Nau, Henery. 1990. *The Myth of Americas Decline*. New York: Oxfrod University Press.

New York Times. 13 March 1996. "Strike Shuts Down 75% of General Motors."

New York Times. 9 March 1996. "The Downsizing of America: A Search for New Answers to Avoid Layoffs."

New York Times. 8 March 1996. "The Downsizing of America: The Politics of Lay-offs."

New York Times. 7 March 1996. "The Downsizing of America: In the Class of '70, Wounded Winners.

New York Times. 6 March 1996. "The Downsizing of America: A Home Town Feels Less Like Home."

New York Times. 5 March 1996. "The Downsizing of America: Big Holes Where the Dignity Used to Be."

New York Times. 4 March 1996. "The Downsizing of America: The Company as Family, No More."

New York Times. 3 March 1996. "The Downsizing of America: On the Battle of Business, Millions of Casualties."

Newman, Katherine. 1985. "Turning Your Back on Tradition: Symbolic Analysis and Moral Critique in a Plant Shutdown." *Urban Anthropology* 44 (1-3): 108-149.

O'Connor, James. 1987. *The Meaning of Crisis: A Theoretical Introduction.* New York: Basil Blackwell.

Payer, Cheryl. 1982. *The World Bank.* New York: Monthly Review Press.

Perrucci, Carolyn et al. 1988. *Plant Closings: International Context and Social Costs.* New York, NY.: Aldine De Gruyer.

Petit, P. 1986. *Slow Growth and the Service Economy.* New York: St. Martin's Press.

Petras, James and Morris Morley. 1995. *Empire or Republic: American Global Power and Domestic Decay.* New York: Routledge.

Petras, James and Steve Vieux. 1994. *From Little Rock to Wall Street: Clinton's Journey Beyond Reaganism.* unpublished manuscript.

Petras, James and Morris Morley. 1990. *US Hegemony Under Siege.* New York: Verso.

Petras, James. 1986. *Latin America: Bankers, Generals and the Struggle for Social Justice.* Totowa: Rowman & Littlefield.

Petras, James. 1984. *Capitalist and Socialist Crises in the Late Twentieth Century.* Totowa: Rowman and Allenheld.

Phillips, Kevin. 1993. *Boiling Point.* New York: Random House.

Phillips, Kevin. 1990. *The Politics of the Rich and Poor.* New York: Random House.

Piore, Michael J. and Charles F. Sabel. 1984. *The Second Industrial Divide.* New York: Basic Books.

Podgursky, Michael and Paul Swaim. 1987. "Job Displacement and Earnings Loss: Evidence from the Displaced Worker Survey." *Industrial Labor Relations Review* 41 (1): 17-29.

Portz, John. 1990. *The Politics of Plant Closings.* Lawrence: University of Kansas Press.

Post Standard. 23 October 1993a. "Workers Reflective as Plant Closing Nears."

Post Standard. 23 October 1993b. "Down and Out a Fisher Guide."

Post Standard. 25 December 1992. "Family Is Unsure What It Will Do When Plant Closes."

Post Standard. 24 December 1992. "Workers Lose Loved Ones-Their Jobs."

Post Standard. 15 December 1992. "GM Plan Could Lesson Fisher Guide Job Losses."

Post Standard. 4 December 1992. "Plant Bottomed Out on GMs Bottom Line."

Pursell, Carroll. 1972. "Economic Concentration and World War II." Pp. 151-171 in *The Military Industrial Complex.* New York: Harper and Row.

Putterman, Julie. 1985. *Chicago Steelworkers: The Cost of Unemployment.* Chicago: Hull House Association.

Quinn, J.B. and C.E. Gagon. 1986. "Will Services Follow Manufacturing into Decline?" *Harvard Business Review* 86(6): 95-106.

Riddle, D. I. 1986. *Service Led-Growth: The Role of the Service sector in World Development.* New York: Praeger.

Ross, Robert and Kent Trachte. 1990. *Global Capitalism: The New Leviathan.* Albany: State University of New York Press.

Rothstein, Lawrence. 1986. *Plant Closings: Power, Politics and Workers.* London: Auburn House Publishing.

Sayer, Andrew. 1986. "Industrial Location on a World Scale: The Case of the Semi-conductor Industry." in *Production, Work, Territory: The Geographical Anatomy of Industrial Capitalism.* edited by Allen J. Scott and Michael Storper. Boston: Allen & Unwin.

Schumpeter, Joseph. 1947. *Capitalism, Socialism, and Democracy.* New York: Harper and Row.

Schwarz, John and Thomas Volgy. 1992. *The Forgotten Americans: Thirty Million Working Poor in the Land of Opportunity.* New York: Norton and Company.

Seitchik, Adam. 1989. *Labor Displacement within the New Family Economy.* (Dissertation) Boston: Boston University.

Serrin, William. 1986. "Part-Time Work, New Labor Trend." *New York Times.* 9 July.

Standard and Poors. 1994. *Industrial Surveys* vol. 1 October.

Statistical Abstracts of the United States. 1993. "No. 651. Displaced Workers, by Selected Characteristics."

Stern, James. 1969. "Evolution of Private Manpower Planning in Armour's Plant Closings." *Monthly Labor Review December.*

Storm, Stephanie. 1995. "This Years Wave of Mergers Heads Toward a Record." *New York Times.* 31 October.

Streeten, Paul. 1982. "Approaches to a New International Economic Order." in *World Development* v. 10, No. 1.

Swinney, Dan and Jack Metzgar. 1987. "Expanding the Fight Against Shutdowns." Pp. 153-160 in *The Imperiled Economy: Book II Through the Safety Net,* edited by Robert Cherry et al. New York: Union for Radical Political Economics.

Targ, Harry R. 1986. *Strategy of an Empire in Decline: Cold War II.* Minneapolis: MEP Publications.

Thomas, E., E. McCabe and J. Berry. 1980. "Unemployment and Family Stress: A Reassessment." *Family Relations 29*: 517-524.

Thrift, Nigel. 1989. "The Geography of International Economic Dsorder." Pp. 16-78 in *A World in Crisis,* edited by R.J. Johnston and P.J. Taylor. Cambridge: Basil Blackwell.

Uchitelle, Louis. 1995. "Labor Costs Show Small Increses." in *New York Times.* 1 Feburary 1995, d1&d5

UNCTAD. 1995. *World Investment Report: Transnational Coporations and Competitiveness.* New York: United Nations.

UNCTAD. 1994. *World Investment Report: Transnational Coporations, Employment and the Workplace.* New York: United Nations.

UNCTAD. 1988. "Services in the World Economy." in *Trade and Development Report.* New York: United Nations. Part Two.

UNCTC. 1988. *Transnational Corporations in World Development.* New York: United Nations.

United Automobile Workers (UAW) 1992. Press release, December 9. Copies can be obtained by contacting the author.

United States Bureau of Census 1992. *County Business Patterns.* Washington DC: United States Government Printing Office.

United States Bureau of Census 1980. *County Business Patterns.* Washington DC: United States Government Printing Office.

United States Bureau of Census. 1994. *County and City Data Book.* Washington DC: United States Government Printing Office.

United States, Congress, Senate, Subcommittee on Labor of the Committee on Labor and Human Resources. 1987. *General Motors Plant Closings.* Report No. S HRG. 100-11. 100th Cong., 1st sess., January 26.

United States Department of Labor. 1994. "Total Hourly Labor Costs in Manufacturing, 1993." USDL-94-261, May 25.

Vernon, Raymond. 1971. *Sovereignty at Bay: The Multinational Spread of U.S. Enterprises.* New York: Basic Books.

Wallace, Michael and Joyce Rothchild. 1988. "Plant Closings, Capital Flight, and Worker Dislocation: The Long Shadow of Deindustrialization." Pp. 1-35 in *Deindustrialization and the Restructuring of American Industry*, edited by Michael Wallace and Joyce Rothchild. London, England: JAI Press.

Wallerstein, Immanuel. 1979. *The Capitalist World Economy*. Cambridge: Cambridge University Press,

Wallerstein, Immanuel and Terence Hopkins. 1982. *World Systems Analysis: Theory and Methodology*. Beverly Hills: Sage Publications.

Wards Automotive Yearbook. 1993. Detroit: Wards Communication.

Warren, Bill. 1980. *Imperialism: Pioneer of Capitalism*. London: Verso.

Weintraub, Sidney. 1979. "The New International Economic Order." *World Development* v. 7.

Womack, James; Daniel Jones and Daniel Roos. 1990. *The Machine That Changed the World,* New York: Maxwell MacMillan International.

Wood, Adrian. 1994. *North-South Trade, Employment and Inequality*. New York: Oxford University Press.

Zajac, James. 1993. "Getting the Welcome Carpet." *Forbes*. 18 July, p. 276-280.

Zippay, Allison. 1991. *From Middle Income to Poor: Downward Mobility Among Displaced Steelworkers*. New York, NY: Praeger.

Index